DATE DUE

DEC 0 1 2008	
NOV 1 7 2009	
MAR 1 6 2012	
MAY 1 4 2012	

DEMCO, INC. 38-2931

The Future of Imprisonment

The Future of Imprisonment

Edited by
Michael Tonry

OXFORD
UNIVERSITY PRESS
2004

OXFORD
UNIVERSITY PRESS

Oxford New York
Auckland Bangkok Buenos Aires Cape Town Chennai
Dar es Salaam Delhi Hong Kong Istanbul Karachi Kolkata
Kuala Lumpur Madrid Melbourne Mexico City Mumbai Nairobi
São Paulo Shanghai Taipei Tokyo Toronto

Published by Oxford University Press, Inc.,
198 Madison Avenue, New York, New York 10016
www.oup.com

Oxford is a registered trademark of Oxford University Press

Library of Congress Cataloging-in-Publication Data

The future of imprisonment / edited by Michael Tonry.
p. cm.
Includes bibliographical references.
ISBN 0-19-516163-7
1. Prisons—United States.   I. Tonry, Michael H.
HV9471 .F88 2004
365′.973′0905—dc21   2003007644

1 2 3 4 5 6 7 8 9

Printed in the United States of America
on acid-free paper

Preface

Not so long ago, serious people thought the prison's days were numbered. "The days of imprisonment as a method of mass treatment of lawbreakers," wrote Norval Morris's mentor, Hermann Mannheim, in 1943, "are largely over." In a 1965 festschrift for Mannheim, Morris wrote that the prison's "origins were makeshift, its operation is unsatisfactory, and its future lacks promise," and "confidently predicted" that, "before the end of this century," the prison, as Mannheim and Morris knew it, would "become extinct."

Neither Mannheim nor Morris was an armchair criminologist. They were in the prisons and jails and courts and probation offices. In the 1940s and the 1960s, smart, sophisticated people, practitioners, policymakers, and professors alike, thought what Mannheim and Morris thought. In the early nineteenth century, the prison was a humanitarian reform, a substitute for capital and corporal punishment and banishment. By the middle of the twentieth century, it seemed clear that many prisons were horrible places that did damage to those sent there with insufficient compensating public gain.

Through the mid-1970s, the prison's days might have looked numbered. The U.S. prison population fell throughout the 1960s and early 1970s, even as crime rates increased. Literatures and theories on penal abolitionism developed in Europe, with American echoes. Labeling theory, with its message that the criminal justice system often causes crime by trying to prevent it, became influential. Mainstream reform organizations including the National Council on Crime and Delinquency proposed a National Moratorium on Prison Construction. Alternatives to incarceration flourished, with ample funding from the Republican administrations of Richard Nixon and Gerald Ford.

People who do not know the history of prisons and penal policy must, looking back, find all that hard to believe. For a quarter century, "prison works" has been the dominant penal ideology. The number of prisoners grew by a factor of seven between 1972 and 2003 and the imprisonment rate by a factor of five. Many politicians propose policies meant deliberately to make conditions in prisons less humane rather than more.

The ideologies and politics of our moment are no more likely to persist than were those of the 1950s. For the lifetimes of those now adults, at least, the prison is likely to remain the primary punishment for serious crimes. This book is an effort to look forward to the prison's twenty-first century future, by looking back to the past 25 years' experience. The aim is to draw lessons that can inform thinking about the prison's future.

The overriding functional questions about the prison are how much imprisonment is too much, who should be sent there, what should happen to them while they are inside, and when, how, and under what conditions should they be released. Those questions provide this book's structure. In the first part, Jeffrey Fagan documents the effects of current high levels of imprisonment on urban neighborhoods and the people who live in them, and Alfred Blumstein explains how current policies came to be as they are. In the second, Richard Frase examines theories of punishment that guide imprisonment decisions, and Marc Miller considers how judges obtain the information they need to decide wisely. In the third part, Franklin Zimring and Gordon Hawkins argue for the strategic importance of controls on punishment, including imprisonment, as a limit on government power, and James Jacobs examines the rise and fall of efforts to improve conditions inside. In the last, Kevin Reitz examines the theory and practice of prison release, and John Monahan reports the current state of the art of knowledge about the prediction of dangerousness.

The themes explored in these essays were developed in Norval Morris's 1974 book *The Future of Imprisonment*. All of the writers are among his great admirers. Some claim him as mentor. Some were his students. Some worked for him. All worked with him. All are grateful to him for his ideas, his help, and his kindness.

This book, like every book, involved lots of work—by the writers, by Sara Harrop, who prepared the manuscript, and by Dedi Felman of Oxford University Press. It would not exist save for urging and periodic reinforcement from James Jacobs and Franklin Zimring. Human beings are multiply motivated in everything we do. Among the motivations of all who worked on this book, the most powerful was our love for Norval Morris.

Contents

Contributors

Alfred Blumstein is J. Erik Jonsson Professor of Urban Systems and Operations Research, H. John Heinz III School of Public Policy and Management, Carnegie Mellon University.

Jeffrey Fagan is professor of law and public health and director of the Center for Violence Research & Prevention, Columbia University.

Richard S. Frase is Benjamin N. Berger Professor of Criminal Law, University of Minnesota.

Gordon Hawkins is a senior fellow at the Earl Warren Institute, University of California, Berkeley, and retired director of the Institute of Criminology, University of Sydney.

James B. Jacobs is Warren E. Burger Professor of Law and director of the Center for Research in Crime & Justice, New York University.

Marc L. Miller is professor of law, Emory University.

John Monahan is Henry and Grace Doherty Professor of Law, University of Virginia.

Kevin R. Reitz is professor of law, University of Colorado.

Michael Tonry is director of the Institute of Criminology, Cambridge University, and Sonosky Professor of Law and Public Policy, University of Minnesota.

Franklin E. Zimring is professor of law, University of California at Berkeley.

The Future of Imprisonment

1

Has the Prison a Future?

Michael Tonry

It is a matter of pride to every American that the new penitentiary system has been established and successfully practiced in this country. That community which . . . persevered in this novel experiment, until success has crowned its perseverance, must occupy an elevated place in the scale of political or social civilization. Francis Lieber (quoted in de Beaumont and de Tocqueville 1833, p. 6)

The falls of Niagara and your penitentiary are two objects I might almost say I most wish to see in America. Charles Dickens (1842, quoted in Shearer and Teeters 1957, p. 114)

The days of imprisonment as a method of mass treatment of lawbreakers are largely over. What remains of it will have to employ much more scientific methods of selection and treatment in order to survive. Hermann Mannheim (1942, p. 222)

It is confidently predicted that, before the end of this century, prison in [its current] form will become extinct, though the word may live on. Norval Morris (1965, p. 268)

Prisons range in security from double-barred steel cages within high walled, electronically monitored perimeters to rooms in unlocked buildings in unfenced fields. They range in pain from windowless rooms of close-confined, sensory-deprived isolation to work camps of no physical adversity whatever. . . . [But it] would be an error to assume that most of these late-twentieth-century mutations of the prison tend toward leniency and comfort. The most common prisons are the overcrowded prisons proximate to the big cities of America; they have become places of deadening routine punctuated by bursts of fear and violence. Norval Morris (1995, p. 227)

There in five quotations is the history of the prison. It began 200 years ago as a humanitarian reform, a substitute for capital and corporal punishment and banishment. It was celebrated. By the middle of the twentieth

3

century, most prisons were widely recognized to be horrible places that damaged those sent there and produced insufficient compensating public gains. In the mid-1960s, Norval Morris reported, "Association with leading prison administrators of the world has revealed a professional attitude they share. . . . All join in dissatisfaction with the prison itself. All enthuse most about methods of keeping criminals out and getting them out" (1965, p. 268). For a brief period in the 1960s and 1970s, prison populations fell, decarceration programs rose, and alternatives to incarceration proliferated.

By the 1980s, the tide had turned. Prison populations in the United States rose at record rates to record heights, passing 2,000,000 in 2003. Punishment policies toughened, compassion for prisoners diminished, and prisons got worse. Early in the twenty-first century, many elected officials in the United States and England subscribe to former English Home Secretary Michael Howard's view that "Prison works." Although on the surface Howard wanted to be understood as saying that imprisonment effectively reduces crime rates, and therefore should be used more, what he presumably really meant was that prison works in political debate as a symbol that effectively demonstrates a politician's concern about crime to the public.

However. Prisons and imprisonment, and our expectations of them, will change, as they have before. Cultural norms and social attitudes change, and political issues go in and out of fashion. What goes up comes down. There are signs that the harshest and most stereotyped attitudes toward crime and criminals in the United States are softening and becoming more nuanced. And even if attitudes have not yet changed enough to permit a radical refashioning of prisons and our expectations of them, the time will come when those subjects are ripe for reconsideration.

For the lifetimes of those now adults, at least, the prison will remain the primary punishment for serious crimes. Serious wrongdoing occurs that violates fundamental norms. Substantively and symbolically appropriate responses are needed. Although there are good reasons to doubt that changes in the severity of punishment have any significant deterrent effects on behavior, no one doubts that having a punishment system, compared with not having one, does have crime-preventive effects.

Those are functional reasons why prisons will remain in use. There is also a good normative reason why we should want to keep them. The alternatives may be scarily worse. In the early nineteenth century, the prison developed as a humane alternative to corporal and capital punishment and banishment. In the twenty-first century it may serve as a humane alternative to biochemical controls on behavior and electrical controls on movement. The technological gap between drugs that allow deeply mentally disturbed people to function in the community and drugs that offset aggressive impulses or excitement is bridgeable. When that bridge is crossed, there will be those who regard the moral autonomy of offenders as less important than the prevention of harm to victims. Delayed-delivery drugs and subcutaneous computer chips are available now. Some crime controllers will be happy to see them used. In the long term, we cannot know how those debates will be resolved, but for a time at least imprisonment may serve as a humane alternative to behavioral controls that may be much more deeply violative of human rights and liberties.

But even if prisons are with us for the foreseeable future, the typical prison need not be a "walled institution where adult criminals in large numbers are held for protracted periods, with economically meaningless or insufficient employment, with vocational or educational training for a few, with rare contacts with the outside world, in cellular conditions varying from the decent to those which a zoo would not tolerate" (Morris 1965, p. 268). Morris's statement four decades ago does not accurately describe all American prisons today, but it describes too many.

We know much more about the operations, functions, and effects of prisons than did the reforming Quakers two centuries ago or did Hermann Mannheim and Norval Morris on either side of the middle of the last century. We could make prisons more effective and less damaging. We could spend less on them and do more with them. In general, American prisons at the outset of the twenty-first century are ineffective and destructive. No doubt they prevent some serious crimes by incapacitating offenders, and no doubt having prisons achieves greater deterrence of crime than if there were none. These crime-preventive effects should not, however, be overstated. Many people sent to prison present very little risk of committing violent crimes, and there is no credible evidence at all that longer prison sentences are better deterrents than shorter ones (or than many community penalties).

The relatively modest preventive gains that prisons can claim come at great cost in money, blighted lives, diminished life chances, and unnecessary damage to children, families, and communities. The tens of billions spent annually on prisons and jails could be better spent on health care, education, and other basic social services. The blighted lives are not only those of prisoners from whom years are taken away but of the prison staff who must live their working lives in depressing, claustrophobic conditions. Some of the diminished life chances are those of prisoners, many of whom come out of prison more deeply socialized into deviant values than when they entered, and for whom imprisonment will mean a lifetime of lesser employment and lower earnings. The diminished life chances, however, also include those of prisoners' children and partners and other residents of the disadvantaged urban communities from which prisoners disproportionately come and to which they return.

Prisoners, and their families, and the rest of us, will benefit if prisons and related institutions can prevent crime more effectively at lower human and economic cost.If we had the will, we have the knowledge to do much better than we now do. In recent decades that will has been lacking. We know how to organize and operate prisons that are less destructive than the current norm. We know how to organize and deliver services that reduce prospects for later offending and increase offenders' chances of living satisfying conventional lives. We know how to supervise offenders in the community in ways that reduce their risk of reoffending. We know how to increase the integration and effectiveness of probation and prison systems that are now typically disjointed and poorly linked.

This essay shows how. It sets out an agenda for prison reform in the first half of the twenty-first century. It reflects three starting points that were in earlier times widely supported in the United States, are widely supported in Europe now, and will, I believe, again come into their own in the United States. First, punishment in individual cases should be no severer or more intrusive than can be justified by reference to the offender's culpability. Second, decisions concerning individual offenses and offenders should be insulated from political and media influence. Third, policy makers should note public attitudes and anxieties but, recognizing the human temptation to strike unwisely in anger, should base policy on substantive analyses and systematic evidence. Taken together, they reflect a view that neither politicians' political self-interest nor the wish to "send a message" to an angry public can justify adoption and implementation of policies that treat individual offenders more harshly than they individually deserve.

Proposals are presented as ukases, briefly stated, briefly explained. The proposals are not utopian, though they are premised on the belief that American prisons need be no worse than those elsewhere. Some are based on new knowledge, some on old knowledge long forgotten or ignored. Before I discuss them, though, two foundations need to be laid. One concerns scope, the other values.

Scope. A primary reason why the prison is a failed institution is that it is commonly conceived too narrowly. Most discussion of prisons focuses on the numbers inside, sentence lengths, prison conditions, and reoffending rates. In other words, prisons are thought of primarily as something free-standing and separate from the rest of the criminal justice system and from the larger community, and concerned primarily with reducing recidivism rates. This is a damaging mistake, which can be shown by comparing how we think about prisons with how we think about hospitals.

Hospitals have two primary missions: saving lives and maximizing patients' physical and mental health. They do not stand alone but are part of a comprehensive health care system. They are expensive, and there is broad agreement that services that can be provided less expensively should be. Another, more important, reason why hospitals do not stand alone is that health care is a comprehensive system. It includes preventive public health programs, service delivery by outpatient facilities, and gatekeeping by primary care physicians. For those released from hospitals, the system includes medication, home care, nursing homes, and hospices. Substantial efforts are made to assure continuity of treatment, both leading to and leading from the hospital's doors.

The preceding paragraph describes institutional arrangements, but that is not the full extent of the health care system. It also includes and takes account of people's private lives. Americans are increasingly conscious of risk factors and many take exercise or plan menus or activities with health effects in mind. Doctors and public health agencies encourage healthy living. Health maintenance organizations invest large sums in preventive programs to encourage people to take care of themselves and reduce their future need for costly care.

The health care system measures its effects in a variety of ways. Curing people and saving lives are not the only measures. The efficiency, costs, solicitude, and humaneness of treatment are others. So is the patient's future quality of life.

Now contrast that with the prison. Prosecutors and judges perform the gatekeeping function, idiosyncratically and without guidance from broadly agreed diagnostic criteria. Probation and parole agencies manage offenders in the community but seldom with meaningful continuity with what will happen or has happened in prison. There are huge inadequacies in provision of proven programs that would not be tolerated in the health care system. Drug abuse treatment is a good example. The primary measures of effective prison management are maintenance of security and cost-control, and of prison's effectiveness are recidivism and parole revocation. It is little wonder that the prison claims few successes other than holding people and incapacitating them from committing crimes in the community.

An agenda for prison reform in the twenty-first century must be premised on recognition that the prison is but one part of a much larger punishment system, and that it affects many things other than recidivism. It affects the quality of life and life chances of prisoners inside the prison and later, to be sure, but also of their children, partners, families, and communities. Thus, an agenda must address institutional arrangements before, during, and after prison, and must address a wide range of consequences for offenders, their loved and loving ones, and their communities.

Values. It is customary to say that punishment implicates two sets of values—retributive (e.g., blameworthiness, proportionality) and instrumental (e.g., deterrence, incapacitation, rehabilitation), but this is wrong. There are three.

There is no question that ideas about blameworthiness and proportionality shape how most people, including judges, prosecutors, victims, and politicians, think about crime and punishment. Nor is there any question that ideas about instrumental effectiveness in preventing crime have influence.

The prevailing sensibilities of a time are what is missing. Sensibilities are important, social scientists would say, as both independent and dependent variables. As independent variables they importantly shape what people think. The 1950s and 1960s, for example, were decades when many people were sympathetic to the disadvantaged and optimistic about the effectiveness of treatment programs. Thus, they were inclined to oppose other than a bare minimum of prison use and to find retributive ideas distasteful. "Law and order" as a mobilizing political issue fell on deaf ears. The 1980s and 1990s were decades when people were unsympathetic to the disadvantaged and pessimistic about treatment programs. That they found harsh prison policies and penalties congenial, had little sympathy for offenders, and supported severe symbolic policies with little concern for how they would affect individuals should come as no surprise.

Sensibilities, however, in one important sense also operate as a dependent variable. The punishment system is enmeshed in the overall social system. Prevailing attitudes about right and wrong and about the relative seriousness of crimes influence legislators and criminal justice practitioners. But what the criminal justice system does also influences prevailing attitudes. That is why some people adamantly oppose drug decriminalization, even of marijuana. They fear it will send the wrong message and weaken social norms against drug use, with the result that more people will become drug users. Feminist activists, conversely, pushed hard in the 1980s for criminal prosecution of domestic violence because, they believed, treating it that way would by example strengthen social norms hostile to violence against women. Similar campaigns have been waged to shape public attitudes through the criminal justice system's handling of drunk driving, child abuse, and white-collar crime.

Scandinavians refer to the norm-reinforcing effects of the criminal justice system as "positive general prevention" (Lappi-Seppälä 2001). They believe that people's socialization as children is the major reason they do and do not commit crimes. Socialization occurs primarily through day-to-day involvement with primary institutions like the family, the school, the church, and the neighborhood. Scandinavians do not expect criminal sanctions to have significant direct instrumental effects, such as through deterrence, but believe it is crucial that sanctions reinforce rather than contradict basic social norms. If, for example, punishments were not proportioned to culpability, if minor crimes were punished more harshly than serious ones, it would create dissonance between basic social norms and the messages emitted by the justice system. Over time this would create normative confusion and undermine important values.

Some might say that retributive ideas and the values embedded in sensibilities are the same thing, but that is a mistake. Norval Morris explained the contrast in terms of a distinction between guilt and blame. By guilt, he meant culpability or desert, a judgment about the moral gravity of an offender's wrongdoing: how culpable in the eyes of God or man was this offender? By blame, he meant the social reactions to the harm an offender caused. In Morris's story "The Brothel Boy," an illiterate, mentally retarded boy raised in a brothel sought intercourse with a young girl. He gave her money, as he had seen countless customers give money to women for sex. She resisted, fell, hit her head on a rock, and a few days later died. "The blame in 'The Brothel Boy' is great," Morris wrote, "the guilt slight" (1992, p. 26). The magistrate handling the brothel boy's case, troubled by the boy's slight guilt, did not believe he deserved to be executed. All elements of the local community, blaming him for the senseless death of a young girl, believed he did. He was.

Social judgments about blame are inexorably part of the backdrop to punishment and the operation of the prison system. In their most powerful forms, they must be resisted lest the system of justice debase into vigilante justice and mob rule. Nonetheless, judgments about blame and the values embedded in prevailing sensibilities cannot be ignored.

The following reform agenda thus assumes that the prison, like the hospital, cannot be sensibly analyzed except in the context of the larger social system of which it is a part and with which it shares core values and common goals. It also takes account of retributive ideas, instrumental goals, and prevailing sensibilities. It assumes, what we should always assume, even if often we cannot live up to it, that offenders, like all human beings, are possessed of basic human rights and are morally entitled to be treated kindly and sympathetically. There but for the grace of God go I, most people, at some point in their lives, rightly think.

What Are Prisons For?

Ukase 1. *Punishment of offenders and prevention of crime should be the prison's aims.* That may seem self-evident, especially since prevention of crime easily encompasses the traditional instrumental goals of deterrence, incapacitation, and rehabilitation. Note, however, what it excludes. Nothing about reparation to victims, victim satisfaction, or responding to public opinion, to mention several other aims sometimes offered.

Reparation to victims is, of course, a good thing. Victim compensation schemes exist for that purpose, and reasonable reparation may often be a legitimate element of a community penalty. If by victim satisfaction is meant a sense that the victim's needs and interests have been respectfully and sympathetically addressed, that also is a good thing. Achieving it has little to do with prisons, however, but instead with how the victim is dealt with by officials ranging from police to parole boards. If by victim satisfaction is meant the victim's approval of a sentence imposed or pleasure in an offender's suffering, they may be understandable things for victims to want, but they should not be aims of imprisonment. The state, not the victim, prosecutes criminals, in part to gain distance from the victim's emotion and wish for revenge. Formal systems of criminal law evolved primarily for that purpose.

Similarly, imprisonment should not aim to express public revulsion at a particular crime or toward a particular offender, even though prevailing sensibilities do shape the penal policies of a time and place. It is important, as the Scandinavians insist, that punishment as a whole reinforce rather than contradict basic social values and norms of right and criminally wrong behavior. These do and should influence the contours of a punishment system. Nonetheless, as the Spanish scholar Montero long ago observed, one of punishment's primary aims is to protect offenders from the emotions and excesses of an outraged community.

Prison has long performed latent functions, serving ends unrelated to principled punishment. "Jobs for the boys" is one. In earlier times this commonly took the form of patronage appointments to posts ranging from guards to wardens and corrections commissioners. Relevant training, experience, or qualifications were often coincidental. Some of that still goes on. More recently, "jobs for the union" has influenced the politics of prison expansion, especially in California. So have "jobs for the community" as parts of the economic development plans of areas buffeted by deindustrialization. Finally, many politicians have proposed more punitive policies not because they would be more just or more effective but as a means of winning electoral support. Human beings should not have to endure the consequences of these, or greater, pains of confinement to provide jobs for guards or governors. Provision of jobs may long have been a function performed by prisons, but it is unjust to offenders and bad social policy.

Ukase 2. *Prisons should facilitate prisoners' self-development.* There are good management reasons to provide a wide range of treatment and work programs in prisons. Prisoners are disproportionately young men at their physical and hormonal peaks. Active days of work and programming occupy their time, focus their attention, and sap their energies, all good things from an order-maintenance perspective. Time passes with mind-numbing slowness in prisons and activities help it pass faster. Programs bring into the prison people who are not primarily concerned with custody and security and thereby contribute to normalizing the prison environment. These things also enhance the morale and enrich the environments of custodial staff, improving their job satisfaction and thereby reducing tensions and burnout. Many prison officials believe that these things by themselves justify provision of a wide range of programming. However, there is another good reason.

Much more than 25 or 50 years ago, there are reasons to believe that participation in treatment, educational, and vocational programs can demonstrably reduce offenders' later offending. Thinking about rehabilitative programs in general and in prison has changed rapidly. In the mid-1950s, rehabilitation loomed large in the rhetoric and programming of imprisonment. "Nothing works" ideas took hold in the mid-1970s, remained influential for two decades, and led to reduction in commitment and funding for treatment programs. Since the mid-1990s, a substantial body of evidence has accumulated that shows, for treatment programs generally and drug treatment particularly, that carefully targeted, well-managed programs can reduce reoffending.

So if there are management benefits from prisoners' participation in programs, and grounds for believing they can improve prisoners' later lives, why not require prisoners to participate in them? It depends on the program. Management considerations, and others discussed later on, justify requiring every prisoner to be gainfully employed 40 hours a week but not requiring them to participate in rehabilitative programs rather than work.

Ordinarily it is not useful to force people to do things for their own good, whether they want to or not. Common experience instructs that motivated people are more successful than unmotivated people, and that learning environments are livelier and more productive when all involved want to be there. It is a waste of scarce resources to provide opportunities to people who do not want them.

There may sometimes be justification for requiring offenders to participate in programs on a trial basis. Their reluctance may come from ignorant preconceptions, or concerns about loss of face, that may dissolve when they see what is really involved. As a practical matter, given the boredom of prison life, many will participate just to have something to do.

The strongest case for a dose of compelled participation concerns drug treatment. Three strong general conclusions can be drawn from the treatment evaluation literature. First, well-targeted, well-delivered treatment programs can reduce drug use and dependency. Second, among criminally active, drug-using people, drug use and crime go together. Reduce the drug use and offending will decline. Third, time in treatment is the best predictor of positive outcomes. These findings provide some grounds for trying to make people participate, but only some grounds and only for a while. People who do not want to participate after an introductory dose will fail, anyway, so it is a kindness to them and a saving of resources not to insist.

Ukase 3. *Prisons should not damage prisoners.* There is more to this than may first meet the eye. Of course, prisons should be safe places where prisoners (and others) are at no greater risk of harm from crime or other causes than they would be in the free community. That goes without saying. In prisons, to prisoners, other harms also are important.

Prison is iatrogenic, like a medicine that cures one ailment while causing another. Whatever good effects prison sentences may have, they foreseeably do damage to prisoners. Here is an incomplete list: separation from children and partners, family breakup, reduced employment and earnings prospects, opportunity-limiting stigmatization, socialization into deviant values, and reduced life expectancy.

Correctional adoption of the Hippocratic oath's "First, do no harm" is impossible. Prisons inherently do harm. But a correctional adaptation would specify, "First, do as little harm as is humanly possible." Much of the damage that prisons do is foreseeable. Minimization of harm should be a governing premise. I return to this in more detail in ukase 17.

How Should Prisons Be Organized?

Ukase 4. *Management of prisons should be the responsibility of a unified corrections agency with responsibility for delivery of all community and institutional punishments.* Advantage cannot be taken of new learning about effective treatment programs without continuity of oversight and programming. Drug abuse treatment is a good example. Drug dependence is a chronic, relapsing condition, not unlike nicotine dependence, alcoholism, or overeating. Time in treatment is powerfully associated with positive outcomes. The implication is that there should be seamless integration of drug treatment programs operated (or purchased) by probation, prison, and parole agencies. The reality, most places, is no integration at all.

The extreme evidence of nonintegration can be seen in the lives of offenders who participate successfully in drug treatment in prison, only to discover after release that no program spaces are available, or that supervising parole officers do not arrange or monitor participation, or that the programs available are poorly run or poorly matched to the individual's treatment needs.

Drug treatment is but one, albeit often, in individual lives, tragic, example of failure of coordination. In general the corrections system does a poor job of maintaining continuities. More generally, because of poor communication across agency boundaries, nonintegrated information systems, and turf concerns, agencies often do not know what they need to know to manage offenders sensitively and responsibly. To address this, Jack Straw, a former English Home Secretary, long promoted "seamless sentencing." Partly he had repressive ideas in mind, but partly also he was proposing that ways be devised to assure that offenders who needed supervision or services received them as they were shifted from one prison to another, or from prison to probation, or from area to another.

Coordinating correctional services is enormously difficult. In 2002, upwards of five million people in the United States were in prison or jail, or on probation or parole. Those numbers break down between federal and state offenders, and among states, but remain everywhere large.

Not all offenders need intensive supervision or extensive services. Once those who do are identified, however, it is close to inexcusable from a public safety perspective, or from the offender's, if they do not receive them. And often they do not receive them because communication between agencies is bad and coordination of service delivery is worse.

In one important sense, failure of coordination is a garden-variety management problem and the solution is to hire better managers. In practice, probation, jail, prison, and parole are often separate agencies managed by people answerable to different political masters. And things are worsened in the United States by divisions of function between state (usually prisons and parole) and local (usually jails, often probation) governments.

A first step, though hardly a solution, is creation of unified corrections systems in which one state-level agency has responsibility for all forms of supervision and custody. Redrawing of organizational charts, of course, is no panacea. Mismanagement and incompetence can occur anywhere. Nonetheless, unified corrections systems have fewer interstices into which people can fall and offer a variety of other advantages. This is not a new idea. A few states, including Delaware and Maine, already operate such systems.

Ukase 5. *Corrections systems should develop capacity for continuing, integrated oversight of services and programs for individual offenders.* The desirability of this is a primary reason for ukase 4. Whether the goal is conceptualized as public safety benefits from reduced reoffending rates or offender benefits from improved prospects for a satisfying life, it makes sense to maximize possible benefits from supervision and services.

Drug treatment follow-through illustrates one benefit from continuity, but there are others. The risks offenders embody and their individual needs and circumstances change. Smart supervision of offenders takes account of those changes, sometimes by imposing closer surveillance or more restrictive conditions, sometimes by loosening control. Unless there is continuity of oversight and availability of a range of resources, those adjustments cannot be made.

Recognition of that is one of the underpinnings of American drug courts and reentry programs. The drug court judge, though advised by probation officers and drug treatment specialists, maintains continuing oversight of offenders. If a drug test is failed, the judge decides what should happen. If residential drug treatment is working, the judge can authorize transfer to a nonresidential program. If an offender has her drug-dependence under control and is successfully getting on with her life, the sentence can be ended early and vice versa. Whenever material circumstances change, the judge can adjust conditions accordingly.

Reentry programs likewise. The old but still-too-common practice of giving released prisoners a one-way bus ticket, some secondhand clothes, and $50 sets them up for failure. Maybe a parole officer will be helpful, maybe not, but often no help is available to help ex-prisoners through the treacherous and paycheck-less early weeks of freedom. Reentry programs try to manage the process, arrange needed services, and continuously adjust to changes in circumstances.

There is nothing radical or especially new in continuous oversight and support. In principle that is what good probation and parole officers always should have done. In practice, correctional balkanization and inadequacy of resources often has meant it does not.

Ukase 6. *Nearly all corrections personnel should be career civil servants.* The only exceptions might be heads of agencies and possibly a few other very senior officials. Even they should be selected on merit grounds by nonpartisan selection committees. Elected officials might be given some discretion to choose, for example, from a vetted short list proposed by a merit selection committee.

At all but the highest levels, the case for civil service career structures is obvious. The argument might be made concerning agency heads that governors should be entitled to appoint people with whom they are personally compatible and whose management style and professional vision they admire. That is legitimate, but the record of patronage appointment of unqualified people to head prison and parole agencies is recent and worrying. Especially in unified corrections systems, appointment of ideologues and amateurs could have disastrous effects. A short-list system would allow choice, but from among substantively qualified people.

Creation of civil service career structures in unified systems offers many advantages. Establishment and observance of consistent and substantive criteria for hiring and promotion is one. Providing career ladders for all employees, including correctional officers, is another. Permitting, or perhaps requiring, upwardly mobile employees to work in different capacities and functions is a third.

Corrections officers on cell blocks who have previously worked in community supervision and in drug treatment will likely possess a richer understanding of their mission than will those who have worked only inside prison walls. This will also facilitate integration and continuity of oversight of individual offenders, since officers will have a better understanding of functions besides the one they are then performing.

And, in the inherent nature of civil service systems, the influence of partisan policies and elected politicians' electoral self-interest will be muted. Crime control policy has been a creature of partisan and ideological politics for a quarter century in the United States. A bit more distance from politics would not be a bad thing.

How Should Prison Sentences Be Set?

Ukase 7. *All sentencing decisions should be guided by presumptive sentencing guidelines.* Presumptive sentencing guidelines, 25 years' experience shows, are the most effective device for assuring reasonable consistency in sentencing while allowing judges to take account of meaningful differences between cases. These have also successfully reduced unwarranted racial, gender, and geographical disparities, provided a tool for implementing changes in sentencing policy, and enabled policy makers to link policy choices to resource allocations.

Sentences should be justly imposed and justifiable. Presumptive guidelines, which require judges to impose a sentence from within a designated range or provide written reasons for imposing some other sentence, make that possible. The adequacy of reasons for departures can be appealed and reviewed by higher courts. If their reasons are sound, judges can tailor sentences to offenders' distinct circumstances.

The requirement that all sentences be guided by presumptive sentencing guidelines implies that all other laws restricting judicial discretion, including probation ineligibility laws, mandatory minimum sentence laws, and three-strikes laws, should be repealed. Ukases 8 and 9 have the same implication. A substantial body of evidence indicates that mandatory sentencing laws have no demonstrable deterrent effects (compared with non-mandatory sentencing laws), often result in unjustly severe penalties in individual cases, and often result in hypocritical circumventions by prosecutors and judges who are unwilling to impose unjust sentences. Laws that do not produce their ostensible goal, but do produce injustice and hypocrisy, have little to be said for them.

Ukase 8. *No sentence may be imposed that is more severe or intrusive than can be justified by reference to the seriousness of the offender's crime or crimes.* This is a requirement of justice: no one should be punished more harshly than he or she deserves. Reasonable people tend to disagree over what sentence should, or justly may, be imposed in a particular case. Reasonable people tend to agree, however, about the comparative seriousness of crimes. From these agreements, rankings of crimes by seriousness can easily be devised. And from these, systems of punishments can be devised that respect the principle of proportionality—all else equal, more serious crimes should be punished more harshly than less serious crimes.

So far, this is common ground. Differences emerge, however, over the phrase "all else equal." Some, like Andrew von Hirsch, argue that little else may justly be taken into account and that the seriousness of the current crime (with some modest adjustments to reflect past criminality) should determine what constitutes a just punishment.

Others, like Norval Morris, argue that it is more helpful to think of punishments that are "not unjust." It is often difficult for a large number of people to reach agreement on the single punishment that a particular offender uniquely deserves. Most people in a place and time can, however, agree on whether a particular punishment is unjustly severe, and sometimes there is widespread agreement about punishments that are unjustly lenient. Within that range, however, between punishments that would be unjustly severe or unjustly lenient, judges may properly take account of legitimate differences between cases.

Morris's view is sometimes called "limiting retributivism." Retributive values set upper and sometimes lower bounds of deserved, or not undeserved, punishments. Within those bounds, Morris would require that judges have a very good reason for imposing a sentence above the lower bound. This is sometimes referred to as the principle of parsimony. Imposing pain on anyone is a bad thing, Morris argues, as did Jeremy Bentham 200 years ago, and there must be a good reason for imposing more pain than is required by the lower bound of deserved punishment. Sometimes, however, rehabilitative, deterrent, or incapacitative considerations provide good reasons.

Ukase 9. *No sentence should be more intrusive or severe than the least restrictive that will serve applicable purposes at sentencing.* This is a different way to express the principle of parsimony. It is a well-established sentencing principle, sometimes referred to as the "least restrictive alternative." It ought to be uncontroversial. Both the American Law Institute's Model Penal Code and the National Council of Crime and Delinquency's Model Sentencing Act so provided. Minnesota's presumptive sentencing guidelines contain a typical formulation: "Sanctions used in sentencing convicted felons should be the least restrictive necessary to achieve the purposes of the sentence."

Note the ukase phrase "purposes at sentencing." Minnesota tried to make the same distinction by referring to "the purpose of *the* sentence" (emphasis added). Both phrases are to be distinguished from "purposes of sentencing," which usually consist of a laundry list of punishment, deterrence, rehabilitation, incapacitation, reparation, and sometimes other purposes. The problem with lists of the latter sort is that they provide no guidance in individual cases because there are too many purposes and often they point in different directions. Purposes at sentencing, by contrast, are those that the judge wishes to try to achieve in an individual case. For a drug-dependent offender, for example, the purposes may be to help the offender break his or her dependence and to provide restitution to a property-crime victim. Probation with a drug-treatment condition and restitution might be the appropriate sentences. For a repeat property offender, the purpose may simply be to impose a punishment that is burdensome. Community service in a well-managed community service program may be appropriate. Incapacitation and alcoholism treatment may be the purposes in the case of a repeat drunk driver and house arrest with electronic monitoring during the evenings and probation with an alcoholism-treatment condition may be appropriate. Imposition of a prison or jail sentence in any of these cases would be unjust if community-based sentences adequately express the governing purposes at sentencing. This does not mean that prison sentences within retributive limits may not be imposed, but merely that they must be justifiable in terms of the purposes to be achieved in the individual case.

Ukase 10. *No prison sentence should be imposed unless the judge has received and reviewed a pre-sentence report (PSR) prepared by a professional corrections officer.* There are economic reasons why it is unrealistic to expect fully elaborated professional pre-sentence reports in every case. However, before a prison sentence is imposed, judges should be given reliable information on the crime, the offender's past record of criminality, and biographical information that will allow the judge to tailor the sentence to the purposes sought to be achieved.

Implementing this ukase would require a change in direction in probation practices. Professionally prepared PSRs were widely seen as highly important in the 1940s – 1970s when support for rehabilitation as a purpose of punishment was high. Support for PSRs declined significantly during the 1980s and 1990s when determinate and truth-in-sentencing came into vogue, and when rehabilitative programs fell into disfavor. Slogans like "Do the Crime, Do the Time" expressed a view that only retributive goals should be taken into account. If that were true, then the only relevant information concerned current and past crimes, and that could be obtained without working up a full PSR.

PSRs need reviving. New evidence about successful drug and other treatment programs shows that well-targeted and well-managed programs can reduce reoffending. That evidence is so strong that other countries, including England and The Netherlands, operate formal accreditation procedures for treatment programs run by probation agencies and prisons. Gaining accreditation requires provision of evaluation evidence that the program is reliably implemented and successfully reduces reoffending.

Judges in America cannot decide whether and for whom to use particular programs without good information about offenders being sentenced. Judges likewise cannot, without rich, reliable information, decide what purposes should guide sentencing decisions in individual cases. And they cannot observe the principle of parsimony and the policy of imposing the least restrictive alternative sentence.

Ukase 11. *Implementation of all sentences, of whatever type, should be continuously overseen by a designated oversight team.* This is the case management implication of ukases 4 (unified corrections systems) and 5 (capacity for integrated and continuing oversight). A mechanism needs to be created to assure that individual offenders do not get lost or fall into cracks, that transitions between programs are well managed, and that needed aftercare or follow-up services and programs are provided. Somebody has to do it. A team might consist of individuals currently working in community supervision, prison, and treatment programs. In a unified system staffed by career civil servants, whose career ladders move them between functions, such a team would bring a wide range of relevant expertise and knowledge.

How Should Prisons Be Run?

Ukase 12. *Prisons should be places of security and safety for prisoners, staff, and visitors.* This, of course, should go without saying. Prisons cannot be made crime-free any more than can the free community, but they should be no less safe than the free community. The most difficult security problem is to free prisons from the influence of long-standing and ad hoc gangs and individual bullies. Citizens in the free community are rightly outraged when gangs and bullies create an atmosphere of intimidation. We should be equally outraged when that happens inside prisons. There can be no perfect solution to this problem, which has bedeviled American prisons for at least 30 years, but the paths to improvement are clear.

One is to create internal environments that are respectful of prisoners and their interests, and where violence is not tolerated. Butner, North Carolina's federal prison, patterned on recommendations in Norval Morris's *The Future of Imprisonment* (1974), provides an object lesson. Admission was limited to prisoners with records of repeated violence, electronic technology provided near-perfect perimeter security, the internal regime was casual and open, and violence resulted in a transfer out. It worked. Evaluations showed that a safe and secure internal environment was achieved. The key was the normalization of prison life—requiring guards to treat prisoners respectfully, allowing prisoners to wear their own street clothes, allowing free unimpeded movement throughout most parts of the prison, permitting but not requiring participation in treatment programs. The next two ukases build on this experience.

Ukase 13. *No prison should house more than 300 prisoners.* Prison managers have recognized for at least a half-century that large prisons are a bad idea. Large numbers produce anonymous and dehumanizing conditions and increase the odds that vulnerable and fragile prisoners will be overlooked and victimized. Large numbers make provision of security harder and allow gangs greater room to maneuver and to recruit from a large population. Large numbers require that much of life, from meals to exercise to health care, must be experienced on an assembly-line basis. The largest prisons are also typically among those that require prisoners to wear uniforms and live a highly regimented life. These are conditions that breed, depending on prisoners' personalities, apathy, desperation, and defiance. They are also environments that breed antisocial values and attitudes. At least since the eighteenth-century time of John Howard, the first famous prison reformer, prisons have been disparaged as schools for crime. Large prisons are the likeliest to fulfill that role.

There is nothing new in the preceding paragraph. Most experienced prison managers would agree with everything in it. Modern mega-prisons have been built not to implement visions of the prison as a constructive social institution but to achieve economies of scale and save money. The challenge is to figure out what to do with prisons designed to house more than 300 prisoners. Older ones can be closed down as prison populations drop. Others can be reconfigured into a series of smaller, separately managed institutions. Those that cannot be reconfigured can be sold to the private sector for conversion into housing or commercial properties (for any purpose other than operating privately owned prisons for more than 300 inmates).

The number 300 is arbitrary. Maybe 200 or 250 is the right number, or possibly something a bit bigger than 300. The key point is that it is difficult to operate prisons much bigger than that that treat prisoners as individuals entitled to respect and concern.

Ukase 14. *Prisoners should enjoy all rights and privileges of free citizens except those inherently infringed by movement controls and security needs associated with imprisonment.* One of the reasons Butner worked, and that many Scandinavian, German, and Dutch prisons feel like places of security and mutual respect, is that prisoners are citizens who are temporarily denied only those rights and liberties that are inherently limited by prison walls. American prisons, including Butner, are not like that, but they should be.

People are sent to prison as punishment for wrongdoing. The punishment is deprivation of their liberty. That is all. The only inherent limits that imprisonment carries with it are to remain in a particular place and to refrain from activities that threaten the safety and security of others. Federal courts could easily, on equal protection grounds, have required that prisoners be accorded all the rights of citizenship of any other citizen, save only those that were unrealizable because of the physical fact of imprisonment. During the early days of the prisoners' rights movement in the 1970s, some federal judges considered adopting such a standard for considering prisoners' complaints. There might, for example, have been a presumption that denial of any general right of citizenship was unconstitutional unless prison officials could convincingly demonstrate that it was inherent in the physical fact of imprisonment. Instead, however, except concerning a few fundamental liberties like free exercise of religion and access to the courts, the Supreme Court adopted the polar opposite presumption: restrictions on liberty are constitutional unless there is no rational basis for them.

Carrying out this ukase is not constitutionally required, but prison managers have authority to do it. What would it mean? It would prohibit petty and stigmatizing indignities like requiring prisoners to wear uniforms or have regulation haircuts. It would forbid censorship of reading and watching materials and access to the Internet. It would imply wide rights of visitation by prisoners' families. It would require that prisoners be able to write letters to editors, to talk with reporters, and to vote. The physical fact of imprisonment requires diminution in none of these liberties and rights of citizenship.

What could be forbidden? The easy examples are escaping and possession of firearms and other dangerous weapons. So could narcotics trafficking, but that is true of all citizens. So, probably, could smuggling of goods into prison (at least if prisoners were able freely to purchase goods from catalogues and receive gifts from loved ones). Some rights that could not be denied, like visitation and communication, might be subjected to reasonable regulation.

This ukase seems radical only in an American context. In many European prisons, prisoners wear street clothes, vote in national elections, and have regular vacation-furloughs. In Germany, historian James Whitman reports, courts forbid prisons from having barred observation windows in cell doors because they violate prisoners' right of privacy.

Ukase 15. *Life within the prison should closely approximate that in the community.* Many prisoners are there partly because they have not learned how to function successfully, even adequately, in the free community. Prisons should help them learn to do so by behaving in prison in ways that most people do in the free community. Go to work everyday. Work 40 hours. Get there on time and stay to day's end. Schedule shopping and personal activities in the evening and on the weekends. Participate in social activities, volunteer work, recreation, and sport in your spare time. Most people do this and if prisoners had to, it would help them develop habits and attitudes that would conduce to success later on.

Much of prison life could be reorganized to parallel the free world. Medical emergencies happen to prisoners, like anyone else, and some prisoners, like other people, attend educational or vocational programs full-time. Most prisoners, though, most of the time could be doing the same kinds of things other people do.

Former Missouri corrections commissioner Dora Schriro proposed and partly implemented such a program—she called it "parallel universe"—in Missouri's prison system. Many prison employees do not like it, because it requires that they change their work schedules in ways and to times they do not like. Prisons, like many institutions, are organized as much or more for the convenience of their staff as to meet the needs of clients or customers. That is why educational and vocational programs often operate weekdays nine to five and why hours of medical clinics and prison shops are about the same. Prisoners therefore must or may often leave work, without penalty, to do things that other people fit into their personal time. There is no reason why it has to be that way. Requiring prisoners to behave in prison as we hope they will in the community cannot be a bad thing.

Ukase 16. *Prisons should provide opportunities for constructive self-change for those prisoners who want it.* This is the application of ukase 2. Substantial evidence, already mentioned, demonstrates that a wide range of educational, vocational training, and treatment programs can reduce reoffending rates. Evaluations demonstrate that some community-based treatment programs are much more cost-effective at preventing crime than is imprisonment. That is an argument for placement of many offenders in treatment programs rather than in prison. For those in prison, though, it is an argument for making programming available to those who want it.

Ukase 17. *Prison walls should be permeable.* This is an implication of ukase 3. Prisons damage people. Two particularly destructive forms this takes are breaking prisoners' ties with their families and loved ones and detaching them from changes in day-to-day life. These harms can be somewhat ameliorated by allowing unlimited visitation rights in prison, by arranging discreet facilities for regular conjugal visits, by allowing annual or semi-annual home furloughs for most prisoners, and by making graduated release programs of interspersed and lengthening furloughs the norm. To many Americans, the last three of these may seem outlandish. They are commonplace in many developed countries and in some underdeveloped countries. Americans have been inclined to treat imprisonment as a form of banishment rather than as a form of temporary deprivation of liberty. We have paid a steep price in broken families, uncared-for children, increased welfare and criminal justice costs, and desocialized ex-prisoners.

How Should Aftercare Be Organized?

Ukase 18. *Supervision and provision of services to released prisoners should continue seamlessly.* Other ukases call for an institutional arrangement that makes this easier to achieve (ukase 5), a mechanism for doing it (ukase 11), and an overall aim to achieve it. It is a waste of time, effort, money, and human life chances not to follow up in the community after release advances prisoners have made in prison toward living law-abiding lives afterwards.

Ukase 19. *Released prisoners should enjoy all rights and privileges of other free citizens, except those inherently limited by the terms of any post-release supervision and for requirements that they participate in mandated treatment programs.* The major implication is that nearly all laws disqualifying ex-prisoners from eligibility for benefit programs, from engaging in particular occupations, and from voting should be repealed. People who complete prison terms have paid their debt to society. They also exit the prison with disabilities—of stigma, of fractured families, of erratic employment records—that most people do not bear. Piling on other disabilities worsens their lives and life chances, and those of their families, and increases the likelihood that they will return to crime. None of that makes any sense. When we recall that nearly half of prisoners are black, and that black Americans have imprisonment rates seven times higher than those of whites, it becomes morally unjustifiable.

Conclusion

The prison has a future in America, like it or not. Prisons in America, however, do not have to be the destructive soul-destroying places they commonly now are. Had America a czar, and were I he, the 19 ukases would create a prison system that was far more respectful of human rights than America's now is, more effective at preventing crime, less destructive of prisoners' and their loved ones lives, and cheaper.

The ukases may to some readers appear radical. They are not. Every proposal made is in operation in one or more Western countries. Some operate today in some American states.

References

American Bar Association. 1994. *Criminal Justice Standards on Sentencing.* 3d ed. Chicago: American Bar Association.

American Law Institute. 1962. *Model Penal Code (Proposed Official Draft)*. Philadelphia: American Law Institute.

de Beaumont, Gustav, and Alexis de Tocqueville. 1833. *On the Penitentiary System in the United States and its Application in France*. Trans. Francis Lieber. Reprint. Carbondale: Southern Illinois University Press, 1964.

Lappi-Seppälä, Tapio. 2001. "Sentencing and Punishment in Finland: The Decline of the Repressive Ideal." In *Sentencing and Sanctions in Western Countries*, ed. Michael Tonry and Richard S. Frase. New York: Oxford University Press.

Mannheim, Hermann. 1942. "American Criminology and Penology in War Time." *Sociological Review* 34:222–234.

Minnesota Sentencing Guidelines Commission. 2002. *Sentencing Guidelines Manual*. St. Paul: Minnesota Sentencing Guidelines Commission.

Morris, Norval. 1965. "Prison in Evolution." In *Criminology in Transition—Essays in Honour of Hermann Mannheim*, ed. Tadeusz Grygier, Howard Jones, and John C. Spencer. London: Tavistock Publications.

———. 1974. *The Future of Imprisonment*. Chicago: University of Chicago Press.

———. 1992. *The Brothel Boy, and Other Parables of the Law*. New York: Oxford University Press.

———. 1995. "The Contemporary Prison, 1965–Present." In *The Oxford History of the Prison*, ed. Norval Morris and David J. Rothman. New York: Oxford University Press.

National Council on Crime and Delinquency, Council of Judges. 1972. "Model Sentencing Act, 2d edition." *Crime and Delinquency* 18:335–370.

Schriro, Dora. 2000. "Correcting Corrections: Missouri's Parallel Universe." In *Sentencing and Corrections: Issues for the Twenty-first Century*. Washington D.C.: U.S. Department of Justice, National Institute of Justice.

Shearer, J., and Negley Teeters. 1957. *The Prison at Philadelphia, Cherry Hill: The Separate System of Penal Discipline, 1829–1913*. New York: Columbia University Press.

von Hirsch, Andrew. 1976. *Doing Justice*. New York: Hill & Wang.

Whitman, James Q. 2003. *Harsh Justice: Criminal Punishment and the Widening Divide between America and Europe*. New York: Oxford University Press.

PART I

How Much Imprisonment Is Too Much?

2

Crime, Law, and the Community: Dynamics of Incarceration in New York City

Jeffrey Fagan

Random Family (LeBlanc 2003) tells the story of a tangled family and social network of young people in New York City in which prison threads through their lives since childhood. Early on, we meet a young man named Cesar, who sold small amounts of crack and heroin in the streets near his home in the Bronx. During one of his many spells in jail, Cesar sees his father pushing a cafeteria cart in the Rikers Island Correctional Facility, New York City's jail. Cesar had not seen his father in many years, but he was not very surprised to see him there. This was neither Cesar's first time at Rikers, nor his first time in jail, and the same was true of his father. Cesar was at Rikers awaiting transfer to a prison in upstate New York, one of several prison spells he would face within his first three decades of life. In addition to seeing his father in jail, Cesar often encountered childhood friends from his Bronx neighborhood as he moved through the state's prisons.

Cesar, his parents and siblings, other family members, his friends, and the women with whom Cesar had children formed a thick social network that shaped the choices, opportunities, and relationships in their lives. Their social mobility, economic choices, and emotional ties were sharply circumscribed by these networks. Prison and jail were routine features of their lives and a nexus of the complex relationships that now spans generations. Although Cesar encountered his father in jail after many years of estrangement, Cesar often saw several of his children and their mothers while in prisons.

This story has been replicated tens of thousands of times in American cities since 1980 (Tonry 1995; Blumstein and Beck 1999; Mauer 2000). The social concentration of incarceration among young, poor minority males is a well-known criminological fact and a feature of contemporary American prisons (Tonry and Petersilia 1999; Bonzcar and Beck 1997). But Cesar's story represents a turn in the persistent story of racial disproportionality and social concentration of imprisonment. The increasing social embedment of both direct and vicarious prison experiences has become part of the developmental ecology of young males in the poorest neighborhoods of urban areas in the United States (Hagan and Dinovitzer 1999).

Recent evidence suggests that the growing social concentration of incarceration is reciprocally tied to the spatial concentration of incarceration in poor urban neighborhoods. Cesar's story suggests that incarceration has become part of the social and psychological fabric of neighborhood life in poor neighborhoods of New York and many other cities. It is in the background of childhood socialization and an everyday contingency for young men as they navigate the transition from adolescence to adulthood. Recent studies show that the risks of going to jail or prison grow over time for persons living in poor neighborhoods, contributing to the accumulation of social and economic adversity for people living in these areas as well as for the overall well-being of the neighborhood itself (Clear, Rose, and Ryder 2001; Lynch and Sabol 2002). As the risks of going to jail or prison grow over time for persons living in these areas, their prospects for marriage or earning a family-sustaining wage diminish as the incarceration rates around them rise, closing off social exits into productive social roles. Over time, incarceration creates more incarceration in a spiraling dynamic.

This chapter illustrates this process using data from New York City on neighborhood rates of incarceration in jail or prison in five waves over a 12-year period beginning in 1986. Rates of incarceration grew slowly in the early 1980s and spiked sharply after 1985 as crime rates rose. Incarceration rates persisted at a high level through the 1990s, declining far more slowly than did the sharply falling crime rates. These analyses show that the use of incarceration, especially prison, seems to have differential effects across the city's neighborhoods and police precincts, but that the overall excess of incarceration rates over crime rates seems to be concentrated among nonwhite males living in the city's poorest neighborhoods.

Thus, the first task of the chapter is to illustrate and explain the growth of incarceration and estimate its effects. The chapter shows that neighborhoods with high rates of incarceration invite closer and more punitive police and parole surveillance, contributing to the growing number of repeat admissions and the resilience of incarceration even as crime rates fall. Incarceration begets more incarceration, and incarceration also begets more crime, which in turn invites more aggressive enforcement, which then resupplies incarceration. It is, quite literally, a vicious cycle. The constant rearrangement of social networks through removal and return of prisoners becomes a systemic part of neighborhood life and its social norms. Incarceration creates a supply of both crime and more incarceration.

Next, the chapter discusses social, economic, legal, and political mechanisms through which spatial concentration transforms a spike in incarceration from an acute external shock into an enduring internal feature of the neighborhood fabric, a dynamic process that then persists regardless of law or policy, and well in excess of the supply of criminals. The chapter illustrates the contributions of law and policy to incarceration dynamics that persist even in eras of declining crime. Then, drawing on new research on the impacts of incarceration, the chapter shows how high rates of incarceration shape the everyday lives both of those directly affected—the children and relatives of inmates, returning prisoners—but also vicariously the neighbors whose lives intersect with the families of inmates and parolees. When high incarceration rates are internalized into the ecology of small, homogeneous neighborhoods, it adversely affects the economic fortunes, political participation, family life, and normative orientation of people living in the social context of imprisonment and its aftermath. The chapter concludes with a discussion of how this concentration distorts the relationships of citizens and law, both to those living in areas affected by these dynamics and to those outside whose views of these neighborhoods and their residents influence their policy preferences.

Crime and Incarceration in New York City

Beginning in the 1980s, the prison population in the United States increased sharply through the late 1990s and continued to rise through 2000 (Cohen and Canela-Cacho 1994; Tonry 1995; Blumstein and Beck 1999; Maurer 2000). The Bureau of Justice Statistics (1996, 1999, 2001) reports that the state prison population more than doubled in the decade from 1980 to 1990, from 295,819 to 684,544. It rose by nearly 50 percent from 1990 to 1995, to 989,004. The growth in the prison population was slower after 1995, but rose nonetheless to 1,181,128 in 2001, even as crime rates were falling nationally.

Incarceration trends in New York City and New York State followed similar trends. New York State's prison population in 1999 was 66,786 inmates, up from 55,000 in 1990 and 27,000 in 1985.[1] Over the past 15 years, approximately 70 percent of the state's prison inmates came from New York City.[2] New York City's average daily jail inmate population was 17,897 in 1999, only slightly lower than the 1990 population of 19,643.[3]

Table 2.1 shows the dynamics of crime, enforcement, prosecution, and sentencing that have contributed to incarceration growth beginning in

Table 2.1. Crime, Arrest, and Punishment, New York City, 1985–1997

	1985	1990	1995	1997	% change 1985–1990	% change 1990–1997
Reported crime						
Total index crimes	602,945	711,556	442,532	356,573	18.0	(49.9)
Violent crimes	135,305	174,689	114,180	92,866	29.1	(46.8)
% violent crimes	22.4	24.6	25.9	26.0	9.8	5.7
Arrests						
Felony arrests	106,530	148,171	135,128	130,309	39.1	(12.1)
Felony drug arrests	21,008	47,838	43,697	41,728	127.7	(12.8)
% felony drug arrests	19.7	32.3	32.3	32.0	64.0	(0.9)
Felony arrests per index crime	0.177	0.208	0.305	0.365	17.5	75.5
Misdemeanor arrests	127,222	118,634	181,565	204,979	(6.8)	72.8
Misdemeanor drug arrests	34,899	33,056	52,892	63,879	(5.3)	93.2
% misdemeanor drug arrests	27.4	27.9	29.1	31.2	1.8	11.8
Prosecution						
Felony prosecution—indictments	30,416	54,837	42,758	37,041	80.3	(32.5)
Violent crime prosecutions	15,745	19,714	13,064	11,239	25.2	(43.0)
% violent crime prosecutions	51.8	36	30.6	30.3	(30.5)	(15.8)
Drug prosecutions	7,702	27,071	22,377	18,964	251.5	(29.9)
% felony drug prosecutions	25.3	49.4	52.3	51.2	95.3	3.6
Convictions	22,093	39,310	34,193	30,812	77.9	(21.6)
Convictions per 100 felony arrests	20.74	26.53	25.30	23.65	27.9	(10.9)
Sentences	75,264	92,261	79,845	93,141	22.6	1.0
Prison	10,802	20,420	18,353	16,490	89.0	(19.2)
Jail	61,839	66,035	55,957	71,508	6.8	8.3
Jail + probation	2,623	5,806	5,535	5,143	121.3	(11.4)
Incarceration ratios						
Prison sentences per 100 index crimes	1.79	2.86	4.15	4.62	59.8	61.5
Prison sentences per 100 felony prosecutions	35.5	37.2	42.9	44.5	4.8	19.6
Prison sentences per 100 convictions	48.9	51.9	53.7	53.5	6.2	3.0
Jail sentences per 100 misdemeanor arrests	50.7	60.6	33.9	37.4	19.5	(38.3)

Source: New York State, Division of Criminal Justice Services, various years.

1985, the year before the onset of the crack epidemic in New York, and continuing through 1997, when crime had declined sharply in New York City.[4] Table 2.1 shows that the number and rate of prison sentences (per arrest and per conviction) rose at a faster pace than did crime from 1985 through 1990, and then declined far more slowly than did crime from 1991 through 1997. Reported index crimes, including violent felonies and major property crimes, rose by nearly 18 percent from 1985 through 1990, but felony arrests rose by nearly 50 percent in this period as did felony prosecutions.

Prosecutions rose, too, perhaps motivated by the increased opportunities for incarceration created by legislation lowering the thresholds for felony drug convictions and mandating prison sentences for "predicate" felony offenders with prior felony convictions (Herman 2000; Nakdai 2001). Convictions, however, rose far more slowly, increasing by less than 10 percent. Even while convictions remained stable, prison sentences nearly doubled during that time, from 10,803 to 20,332. Jail sentences remained stable, a reflection of the stable rate of misdemeanor arrests. It appears, then, that sentencing accounted for the growth in imprisonment during this time, with prison sentences growing at a faster rate than the crime rate, the felony arrest rate, and the rate of convictions. The narrowing of discretion in sentencing by the legislature contributed significantly to the doubling of incarceration rates during this period.

The effects of the predicate felony law can be seen in table 2.2. Fagan, West, and Holland (forthcoming) analyzed the prior criminal records of a 25 percent sample of prison admissions of convicted offenders from New York City over five waves from 1985 to 1996. The percent with prior arrests, prior convictions, and prior jail sentences rose slightly over the period. For example, 48 percent of the prison admissions in 1985 had prior jail sentences; by 1996, 55 percent had prior jail sentences. The largest increase was in prior prison sentences. In 1985, 26 percent of the new admissions to prison had served prior prison sentences; by 1993 the

Table 2.2. Proportion of Prison Admissions by Prior Criminal Justice Involvement, 1985–1996

Year	Prior arrests	Prior convictions	Prior jail sentences	Prior prison sentences
1985	.77	.67	.48	.26
1987	.77	.68	.51	.24
1990	.78	.68	.53	.26
1993	.80	.71	.55	.38
1996	.80	.72	.55	.39

Source: New York State, Division of Criminal Justice Services, various years.

proportion had risen to 38 percent, and it was 39 percent in 1996. Over time, the prison admissions were drawn from the ranks of previously incarcerated prisoners. The recycling of prisoners was a driving force in maintaining high prison populations even in an era of sharply declining crime rates.

Drugs and Incarceration

Most of the growth in felony arrest and prosecution was for drug offenses, which were the primary targets of sentencing legislation during this time. Felony drug arrests more than doubled during this period, while misdemeanor drug arrests remained stable. Table 2.1 shows that the number of drug prosecutions rose by nearly 400 percent from 1985 to 1990, a pace twice as great as the rise in felony drug arrests. Although convictions rose far more slowly during this time, the rate of prison sentences per 100 convictions rose from 71.2 to 93.8. Since drug offenses accounted for much of the growth in prosecution, it is safe to assume that the rise in prison sentences per conviction was due mainly to the growth of drug convictions.

Several features of drug law and policy contributed to the disproportionate share of drug offenders among the newly incarcerated. First, New York implemented a series of intensive street-level enforcement initiatives during this time, each focusing on aggressive buy-and-bust tactics to snare drug sellers and some buyers. One initiative was Operation Pressure Point (OPP), launched in the mid-1980s (Zimmer 1987), focusing on outdoor retail drug markets in the Lower East Side neighborhood of Manhattan. Following the onset of the crack epidemic, a second initiative replicated the Pressure Point strategy in neighborhoods across the city. In 1988 a relatively small Crack Squad within the Narcotics Division of the NYPD was expanded to become the Tactical Narcotic Teams (TNT) (Sviridoff et al. 1992). TNT teams were deployed mainly in minority neighborhoods where the visible crack trade made an inviting target that produced thousands of felony drug arrests (Fagan and Chin 1989). These were among the poorest neighborhoods in the city, with median incomes well below poverty and areas where nonwhites lived under conditions of intense racial segregation (Letwin 1990).[5]

Second, drug sentencing laws were amended during this time to mandate longer sentences for possession of even small amounts of cocaine (Fagan and Chin 1989; Belenko 1993; Sviridoff et al. 1992; Letwin 1990). By 1987 the New York State legislature had enacted broad changes in sentencing for many drug offenses, including mandatory incarceration and lengthened sentences for even small amounts of drugs.[6] "Predicate felony" laws passed during this time also contributed to the rise in imprisonment by mandating prison sentences for felony offenders with any prior felony conviction.[7] Coming on top of the already harsh, deterministic "Rockefeller Drug Laws,"[8] the predicate felony statutes in practice elevated the prison population by indexing the incarceration rate to the arrest rate by denying judicial discretion in sentencing repeat offenders.[9] The effects of the predicate felony statutes landed most heavily on drug offenders and violent offenders (Herman 2000). The intersection of these policies, fueled by calls for ever tougher enforcement against drug dealers, was the engine behind New York's historic expansion of its prison population during this time (Letwin 1990).

The increasing share of prison admissions for drug crimes can be seen in figure 2.1. Fagan, West, and Holland (forthcoming) showed that the percentage convicted on drug sale charges nearly tripled from 1985 to 1996, from 16.9 to 47.9 percent. For drug possession, the increase was more than double, from 5.4 to 11.2 percent. The proportion convicted for violent crimes declined by more than half during the same period, from 47.5 to 21.5 percent. The decline for property crimes was also nearly 50 percent. Drug enforcement, then, was the engine for first the growth and then the stability of incarceration in New York City for over a decade,

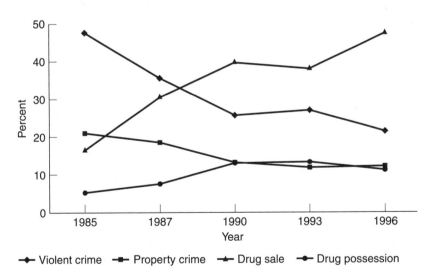

Fig. 2.1 Percentage of prison admissions by offense type, New York City, 1985–1996.

Source: New York State, Division of Criminal Justice Services, 25 percent sample of prison admissions over five waves, 1985–1996.

even as other felony crime rates declined sharply. The durability of drug enforcement as a source of prison populations over time and across distinctly different crime "eras" suggests that just as incarceration shifts from an externality to an endogenous feature of neighborhood social organization, so too does drug enforcement become an endogenous feature of the social organization and political economy of law enforcement.[10]

Incarceration Growth and Declining Crime

Figure 2.1 shows that even as crime began its historic decline in New York City in 1991 and accelerated by 1994, drug arrests remained at their 1990 levels, and convictions for drug sale and possession continued to fuel incarceration rates. From 1990 to 1995, reported index crimes declined by more than 40 percent, from 711,556 to 442,532. Within two more years, index crimes dropped further to 356,573, an overall decline of nearly 50 percent from its peak in 1990. Yet felony arrests declined by 12 percent, only a fraction of the decline in crime.

The engine for the growth and stability of the incarceration rate in an era of declining crime was the replacement of drug enforcement programs such as OPP and TNT with new initiatives that embedded politically popular theories of zero-tolerance and order-maintenance policing (Livingston 1997; Fagan and Davies 2000) into drug enforcement. For example, "Operation Condor," launched in 1999, was an initiative of the New York City Police Department that used overtime pay to motivate police officers to use both "buy-and-bust" tactics and reverse stings to make drug arrests (Flynn and Rashbaum 2003). At its height, the program paid for an additional 1,000 officers on the street each day. As in other zero-tolerance policies, Condor was designed to detect more serious offenders among drug purchasers and sellers who were caught in Condor's stings.

Operation Condor produced tens of thousands of drug arrests across the city each year, but its tactics raised complaints from minority citizens about its racial disproportionality and the excessive use of a full criminal justice process (including the use of pretrial detention rather than summons) for low-level drug offenders whose crimes were mostly nonviolent and who posed minimal public safety threat (Rashbaum 2000). Large numbers of individuals were brought in on drug charges ranging from misdemeanor marijuana possession to possession of controlled substances (powder cocaine, crack, or heroin). The death of Patrick Dorismond, an unarmed citizen who was approached by undercover police officers who tried to sell him marijuana during an Operation Condor arrest, heightened racial tensions between minority citizens and the police (Rosen 2000).

Thus, the felony arrest rate per index crime rose by 73 percent from 1990 to 1997, a product of aggressive "retail" law enforcement and a policy to narrow discretion and use formal and full criminal processing of all arrests (Bratton and Knobler 1998). While prosecutions declined by nearly one-third during this period, the rate of convictions per arrest rose by nearly 30 percent. Thus, as the supply of arrestees and felony defendants grew smaller, the number of persons sentenced to prison declined by 19.1 percent from 1990 to 1995. The imbalance in declines—incarceration declining more slowly than the crime rate—again reflects the narrowing of discretion in sentencing and the continuing rise in incarcerations per felony prosecution.

The Spatial Concentration of Incarceration in New York

Research in a small number of cities shows that incarceration has been spatially concentrated in specific neighborhoods (Rose and Clear 1998; Maurer 2000; Lynch and Sabol 2002). In one study, incarceration rates within high incarceration neighborhoods increased exponentially over a two-year period (Clear et al. 2003). Lynch and Sabol (2002) calculated incarceration rates by neighborhood, focusing on concentration of prisoners spatially and temporally, and reported similar concentration. Before the research reported here, no studies examined the spatial concentration of incarceration over a longer period, across crime eras, political and policing regimes, and spanning age cohorts.

In New York City, arrests and incarcerations, both for drug and nondrug crimes, have long been spatially concentrated in the city's poorest neighborhoods. A study completed a decade ago, in the midst of the city's incarceration run-up from the mid-1980s, showed that just seven of New York City's 55 community board districts accounted for over 72 percent of all the state's prisoners (Clines 1992).[11]More recent studies, using arrest and incarceration records from the state's Division of Criminal Justice Services, showed that incarceration rates are highest in police precincts with the highest rates of poverty, single-parent families, and population concentrations of youths and nonwhites (Fagan, West, and Holland forthcoming). In these studies, African Americans account for over 50 percent, and Hispanics over 40 percent, of all NYC prison admissions, but they constitute only 25.6 percent and 23.7 percent, respectively, of the city's population. The city's patterns of racial residential segregation all but ensure that incarceration will be spatially and socially concentrated in the city's poorest neighborhoods (DeGiovanni and Minnite 1991).

To illustrate the spatial concentration of incarceration and its persistence over time in specific areas of New York, Fagan, West, and Holland (forthcoming) recorded the residential addresses of a 25 percent sample of persons admitted to prison from New York City over six waves beginning in 1985.[12] These addresses then were assigned first to the city's 75 police precincts. These addresses were also assigned to one of 330 neighborhoods, spatial units constructed by Jackson and Manbeck (1998) based on interviews with neighborhood residents and physical examination of naturally occurring neighborhood boundaries.[13] The maps shown in figures 2.2 and 2.3 show the concentration of incarceration over time. Figure 2.2 shows the changes in incarceration rates per neighborhood at three points in time: 1985, 1990, and 1996. Figure 2.3 shows the concentration of incarceration by police precincts for the same three time periods. Each spatial unit is meaningful in understanding the concentration of crime and enforcement. Neighborhoods reflect small social areas where the effects of local social and economic contexts are influential both on social control and on crime opportunities (Sampson, Morenoff, and Ganon-Rowley 2002). Precincts are the administrative unit at which enforcement policies are implemented and managed, and also where police units form small organizational cultures and knowledge of local crime problems and actors.

Both figures show that incarceration rates spread outward from a small number of precincts or neighborhoods from 1985 to 1990 and also intensified in the areas with the highest incarceration rates five years earlier. By 1996, when crime rates had declined across neighborhoods and police precincts in the city, incarceration remained very high in most of the areas where it was highest in 1990 and declined only slightly in a few others. There were virtually no places that had high incarceration rates in 1990 that became low incarceration areas by 1996. In some areas, such as the Washington Heights area in the northwest part of Manhattan and southeastern Queens, incarceration rates rose during this period of general crime decline. Overall, both figures show the stability of incarceration from 1990 to 1996, at the same time that felony crimes had declined by nearly 50 percent.

The Growth of Incarceration

To better understand how incarceration contributed to the stability or growth in incarceration, Fagan and colleagues (forthcoming) estimated models to assess the effects of incarceration on crime and subsequent incarceration over a 12-year period beginning in 1985. If incarceration rises and falls in a metric animated by crime rates, we would expect that

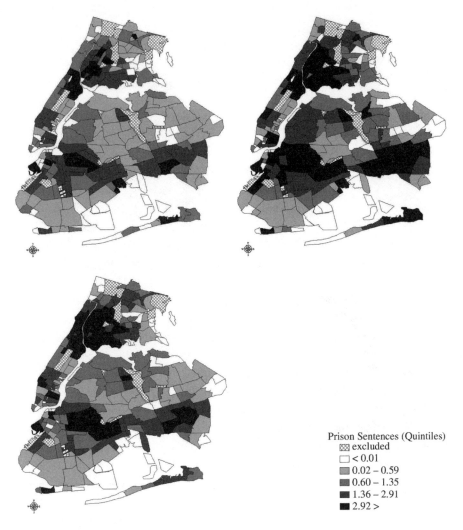

Prison Sentences (Quintiles)
▨ excluded
☐ < 0.01
▨ 0.02 – 0.59
▨ 0.60 – 1.35
▨ 1.36 – 2.91
■ 2.92 >

Fig. 2.2 Prison rates, neighborhood level. Rate of incarceration, neighborhoods, per 1,000 persons >15 years old (25 percent sample of persons sentenced to prison: 1985 (top left), 1990 (top right), 1996 (bottom left).

Source: New York State, Division of Criminal Justice Services, 25 percent sample of prison admissions over five waves, 1985–1996.

incarceration rates would be predicted by crime rates, net of arrests. That is, arrests should rise and fall with crime, and the effects of arrest on incarceration after controlling for crime rates would not be statistically significant. If arrests predict incarceration after controlling for crime, we might conclude that enforcement at some tipping point becomes an endog-

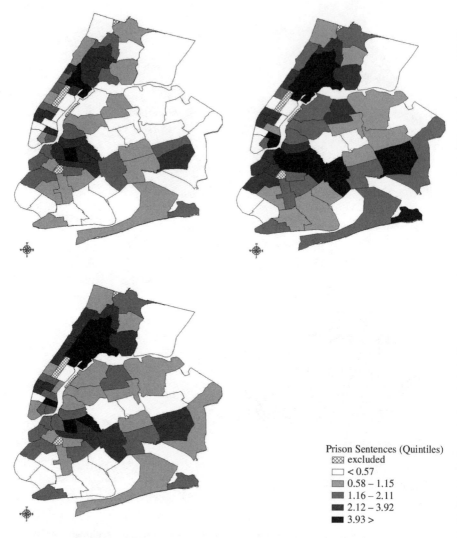

Prison Sentences (Quintiles)
▨ excluded
☐ < 0.57
▨ 0.58 – 1.15
▨ 1.16 – 2.11
■ 2.12 – 3.92
■ 3.93 >

Fig. 2.3 Prison rates, precinct level. Rate of incarceration, NYPD precincts, per 1,000 persons >15 years old (25 percent sample of persons sentenced to prison: 1985 (top left), 1990 (top right), 1996 (bottom left).

Source: New York State, Division of Criminal Justice Services, 25 percent sample of prison admissions over five waves, 1985–1996.

enous process that intensifies punishment beyond what we would predict from its crime rate. In this dynamic, law enforcement produces the supply of persons for incarceration in a process independent of crime. Incarceration thus is grown from within, not imposed from the outside.

Accordingly, these analyses examined how law enforcement patterns, including enforcement aimed at combating drug-related crime, contributed to temporal patterns of incarceration.[14] The results are shown in table 2.3. The homicide victimization rate is the measure of the prior year's crime rate, since it is the only crime measure that can be computed for either precincts or for the smaller neighborhood areas. Both drug arrest rates and arrest rates for other felonies are the enforcement measures in the precinct models. Unfortunately, felony arrest rates were available only for the precinct models and not for the neighborhood models.[15] Jail admissions are included as a control for the levels of misdemeanor crime in the neighborhood, and as a proxy for the generalized aggressiveness of law enforcement (see, e.g., Sampson and Cohen 1988). The models were estimated with both main effects and interactions with time. The latter show the contributions of the crime measures to changes in incarceration rates over time. The exponentiated coefficients show the rate of increase or decrease in incarceration for each unit of change in the predictors. These models were run with controls for the social structural characteristics, but only the main effects are shown.[16] The results in table 2.3 suggest that incarceration increased steadily over the 12-year period, even during years when the base rate of crime was declining.

Table 2.3 shows that the processes that contribute to incarceration differ depending on whether we consider incarceration as a function of the

Table 2.3. Poisson Regression of Incarceration by Neighborhood or Precinct Crime Rates, Controlling for Social Structure, New York City, 1985–1996

	Precincts				Neighborhoods			
	Estimate	T	p(t)	Exp(B)	Estimate	t	p(t)	Exp(B)
Intercept	−12.61	−2.26	c	0.000	−4.810	−1.31		0.008
Time	0.041	0.66		1.042	−0.029	−0.71		0.971
Jail one year lag	−0.002	−1.54		0.996	0.001	3.39	a	1.000
(Log) felony arrest rate*	1.871	1.67		3.658	n/a	n/a		n/a
(Log) homicide rate	2.788	0.67		1.625	−0.691	−0.25		0.501
(Log) drug arrest rate*	−1.584	−1.80		0.334	−1.565	−2.78	b	0.337
Interactions with time								
Jail one year lag	0.0002	1.64		1.000	0			1.000
(Log) felony arrest rate*	−0.017	−1.38		0.983	n/a	n/a		n/a
(Log) homicide rate	−0.028	−0.62		0.972	0.009	0.29		1.009
(Log) drug arrest rate*	0.023	2.29	c	1.023	0.022	3.41	a	1.022
2 log likelihood		301.5				3135.5		

p(t): a: $p < .05$, b: $p < .01$, c: $p < .001$

implementation of enforcement policies in larger administrative units such as police precincts, or if we assess factors in small homogeneous social areas where enforcement interacts more dynamically with social structure and neighborhood social organization. The precinct model in table 2.3 shows the influence of drug arrests on incarceration over time, after controlling for the social composition of the precinct and both crime and arrest rates. The interaction of time with drug arrests ($t = 2.29$, $p < .05$) suggests that the only factor explaining changes in incarceration rates over time is the drug arrest rate. Incarceration rates rise by 2.3 percent relative to changes in the drug arrest rate. For precincts, then, the recurring drug enforcement efforts continue to produce higher imprisonment rates over time even as crime is falling. In this model, the housing structure was the only significant social factor contributing to the growth of incarceration (data not shown). This measure included the percent of the local population living in public housing. Special efforts targeting drug selling in public housing were part of the city's strategy to control drug selling and its related violence (Fagan, Holland, Davies, and Dumanovsky 2003).[17] Accordingly, the targeting of public housing turned such locations into "hot spots" of incarceration.

The neighborhood model in table 2.3 shows that drug enforcement again was a significant contributor to imprisonment. The drug arrest rate is significant in two ways: as a main effect and again in an interaction with time. The main effect suggests that the rate of drug enforcement predicts differences between neighborhoods in incarceration averaged over the entire 12-year period. The significant interaction of time with drug arrests indicates that drug arrests contributed to the growth of incarceration over time in the city's neighborhoods. Among the social factors, the incarceration rate was higher over time in neighborhoods with higher concentrations of youth population (below 15 years of age) (data not shown).

Not only does enforcement contribute to the concentration of incarceration within police precincts, well beyond what crime rates would predict, but incarceration tends to increase crime rates over time (Fagan, West, and Holland forthcoming, table 8). There were positive and significant effects of prison admissions on felony arrest rates at the precinct level in the following year, controlling for the social composition of the precinct. Each prison admission increased the likelihood of a felony arrest by a factor of nearly two. Drug enforcement was not a significant predictor of crime rates over time. The pattern of interactions with social factors suggests that imprisonment is concentrated in precincts that are characterized by poverty, high percentages of nonwhite residents, and racial segregation. The limitations on measurement of crime rates within neighborhoods precluded analyses of the effects of incarceration on neighborhood crime rates.[18]

The Reciprocity of Crime, Law, and Incarceration

Systemic theories of neighborhood and crime regard social control as essential to regulating crime rates by residents and visitors (Bursik and Grasmick 1993). Social ties and interactions among neighborhood residents are essential components of a dynamic theory of neighborhood social control (Sampson, Raudenbush, and Earls 1997). Most theories of social organization and social control, whether in high or low crime areas, do not consider incarceration to be an endogenous factor in the dynamics of social control within neighborhoods. For example, Morenoff, Sampson, and Raudenbush (2001) show that social organization and social control are dynamic processes that are embedded in small social areas and that influence local crime rates. They concentrate on informal social control and are agnostic on the effects of criminal justice practices. Only Rose and Clear (1998) and Clear et al. (2003) have explicitly considered how incarceration affects future crime and incarceration, both empirically and theoretically.

The evidence from New York suggests that at some tipping point, the removal to incarceration of neighborhood residents is internalized into the ecology of crime, law, and social control in neighborhoods. The concentration of offenders invites closer and more punitive parole surveillance, a strong influence on incarceration trends (Irwin and Austin 1994; Petersilia 1999). Incarceration begets more incarceration, and incarceration also begets more crime, which in turn invites more aggressive enforcement, which then resupplies incarceration. It is, quite literally, a vicious cycle. From 1985 to 1990, when crime rates were increasing, drug enforcement was the engine for incarceration. Once crime declined, incarceration remained stable, independent of the declining crime rate and animated by enforcement policies, especially drug enforcement and the drug component of parole supervision. It seems that over time, and after the onset of a dynamic process of enforcement and incarceration becomes stable within a social area, incarceration transitions from an externality to social organization into an integral part of local social networks and part of the dynamics of crime and social control. The constant rearrangement of social networks through removal and return of prisoners becomes a systemic part of neighborhood life and its social norms. In other words, incarceration creates a supply of both crime and more incarceration. The ecological dynamics of this process are examined next.

Incarceration and Neighborhood Ecology

As local incarceration rates increased and concentrated spatially, incarceration and crime became embedded in the social organization of neighborhoods like Cesar's in the Bronx. The effects of concentrated imprisonment can be observed in the everyday lives both of those directly affected—the children and relatives of inmates, for example—but also vicariously on their neighbors whose lives intersect with the families of inmates and parolees. When high incarceration rates are internalized into the ecology of small, homogeneous neighborhoods, it adversely affects their economic fortunes, political participation, family life, and normative orientation.

The Economic Fortunes of Returning Prisoners and Their Neighbors

The economic impacts of incarceration on neighborhoods derive in large part from the accumulation of individual economic deficits. Young men returning from prison have attenuated access to steady jobs, and when working, they have far slower wage growth than similarly situated young men who have not been imprisoned. For example, Western (2002) showed that incarceration is a turning point that reduces the earnings, wage growth, and job mobility of young men. His research examined the economic fortunes of a national probability sample of young males from 1979 to 1998. Western's work and also local studies by Crutchfield and Pitchford (1997) suggest that the concentration of incarceration produces a concentration of young males whose job and earnings prospects are diminished. In fact, Western shows that the wages of ex-inmates actually declined over time, a combination of both their incarceration experience and the penalty of a low education. These gaps exist at the margins of the unskilled labor market, the labor market segment most vulnerable to downturns in the overall economy.

The translation of incarceration growth into neighborhood disadvantage, subsequent crime, and reincarceration is hardly surprising under these circumstances, but there are several causal stories that may explain these effects. One story is the accumulation of individual effects. Employment problems of ex-offenders are an obvious risk for persistent crime once they return from prison. Ex-offenders often are relegated to spot labor markets with little prospect of stable earnings or growth in wages (Nagin and Waldfogel 1998). Work is one of the critical factors in desistance from crime (Fagan and Freeman 1999; Sampson and Laub 2001). These effects are strongest for young men in their late 20s and early 30s

(Uggen 2000). Incarceration experiences also limit both residential and job mobility (Western 2002).

A second story may be spatial. The concentration of incarceration among nonwhites and its spatial concentration interact with other concentration effects—residential segregation and antecedent racial wage gaps—to intensify the social isolation and economic disadvantage that contribute to crime. Concentrations of ex-inmates may stigmatize neighborhoods and deter businesses from hiring locally or locating in such areas (Wilson 1996; Kirschenman and Neckerman 1991). The concentration of ex-offenders within social areas can also deplete the area's leverage or bridging social capital that is essential to making connections into referral networks that link people to jobs, in turn frustrating efforts of ex-inmates to forge links to legitimate employment. The social and economic isolation of ex-inmates may sever them from social networks that can link them to both trades and public sector employment (Granovetter 1973, 1974).[19] When neighborhoods fill with ex-offenders, stable middle-class wage earners may leave, fearing crime and severing the ties of those left behind to local labor markets and job referral networks (Wilson 1996).

A third story might be the reaction of employers to persons with criminal histories whose job prospects were already limited, or their reactions to persons from neighborhoods where incarceration is common (Western, Kling, and Weiman 2001). Employers with imperfect information simply assume that African American job applicants have a greater likelihood of prior criminal involvement, and these fears motivate a higher rate of conducting background checks for African American job seekers than other groups.[20]

And a fourth may be the aftermath of incarceration itself: the inability to gain job skills or other human capital while locked up and the psychological self-stigma of prisonization (Irwin 1970). Incarceration also creates illegal work opportunities in criminal networks that compete well with the low-wage legal work slots available to ex-prisoners. Removal of men to prison has a churning effect on illegal labor queues; in the context of limited access to legal work, the replacement process often is quite efficient (Hagan 1993; Hagedorn 1998; Sanchez-Jankowski 1991). All these mechanisms lead to a common outcome: the attenuation of work opportunities, both for individuals and for aggregates living in the areas where incarceration rates are highest. The disappearance of work elevates the risk of crime by creating incentives to join in illegal economies.

Incarceration and Family Life

Imprisonment creates adverse conditions for the families of inmates. These adversities are revisited on the communities where incarceration is concentrated through weaker supervision of children and adverse emotional impacts on children. The burdens of incarceration on families are several. Loss of material support strains family resources. These strains are real regardless of whether the lost income was from legal or illegal sources. Visits to prison, gifts to prisoners, and, in some cases, litigation costs, further burden families. In some cases, litigation costs for appeals and preparation for parole hearings also drain resources that already were limited. The shift of financial burden to single parents, grandparents, or other relatives creates strains for people like Jessica, Cesar's half sister, who lost Cesar's contributions to family childcare costs when he went to prison. The incomes of families like Cesar's have little margin for additional everyday costs (MacLanahan and Sandefur 1994). Burdens for childcare or financial support also may shift to younger siblings, who may leave school to earn money, marry early to escape the strains of disrupted family life, or turn to the underground economy or crime to compensate for lost family income (Hagan and Wheaton 1993). Some families may experience the opposite effect: relief from the removal of a family member who was a financial and emotional drain on other family members (Edin and Lein 1997).

The ability of remaining parents or other family members to supervise children also is compromised by incarceration of a family member (MacLanahan and Bumpass 1998). The removal of young adults from the community means fewer adults to monitor and supervise children. Inadequate supervision leads to increased opportunities for children to become involved in delinquency and crime (Sampson and Laub 1994). Although some of the inmates who were fathers or mothers may have been less than ideal parents, several studies suggest that they often played an active and positive role in their children's lives before prison (see Hagan and Dinovitzer 1999 for a review).

The loss of affection and support from an incarcerated parent can spark mental health problems in children that may have negative developmental consequences and add to their risks for crime. It also further strains the emotional reserves of the remaining parent or relatives to supervise or care for them (Garfinkel, MacLanahan, and Hanson 1998), raising the risks of the children's entry into delinquency. The aggravation of children's risks further corrodes the ability of neighborhoods to sustain social control of children. The multiplicative effects of family economic and emotional strain and children's emotional reaction to loss of a parent compound the consequences of incarceration.

Imprisonment, then, has the perverse effect of weakening families while trying to protect them from crime. The cumulative effect of incarceration is to limit the contributions of families to the process of informal social control that characterizes low crime rates in even the poorest communities (Sampson, Morenoff, and Ganon-Rowley 2002). The accumulation of these deficits at some threshold undermines the capacities of families—and the neighborhoods they constitute—to exercise social control. This dynamic invites a recurring cycle of crime – enforcement – imprisonment, which, after the initial shock to a neighborhood, transforms into an endogenous feature of neighborhood life.

Law and Social Norms

Social control in neighborhoods is compromised by the concentration of incarceration, again in several ways. First, high rates of imprisonment raise questions of the legitimacy of government and undermine incentives to comply with the law (Sherman 1993; Fagan and Meares forthcoming; Tyler 1990; Tyler and Huo 2002). The racial and neighborhood asymmetry in punishment offers a stark contrast to the claims of legal actors that law is fair and legitimate. Tyler's work shows that experience-based assessments of both distributive fairness and procedural fairness matter a great deal to perceptions of legitimacy and compliance, especially among African Americans who are the most overrepresented racial group in New York prisons as well as nationally. The disproportionate imprisonment of people from the same neighborhoods is linked to notions of distributive and procedural justice in a fairly direct way. If people from a neighborhood do not believe that the prison sentences that their neighbors receive are fairly distributed, then they may conclude that the policy that produces the unfair distribution is illegitimate (Fagan and Meares forthcoming). If neighborhoods residents see many of their neighbors taken away through a process that they see as unfair, then it is not hard to see that some may be likely to defy the law or at the least reject its underlying social norms.

Second, when arrest and incarceration rates are high, the social meaning of criminal sanctions is eroded by the concentration of "stigmatized" persons within neighborhoods, leading to both defiance of social norms and "counterdeterrence" (Nagin 1999), and undermining the deterrent effects of imprisonment. Tyler's work, for example, shows that legitimacy and perceptions of procedural fairness have a greater impact on compliance than does the fear of sanctions (see also Paternoster et al. 1997).[21] High rates of imprisonment within a small social area undermine the moral communication of punishment, while simultaneously eroding its contingent value. In contrast to the individual who complies with the law because he or she is responding to externally imposed punishments, the individual who complies for normative reasons does so because he or she feels an *internal* obligation. High rates of incarceration also affect the narratives about punishment among neighbors, and the ways that they talk about the legitimacy of government with children, neighbors, and friends.

Incarceration also carries stigma costs that lead to more imprisonment. Stigma may attach to both individuals and collectivities such as neighborhoods. The famous study by Schwartz and Skolnick (1962) demonstrated the stigma effect for individuals seeking work with a criminal record, a mechanism updated in studies by Sullivan (1989) and Sanchez-Jankowski (1991). Hagan and Palloni (1990) showed how the intergenerational relationship of incarceration of parents and later crime by children is mediated by stigma effects that mark individuals for closer and perhaps harsher attention by legal authorities. Neighborhoods are stigmatized for closer attention by police, increasing the likelihood of detection of crimes independent of the crime commission rate, and also harsher treatment by legal actors of persons in stigmatized neighborhoods (see, e.g., Smith 1986 and Hagan 1993). Parole officers may concentrate their efforts in neighborhoods with higher concentrations of ex-offenders, in no small part because they may anticipate a higher likelihood of detecting prohibited behavior (Simon 1993; Petersilia 1999).

Social norms also may be disrupted by the constant churning effects of removal of persons to jail or prison followed by their return. The "prisonization" of local "street" culture in style and appearance reflects the diffusion of prison culture to neighborhoods, the salience of prison-style behavioral affect or scripts in the face of high imprisonment rates (Vigil 1988; Moore 1996), and the reification of these styles and norm sets in popular culture (Anderson 1999). While conventional norms live side by side with oppositional styles, the outward appearances of defiance or antisocial posturing may invite closer scrutiny by legal authorities and evoke stronger reactions that lead to harsher punishment (Fagan 2002).

Political Participation and Citizenship

Convicted felons are disqualified from several forms of political participation and citizenship: jury service, the right to vote, and the right to hold elective office. In some states, disenfranchisement is time-limited, but in some other states felons are disenfranchised for life (Mauer 2000). Disenfranchisement disproportionately and severely affects African American males, consistent with their distorted presence in the incarceration population: of the 3.9 million American felons who are disenfranchised, nearly 1.4 million were African American males, representing 13 percent of all black males (Mauer 2000). Patterns of racial residential segregation and the concentration of incarceration in poor, predominantly minority neighborhoods in New York and other cities ensure that disenfranchisement will limit the ability of residents of those neighborhoods to influence local services and policies that both directly and indirectly affect crime and social control. For example, Uggen and Manza (2002) show that the outcomes of at least seven recent senatorial elections and one presidential election have been influenced by felon disenfranchisement, thus limiting the influence of disadvantaged citizens. In smaller areas, especially local electoral districts, the concentration of ex-felons may weaken leverage and access to important services that can moderate the risks of crime, including better schools, trash removal, health care, and economic development funds. It also disempowers those neighborhoods in zoning decisions and leverage to influence policing and other services. Barriers to political participation may also weaken policy leverage that might moderate police surveillance and enforcement practices that intensify incarceration patterns.

The denial of the vote and collateral limits on participation in government also may affect the way that neighbors in high incarceration neighborhoods evaluate the legitimacy of law and government. These evaluations in turn may corrode social ties and incentives to comply with law or engage in social regulation. Both for returning prisoners and their neighbors, this denial of opportunities attaches to people with whom they may share a perception of "linked fate" (Fagan and Meares forthcoming). If they or their neighbors are unable to engage in law through activities such as jury duty, such social exclusion can undermine perceptions of the legitimacy of law, or even breed resistance to participation in everyday citizen – law interactions such as cooperation with police in investigations. Denial of the vote is also a powerful symbol of the power of the state to punish and a clear stigma; when that power is perceived as illegitimate or its use capricious, it has a potentially corrosive affect on societal ties. The vicarious effects of reduced political participation may extend not just to neighbors, but also intergenerationally to weaken the legal socialization of children and adolescents toward law and legal actors. Felons are denied access to federal education grants, a form of social exclusion that deepens the embeddedness of incarceration within families and across generations.

The denial of the vote and other privileges to felons, then, is not simply a recurring form of stigma, infamy, or punishment (Fletcher 1999). When incarceration rates produce a critical mass of ex-felons to alter elections, the fates not just of those persons but of the persons who live near or next to them are harmed. The effects of disenfranchisement on political outcomes are yet another dimension of the endogeneity of incarceration in poor neighborhoods and its capacity for self-replication. The exclusion of felons from political participation exacts a political economic cost for them and for their neighbors in the social areas where incarceration rates are highest.

Conclusion

The racial-spatial concentration of incarceration in disadvantaged urban neighborhoods in New York accrued rapidly in the late 1980s and was sustained through the decade of the 1990s even as crime rates fell by one-half or more. The persistence and concentration of incarceration seem to be products not of crime, but of the internalization of incarceration in the ecology of many neighborhoods, and the endogeneity of drug enforcement in the social organization and political economy of the city's legal institutions.

The spatial concentration of incarceration has grown more acute in neighborhoods that already were socially and economically disadvantaged, areas where nonwhites were the dominant population group. Analyses of incarceration trends in New York City by neighborhood and police precinct suggest that the risks of going to jail or prison seem to grow over time for persons living in these areas regardless of the supply of offenders, and their ability to address the social and economic dimensions that contribute to incarceration diminishes as the size of the ex-inmate population grows. Changes in law that narrowed judicial discretion and structured sentencing toward mandated imprisonment ensured that even a drastically smaller crime rate would produce a stable flow of prison admissions.

The spatial concentration of incarceration distorts neighborhood social ecology and attenuates these neighborhoods' economic fortunes. The initial shock of spiking incarceration rates transforms over time into an endogenous or internal neighborhood characteristic that endures in defiance of a declining supply of offenders. In fact, incarceration seems to provide a steady supply of offenders for more incarceration through four mechanisms. The interaction of these four mechanisms produces a multiplier effect that further embeds incarceration into neighborhood life.

First, higher rates of incarceration invite heightened levels of surveillance and policing, making detection of wrongdoing more likely. By transforming neighborhoods into the subjects of enforcement, the likelihood of incarcerative punishment increases as a result of living in a stigmatized place. Second, the declining economic fortunes of residents further concentrates economic disadvantage within persons and discourages local businesses from locating in these areas. Beyond material deficits, the absence of local economic activity deprives these areas of everyday economic interactions that help regulate social interactions. Third, social control is not sustainable when kinship networks are strained materially to support children whose fathers are incarcerated, and when marriage rates decline due to the absence of marriageable males. Social control is compromised, and their prospects for marriage or earning a living wage diminish as the incarceration rates around them rise.

Voter disenfranchisement of convicted felons creates a fourth dynamic that adversely affects the political economy of neighborhoods with high incarceration rates. The inability to influence political processes weakens leverage and access to important services that can moderate the risks of crime, from educational resources to trash removal and recreation. It is no secret that incarceration policy is embedded in a political process that benefits both corrections professionals and lawmakers.[22] While lawmakers derive political benefits from sustaining high rates of incarceration, the accumulation of disenfranchised voters in their districts defangs putative reelection challenges. In this way, disenfranchisement weakens political leverage over both state law and local policies that might moderate the practices that intensify incarceration patterns. Disenfranchisement further deprives residents of opportunities to engage in law through activities such as jury duty or motivates resistance to everyday citizen – law inter-actions such as cooperation in investigations. Finally, the racial-spatial concentration of incarceration intensifies racial residential segregation, depressing real estate values, and frustrating residents' efforts to build capital through home ownership.

The social exclusion of America's correctional population poses a challenge to democracy that demands political and social attention. There has been no civic debate on the political and social consequences of the production of incarceration, nor has there been reflection on the laws and policies that sustain incarceration over time and detach it from the social problems it was meant to address. With nearly five million Americans under criminal justice supervision and more than two million in prison or jail, such a debate is long overdue and critical to the moral and political health of the nation.

Notes

Thanks to Jan Holland for expert mapping, Valerie West for her contributions to the data analysis, Tamara Dumanovsky for assembling the datasets, and Steven Glickman for assembling the relevant New York Penal Law chapters. This research was supported in part by generous grants from the Robert Wood Johnson Foundation and the Russell Sage Foundation. The New York State Division of Criminal

Justice Services graciously provided data on prison admission. All opinions and errors are solely mine.

1. http://criminaljustice.state.ny.us/crimnet/ojsa/cjdata.htm#Under%20 Custody%20Pop.

2. In 1987, 75 percent of all NYS prison admissions originated from cases disposed in New York City, 69 percent in 1990, and 69 percent in 1994. NYS Division of Criminal Justice Services (DCJS) and National Corrections Reporting Program (NCRP).

3. New York City Department of Correction (DOC). Online data report. Available: http://www.ci.nyc.ny.us/html/doc/html/avrdaily.html.

4. New York City's crime decline has been well documented and studied extensively. See, e.g., Curtis (1998), Karmen (2000), Fagan, Zimring, and Kim (1998), and Kelling and Souza (2001). There are disagreements over the sources of the decline. Curtis attributes the decline to shrinking demand for drugs, while Karmen attributes the decline to the interaction of social forces including employment, demography, and policing strategy. Fagan et al. view the crime decline as indexed to an epidemic of gun violence that receded sharply after 1991. Kelling and Souza see the crime decline as the result of aggressive policing of social and physical disorder, which in turn had prophylactic effects on crime rates.

5. The TNT report by Letwin (1990) described four such areas:

Manhattan North TNT Target Area 2 (February 15–2009May 14, 1989): This section of northwest Harlem is a densely populated neighborhood of multiple dwellings and vacant buildings made up of two community districts, Districts 9 and 10. District 9 is 48.6 percent Black, 22.9 percent White and 22.7 percent Hispanic. District 10 is 91.6 percent Black, 6.5 percent Hispanic, 1.3 percent "Other" and 0.6 percent white. In District 9 the median household income is $13,500, which is approximately 33 percent lower than the city average, and in District 10, the median household income is $8,600, 60 percent below the average.

Manhattan North Target Area 1 (November 14, 1988–February 14, 1989): This section of East Harlem is also a densely populated neighborhood of tenements and walkup apartment buildings. The population is 43.8 percent Black, 42.4 percent Hispanic, and 10.7 White. The median household income is $8,300, less than half of the city median of $20,000.

Brooklyn North TNT Target Area 1 (January 2–May 2, 1989): This East New York neighborhood of one and two-family homes and apartment buildings is densely populated, and includes a number of large housing projects. The population is 42.7 percent Black, 29.1 percent Hispanic, 19.8 percent white, and 8.4 percent "Other". In this target area, the median household income is $13,500, 33 percent below the city average.

Bronx TNT Target Area 1 (February 15–May 21, 1989): The South Bronx– Hunts Point area is a neighborhood of large residential buildings and significant industrial and commercial areas, with a population that is 67.8

percent Hispanic, 28.3 percent Black, 1.2 percent White and 2.8 percent "Other." The median household income, at $6,000, is 70 percent below the citywide average, and the lowest in the borough. (pp. 801–804)

6. See N.Y. Penal Law, § 220; Donnino (1989). With respect to cocaine, in 1988, "criminal possession of a controlled substance in the fifth degree" was amended to add the knowing and unlawful possession of "five hundred milligrams or more of cocaine" (L. 1988, c. 178; Penal Law, § 220.05(5)). The purpose of the amendment was to take into account the widely used form of cocaine known as "crack." Crack is a concentrated form of cocaine that is exceptionally potent and addictive. The desired effect from the use of the crack may be obtained by the use of a substantially smaller quantity than would be required to obtain the same effect from the traditional form of cocaine. Thus, crack is generally sold to users in vials containing a small quantity of the drug. To the extent the distinction between misdemeanor and felony possession rests philosophically on a distinction between minor use, and either significant use or the likelihood that the possessor was selling or sharing the drug, the aggregate weight standard for cocaine was deemed unrealistically high as the threshold for liability for felony possession of crack. Thus, criminal possession of a controlled substance in the fifth degree, a class D felony, was amended to encompass the possession of 500 milligrams or more of cocaine. In part because of the chemical properties of crack, and because of a growing belief that liability for possession of a controlled substance should be based solely on the quantity of the drug possessed, liability for the possession of the 500 milligrams of cocaine is premised on the "pure" or actual weight of the drug, not the aggregate weight of the substance containing the drug. The remaining crimes of criminal possession and sale of cocaine, however, utilize the aggregate standard (see and compare N.Y. Penal Law, §§ 220.06(5); 220.09(1); 220.16(12); 220.18(1); 220.21(1)).

7. See N.Y. Penal Law, § 70.06(1). The law defines a predicate felony offender as a second violent felony offender whose previous felony conviction occurred within the past 10 years. Prior felony convictions that resulted in a suspended sentence, a probation sentence, a sentence of conditional or unconditional discharge, or any other sentence, were considered eligible for predicate felony sentencing upon a second felony conviction. Sentencing for predicate felons reverts to the minimum standards.

8. N.Y. Penal Law, §§ 220.00–220.65, "New York State Substance Abuse Control Act." The 1973 Act distinguished between degrees of possession and sale by weight of the prohibited substance, a departure from previous laws that classified only certain drugs such as heroin, morphine, and cocaine into degrees, which were differentiated by the quantity of the preparation, compound, mixture, or substance containing the drug. Under this system, drug offenses are graded according to the dangerousness and the quantity of the drug involved. Dangerousness of a drug is determined by consulting detailed schedules of controlled substances, with the drugs considered most harmful listed in schedule I, and those classified as the least harmful in schedule V. The 1973 Act made the possession or sale of a specified amount of a broader variety of drugs a felony, thus, three

categories of drug possession and three categories of sale required mandatory imprisonment carrying minimum ranges of one to life (A-III), six to life (A-II), or 15 years to life (A-I).

9. See, e.g., Lynch (2001) for a rich case study illustrating the tensions between the intent and impact of structured sentencing laws that deny judges the latitude to weigh culpability in the context of complex life histories of even repeat drug offenders.

10. In this context, an endogenous factor is something that is grown from within the neighborhood, rather than being imposed from an external factor such as political policy or an economic shock.

11. The seven neighborhoods are Community Districts, 55 areas of the city that are heterogeneous administrative units responsible for funneling community views into citywide policy making. The seven areas are: the Lower East Side, the South Bronx, Harlem, Brownsville, Bedford-Stuyvesant, East New York, and South Jamaica. These are among the poorest areas of the city, according to the Community Profiles of the Department of City Planning. See: http://www.ci.nyc. ny.us/html/dcp/html/lucds/cdstart.html.

12. These data were provided by the New York State Division of Criminal Justice Services from its TRENDS database. In addition to address, each record included the arrest and conviction charge, prior arrests and convictions, and basic demographic information. See Fagan, West, and Holland (forthcoming) for details.

13. Each neighborhood comprises several census tracts. Jackson and Manbeck drew these boundaries based on an exhaustive process of interviews with local residents and their own observation of physical boundaries. The final sample of neighborhoods is 276, after elimination of areas with no population, such as parks and heavily industrialized areas. See www.infoshare.org for neighborhood indicators and boundary maps depicting these relatively new spatial units.

14. These analyses estimated the growth or recession of incarceration using mixed effects repeated measures Poisson regression models with an overdispersion parameter adjustment (Singer 1998; Littell et al. 1996). Since the dependent variable in each analysis is a count of incarceration events, each model is specified according to a Poisson distribution. Incarceration counts, offset by the area population, are estimated as a function of the social and economic characteristics of the area plus drug arrest activity (lagged by one wave). All effects except time are fixed; time is both a random effect to account for the panel structure of the data, and a fixed effect to account for the specific year within the panel. The latter estimation is important because of specific period effects nested in the model, including the sharp increase and decline in several of the predictors (especially crime) over the panel. Time is specified in three ways. First, in order to determine the direct influence of the years comprising the study, time is treated as a fixed effect. Second, variation between spatial units (precincts, neighborhoods) over time is estimated by treating time as random effect and interacting it with each of the predictors. Finally, variation within tracts over time is captured using time as a repeated measure. These analyses used a first order autoregressive

covariance structure to estimate within-unit change over time. All models were run in using the GLIMMIX macro in the SAS Generalized Linear Model procedure (Singer 1998). Details of the modeling procedure are discussed in Fagan, West, and Holland (forthcoming).

15. Felony arrest rates were obtained from a different data source than were the drug arrests. Drug arrests were obtained from the state Division of Criminal Justice Services and the residence of the arrestee was geocoded and assigned to a precinct or neighborhood. Felony arrest rates were obtained from the New York City Police Department, and residential addresses were not available from these archives.

16. See Fagan, West, and Holland (forthcoming) for details.

17. Throughout the 1990s, police in New York and several other cities targeted public housing for more intensive drug enforcement (Popkin et al. 2000), financed by the federal government's Drug Elimination Program. In New York, beginning in 1990, this program channeled approximately $35 million per year to the New York City Housing Authority, about half of which went to the Police Department's Operation Safe Homes (OSH). OSH, in turn, used these funds almost exclusively to expand drug enforcement in public housing, using the same tactics that characterized earlier street-level enforcement strategies such as TNT.

18. Beginning in 1994, the New York City Police Department launched a computerized crime mapping system, COMPSTAT (Bratton and Knobler 1998). Crime data before that date cannot be located to specific addresses other than through manual geocoding of complaint and arrest records, or manual coding of the records of arrestees. Even after the launch of COMPSTAT, these data were unavailable for research purposes, but were used internally for strategic analysis of enforcement practices. One reason is that the spatial coordinates were obtained only for the initial crime complaint, which often was unverified at the time it was incorporated into the database. NYPD officials were reluctant to release these data, since many of the complaints had not been investigated. For example, a complaint of a gunshot might turn out on investigation to be a car backfiring. Or a burglary could simply be a missing personal item that was later recovered. Once verified, complaints were entered into the city's crime counts, but for unstated reasons, the geographical coordinates of the crime location were not carried forward or aggregated.

19. This is not a recent or strictly American phenomenon. From London data in the nineteenth century, Hagan and Palloni (1990) show that incarceration tends to complicate efforts of ex-offenders to forge social linkages to legal work, increasing their chances of further incarceration.

20. Holzer, Raphael, and Stoll, analyzing data from a survey of employers, show that:

[h]igh criminal conviction rates among certain sub-groups of the population may indirectly affect the labor market prospects of members of that population who do not have criminal histories. When information is imperfect, employers are likely to infer the likelihood of a past criminal conviction based on such traits as gender, race, and age. To the extent that employers

are reluctant to hire workers with criminal histories, employers may statistically discriminate against individuals from demographic groups with high incarceration rates. Under such circumstances, the effect of employer-initiated criminal background checks on the hiring of groups with disproportionately high rates of past criminal convictions is theoretically ambiguous. (p. 1)

21. See also Paternoster et al. (1997), who showed that rearrest rates for domestic violence were lowest among offenders who rated their handling by police as procedurally fair.

22. In New York, state legislators and the governor received large campaign contributions from private corrections contractors, they are provided personal services such as chauffeurs and are assigned campaign workers (from the contractors' payrolls) for their reelection campaigns (Levy 2003). These contractors, such as the Correctional Services Corporation (CSC), currently have contracts of $22 million to operate adult correctional facilities for the State of New York. According to the *New York Times* report, approximately $30,000 in campaign contributions were given to the Republican State Committee both by CSC and private contributions made by CSC on behalf of its employees. In addition to gifts, campaign contributions, and logistical support, several state legislators living in New York City received free transportation back and forth to the state capital in Albany, approximately 150 miles from the city, in vans used by corrections officers to shuttle prisoners back and forth to court hearings in the city. In exchange for these services, letters were written in 1997–98, e.g., to the Governor's Office requesting that the contracts to CCA be continued or expanded. See also Dyer (2000).

References

Anderson, Elijah. 1999. *The Code of the Street: Decency, Violence and the Moral Life of the Inner City*. New York: Norton.

Belenko, Steven. 1993. *Crack and the Evolution of Anti-Drug Policy*. Westport, Conn.: Greenwood.

Blumstein, Alfred, and Allen J. Beck. 1999. "Population Growth in U.S. Prisons, 1980–1996." In *Prisons, Crime and Justice: A Review of Research,* vol. 26, ed. Michael Tonry and Joan Petersilia. Chicago: University of Chicago Press.

Bonzcar, Thomas P., and Allen J. Beck. 1997. *Lifetime Likelihood of Going to State or Federal Prison*. Bureau of Justice Statistics Bulletin, NCJ 160092. Washington, D.C.: U.S. Department of Justice.

Bratton, William, and Peter Knobler. 1998. *Turnaround: How America's Top Cop Reversed the Crime Epidemic*. New York: Random House.

Bureau of Justice Statistics. 1996. "Correctional Populations in the United States, 1995." NCJ 163916. Washington, D.C.: U.S. Department of Justice.

———. 1999. "Correctional Populations in the United States." NCJ 170013. Washington, D.C.: U.S. Department of Justice.

———. 2002. "Prisoners in 2001." NCJ 195189. Washington, D.C.: U.S. Department of Justice.

Bursik, Robert J., Jr., and Harold G. Grasmick. 1993. *Neighborhood and Crime: The Dimensions of Effective Community Control*. New York: Lexington Books.

Clear, Todd R., Dina R. Rose, and Judith A. Ryder. 2001. "Incarceration and the Community: The Problem of Removing and Returning Offenders." *Crime and Delinquency* 47:335–351.

Clear, Todd R., Dina R. Rose, Elin Waring, and Kristen Scully. 2003. "Coercive Mobility and Crime: A Preliminary Examination of Concentrated Incarceration and Social Disorganization." *Justice Quarterly* 20:33–64.

Clines, Francis X. 1992. "Ex-inmates Urge Return to Areas of Crime to Help." *New York Times*, December 23, at A1.

Cohen, Jacqueline, and Jose Canela-Cacho. 1994. "Incarceration and Violent Crime." In *Understanding and Preventing Violence*, vol. 4, ed. Albert J. Reiss, Jr. and Jeffrey A. Roth. Washington, D.C.: National Academy Press.

Crutchfield, Robert D., and Susan R. Pitchford. 1997. "Work and Crime: The Effects of Labor Stratification." *Social Forces* 76:93–118.

Curtis, Richard. 1998. "The Improbable Transformation of Inner-City Neighborhoods: Crime, Violence, Drugs and Youth in the 1990s." *Journal of Criminal Law and Criminology* 88:1223–1257.

DeGiovanni, Frank F., and Lorraine C. Minnite. 1991. "Patterns of Neighborhood Change." In *Dual City: Restructuring New York*, ed. John H. Mollenkopf and Manuel Castells. New York: Russell Sage Foundation Press.

Donnino, William C. 1989. "Practice Commentaries." In *McKinney's New York Penal Law*. New York: West Publishing.

Dyer, Joel. 2000. *The Perpetual Prisoner Machine: How America Profits from Crime*. Boulder, Colo.: Westview Press.

Edin, Katherine, and Laura Lein. 1997. "Work, Welfare and Single Mothers' Economic Survival Strategies." *American Sociological Review* 602:253–266.

Fagan, Jeffrey, 2002. "Law, Social Science and Racial Profiling." *Justice Research and Policy* 4:104–129.

Fagan, Jeffrey, and Ko-lin Chin. 1989. "Initiation into Crack and Cocaine: A Tale of Two Epidemics." *Contemporary Drug Problems* 16:579–618.

Fagan, Jeffrey, and Garth Davies. 2000. "Street Stops and Broken Windows: *Terry*, Race and Disorder in New York City." *Fordham Urban Law Journal* 28:457–504.

Fagan, Jeffrey, and Richard B. Freeman. 1999. "Crime and Work." In *Crime and Justice: A Review of Research*, vol. 25, ed. Michael Tonry. Chicago: University of Chicago Press.

Fagan, Jeffrey, Jan Holland, Garth Davies, and Tamara Dumanovsky. 2003. "Drug Control in Public Housing: The Crime Control Returns of the Drug Elimination Program." Final Report, Grant 034898 from the Substance Abuse Policy Research Program, Robert Wood Johnson Foundation. New York: Columbia University, Mailman School of Public Health.

Fagan, Jeffrey, and Tracey Meares. Forthcoming. "Punishment, Deterrence and Social Control: The Paradox of Punishment in Minority Communities." *Punishment and Society*.

Fagan, Jeffrey, Valerie West, and Jan Holland. Forthcoming. "Reciprocal Effects of Crime and Incarceration in New York City Neighborhoods." *Fordham Urban Law Journal.*

Fagan, Jeffrey, Franklin E. Zimring, and June Kim. 1998. "Declining Homicide in New York: A Tale of Two Trends." *Journal of Criminal Law and Criminology* 88:1277–1324.

Fletcher, George. 1999. "Disenfranchisement as Punishment: Reflections on the Racial Use of Infamia." *U.C.L.A. Law Review* 46:1895–2005.

Flynn, Kevin, and William Rashbaum. 2003. "As a Force Cuts Back, How Small Is Too Small?" *New York Times,* January 12, at B1.

Garfinkel, Irwin, Sara MacLanahan, and Thomas L. Hanson. 1998. "A Patchwork Portrait of Non-Resident Fathers." Working Paper no. 98–25. Princeton: Princeton University.

Granovetter, Mark. 1973. "The Strength of Weak Ties." *American Journal of Sociology* 78:1360–1380.

———. 1974. *Getting a Job: A Study of Contracts and Careers.* Cambridge, Mass.: Harvard University Press.

Hagan, John. 1993. "The Social Embeddedness of Crime and Unemployment." *Criminology* 31:465–492.

Hagan, John, and Ronit Dinovitzer. 1999. "Collateral Consequences of Imprisonment for Children, Communities, and Prisoners." In *Prisons, Crime and Justice: A Review of Research,* vol. 26, ed. Michael Tonry and Joan Petersilia. Chicago: University of Chicago Press.

Hagan, John, and Alberto Palloni. 1990. "The Social Reproduction of a Criminal Class in Working Class London, circa 1950–80." *American Journal of Sociology* 96:265–299.

Hagan, John, and Blair Wheaton. 1993. "The Search for Adolescent Role Exits and the Transition to Adulthood." *Social Forces* 71:955–980.

Hagedorn, John. 1998. "Gang Violence in the Post-Industrial Era." In *Youth Violence, Crime and Justice: A Review of Research,* vol. 24, ed. Michael Tonry and Mark Moore. Chicago: University of Chicago Press.

Herman, Susan. 2000. "Measuring Culpability by Measuring Drugs? Three Reasons to Re-evaluate the Rockefeller Drug Laws." *Albany Law Review* 63:778–798.

Holzer, Harry, Steven Raphael, and Michael Stoll. 2001. *Perceived Criminality: Criminal Background Checks and the Racial Hiring Practices of Employers.* JCPR Working Paper 295. Chicago: Joint Center for Poverty Research, Northwestern University/University of Chicago.

Irwin, John. 1970. *The Felon.* Englewood Cliffs, N.J.: Prentice-Hall.

Irwin, John, and James Austin. 1994. *It's about Time.* Belmont, Calif.: Wadsworth Press.

Jackson, Kenneth, and John Manbeck. 1998. *The Neighborhoods of Brooklyn.* New Haven: Yale University Press.

Karmen, Andrew. 2000. *New York Murder Mystery.* New York: New York University Press.

Kelling, George, and William Souza, Jr. 2001. *Do Police Matter? An Analysis of the Impact of New York City's Police Reforms*. New York: Manhattan Institute.

Kirschenman, Joleen, and Kathryn M. Neckerman. 1991. "We'd Love to Hire Them, But . . . : The Meaning of Race for Employers." In *The Urban Underclass*, ed. Christopher Jencks and Paul E. Peterson. Washington, D.C.: Brookings Institution.

LeBlanc, Adrian Nicole. 2003. *Random Family*. New York: Scribner.

Letwin, Michael Z. 1990. "Report from the Front Line: The Bennett Plan, Street-Level Drug Enforcement in New York City, and the Legalization Debate." *Hofstra Law Review* 18:795–835.

Levy, Clifford J. 2003. "Prison Company's Courtship Provokes New York's Scrutiny." *New York Times*, February 17, at A1.

Littell, R. C., G. A. Milliken, W. S. Stroup, and R. D. Wolfinger. 1996. *SAS System for Mixed Models*. Cary, N.C.: SAS Institute.

Livingston, Debra. 1997. "Police Discretion and the Quality of Life in Public Places: Courts, Communities, and the New Policing." *Columbia Law Review* 97:551–649.

Lynch, Gerard E. 2001. "Sentencing Eddie." *Journal of Criminal Law and Criminology* 91:547–566.

Lynch, James P., and William J. Sabol. 2002. "Assessing the Longer-Run Consequences of Incarceration: Effects on Families and Employment." In *Crime Control and Criminal Justice: The Delicate Balance*, ed. D. F. Hawkins, Samuel Myers, and R. Stone. Westport, Conn.: Greenwood.

MacLanahan, Sara, and Larry Bumpass. 1998. "Intergenerational Consequences of Family Disruption." *American Journal of Sociology* 94:130–152.

MacLanahan, Sara, and Gary Sandefur. 1994. *Growing Up with a Single Parent: What Hurts, What Helps*. Cambridge, Mass.: Harvard University Press.

Mauer, Marc. 2000. *Race to Incarcerate*. New York: New Press.

Moore, Joan W. 1996. "Bearing the Burden: How Incarceration Policies Weaken Inner-City Communities." In *The Unintended Consequences of Incarceration*, ed. Karen Fulbright. New York: Vera Institute of Justice.

Morenoff, Jeffrey D., Robert J. Sampson, and Stephen W. Raudenbush. 2001. "Neighborhood Equality, Collective Efficacy, and the Spatial Dynamics of Urban Violence." *Criminology* 39:517–558.

Nagin, Daniel. 1999. "Criminal Deterrence Research at the Outset of the Twenty-First Century." In *Crime and Justice: A Review of Research*, vol. 25, ed. Michael Tonry. Chicago: University of Chicago Press.

Nagin, Daniel, and Joel Waldfogel. 1998. "The Effect of Conviction on Income through the Life Cycle." *International Review of Law and Economics* 18:25–40.

Nakdai, Lisa R. 2001. "Are New York's Rockefeller Drug Laws Killing the Messenger for the Sake of the Message?" *Hofstra Law Review* 30:557–587.

New York City, Department of Correction (DOC). Online data report. Available: New York State, Division of Criminal Justice Services (DCJS). Criminal Justice Indicators. Online data reports. Available: http://criminaljustice.state.ny.us/crimnet/ojsa/areastat/areast.htm.

Paternoster, Raymond, Lawrence Sherman, Bobby Brame, et al. 1997. "Do Fair Procedures Matter? The Effect of Procedural Justice on Spouse Assault." *Law and Society Review* 31:163–197.

Petersilia, Joan. 1999. "Parole and Prisoner Re-Entry in the United States." In *Prisons, Crime and Justice: A Review of Research,* vol. 26, ed. Michael Tonry and Joan Petersilia. Chicago: University of Chicago Press.

Popkin, Susan J., Victoria E. Gwiasda, Lynn M. Olson, and Dennis P. Rosenbaum. 2000. *The Hidden War: Crime and the Tragedy of Public Housing in Chicago.* New Brunswick, N.J.: Rutgers University Press.

Rashbaum, William. 2000. "Police Suspend Extra Patrols for 10 Days." *New York Times,* October 10, at B1.

Rose, Dina R., and Todd R. Clear. 1998. "Incarceration, Social Capital and Crime: Examining the Unintended Consequences of Incarceration." *Criminology* 36: 441–479.

Rosen, Jeffrey. 2000. "Excessive Force: Why Patrick Dorismond Didn't Have to Die," *New Republic,* April 10.

Sampson, Robert J., and Jacqueline Cohen. 1988. "Deterrent Effects of the Police on Crime: A Replication and Theoretical Extension." *Law and Society Review* 22:163–189.

Sampson, Robert J., and John H. Laub. 1994. "Urban Poverty and the Family Context of Delinquency: A New Look at Structure and Process in a Classic Study." *Child Development* 65:523–539.

———. 2001. "Understanding Desistance from Crime." In *Crime and Justice: A Review of Research*, vol. 28, ed. Michael Tonry. Chicago: University of Chicago Press.

Sampson, Robert J., Jeffrey D. Morenoff, and Thomas Ganon-Rowley. 2002. "Assessing 'Neighborhood Effects': Social Processes and New Directions in Research." *Annual Review of Sociology* 28:443–478.

Sampson, Robert J., Stephen W. Raudenbush, and Felton Earls. 1997. "Neighborhoods and Violent Crime: A Multilevel Model of Collective Efficacy." *Science* 277:918–924.

Sanchez-Jankowski, Martin. 1991. *Islands in the Street: Gangs and American Urban Society.* Berkeley: University of California Press.

Schwartz, Richard D., and Jerome H. Skolnick. 1962. "Two Studies of Legal Stigma." *Social Problems* 10:133–142.

Sherman, Lawrence. 1993. "Defiance, Deterrence, and Irrelevance: A Theory of the Criminal Sanction." *Journal of Research in Crime and Delinquency* 30:445–473.

Simon, Jonathan. 1993. *Poor Discipline: Parole and the Social Control of the Underclass, 1890–1990.* Chicago: University of Chicago Press.

Singer, Judith. 1998. "Using SAS PROC MIXED to Fit Multilevel Models, Hierarchical Models, and Individual Growth Models." *Journal of Educational and Behavioral Statistics* 24(4):322–354.

Smith, Douglas A. 1986. "The Neighborhood Contexts of Police Behavior." In *Communities and Crime*, ed. Albert J. Reiss, Jr. and Michael Tonry. Chicago: University of Chicago Press.

Sullivan, Mercer. 1989. *Getting Paid*. Ithaca, N.Y.: Cornell University Press.

Sviridoff, Michele, Susan Sadd, Richard Curtis, Randolph Grinc, and Michael E. Smith. 1992. "The Neighborhood Effects of Street-Level Drug Enforcement: Tactical Narcotics Teams in New York." Final Report Grant #89-IJ-CX-0056, National Institute of Justice. New York: Vera Institute of Justice.

Tonry, Michael. 1995. *Malign Neglect: Race, Crime, and Punishment in America.* New York: Oxford University Press.

Tonry, Michael, and Joan Petersilia. 1999. "American Prisons at the Beginning of the Twenty First Century." In *Prisons, Crime and Justice: A Review of Research,* vol. 26, ed. Michael Tonry and Joan Petersilia. Chicago: University of Chicago Press.

Tyler, Tom R. 1990. *Why People Obey the Law.* New Haven: Yalue University Press.

Tyler, Tom R., and Yuen J. Huo. 2002. *Trust in the Law: Encouraging Public Cooperation with the Police and Courts.* New York: Russell Sage Foundation.

Uggen, Christopher. 2000. "Work as a Turning Point in the Life Course of Criminals: A Duration Model of Age, Employment and Recidivism." *American Sociological Review* 65:529–546.

Uggen, Christopher, and Jeff Manza. 2002. "Democratic Contraction? Political Consequences of Felon Disenfranchisement in the United States." *American Sociological Review* 67:777–803.

U.S. Dept. of Justice, Bureau of Justice Statistics. National Corrections Reporting Program, 1985, 1990, and 1996: United States [computer file]. Conducted by U.S. Dept. of Commerce, Bureau of the Census. ICPSR ed. Ann Arbor, Mich.: Inter-university Consortium for Political and Social Research [producer and distributor].

Vigil, Janes Diego. 1988. *Barrio Gangs: Street Life and Identity in Southern California.* Austin: University of Texas.

Western, Bruce. 2002. "The Impact of Incarceration on Wage Mobility and Inequality." *American Sociological Review* 67:526–546.

Western, Bruce, Jeffrey R. Kling, and David F. Weiman. 2001. "The Labor Market Consequences of Incarceration." *Crime and Delinquency* 47:410–427.

Wilson, William J. 1996. *When Work Disappears: The World of the New Urban Poor.* New York: Knopf.

Zimmer, Lynn. 1987. "Operation Pressure Point: The Disruption of Street-Level Drug Trade on New York's Lower East Side." New York: Center for Crime and Justice, New York University School of Law.

3

Restoring Rationality in Punishment Policy

Alfred Blumstein

One of the dominant features of Norval Morris's concerns over his entire professional career was seeking ways to maintain a level of reasonableness and rationality in the punishment process. This is clearly reflected in his *The Honest Politician's Guide to Crime Control* (1970) with Gordon Hawkins. His volume with Michael Tonry, *Between Prison and Probation: Intermediate Punishments in a Rational Sentencing System* (1990), called attention to the many opportunities possible with community-based treatment. Given the punitive context of the times, they obviously felt that they had to label such treatments as "punishment" in order to make it politically acceptable for their proposals to be implemented. Yet however much they worked at it, intermediate punishments—to create meaningful alternatives between the intensity of prison and the extreme casualness of most probation—still have a hard time getting much attention in most jurisdictions. Perhaps states facing severe budget problems will begin to give them more attention in the near future.

There is unbounded potential for increases in punishment. The scope of the criminal law is sufficiently broad that almost everybody violates some aspect of it at some time in their lives; and a reasonable number of people, especially when they are young, violate some serious aspects with high frequency. The fundamental challenge to a just society is finding ways to moderate the imposition of punishment for those guilty of the most serious violations and to maintain a range of sanctions from warnings to supervised probation with various intensities of supervision along with support to direct their behavior into the most socially useful directions. Incarceration should be seen as a last resort, for those who engage in the most serious acts and who cannot be trusted to function in the community. All punishments should be seen as limited, to control the offending individual for a limited period of time, all the while trying to help him into a more civil and productive mode. This limitation has been particularly difficult to foster in the political environment of the last quarter century.

During the past 25 years the United States more than quadrupled its incarceration rate. That quadrupling is particularly astonishing when seen in light of the impressive stability and trendlessness of the incarceration rate that prevailed from at least the mid-1920s to the mid-1970s. If this were attributable to a massive increase in violent crime, then that growth might be understandable as a response to contain that epidemic. If it was merely an increase in punitiveness, the question arises of what political forces were at work to generate that major shift.

Those political forces first showed themselves when the leading edge of the post–World War II baby boom entered their high-crime teenage years in the early 1960s. This shift brought criminal justice policy vigorously into the political arena, where there was a strong payoff to those who displayed their toughness and a real vulnerability of those who could be labeled "soft on crime." These political developments were important factors contributing to the growth in incarceration.

They were accompanied by a growing public concern over the problems of drug abuse, especially as it might affect their children. That concern was also accompanied by a political response that turned to the only approach that seemed to satiate public pressure—tougher sanction policies. This assumed that the problem of drug abuse could be effectively addressed through massive incarceration of all drug sellers and ignored the resilience of the drug markets in responding to the articulated demand.

There are some recent indications that the nation seems to be moving away from an often-mindless punitiveness toward more rational considerations in its punishment policies. To some extent, this is facilitated by the decrease in crime rates and the associated loosening of public pressure in the political arena to "do something" about crime. This is most evident in the revision to thinking about incarceration as the first choice in dealing with the drug problem and growing attention to the consideration of treatment as more appropriate. There is even some movement to repeal the mandatory-minimum sentencing laws that were enacted in response to the political demand for toughness.

Even more important and influential than the rethinking of excessive policies has been the severe revenue shortfall confronting virtually all the states. As they face the requirements for balancing their budgets, attention is quickly directed at the corrections budgets, which had been the areas of major growth during the previous two decades. That could well be the place to find reductions. The interplay of these factors when reconsidering the excesses of the past and balancing their budgets may offer some hope that U.S. incarceration policy and practice may be moving toward restoring rationality.

In this essay, I explore the reasons for the shift toward greater punitiveness over the past quarter century and consider the degree to which we are seeing a diminution in that trend and an associated reemergence of rationality in the punishment process. That requires looking at factors in the crime situation and how they interact with crime policy. Inevitably, that leads to some policy implications that might enhance the rationality of the process.

Growth of Incarceration over the Past 25 Years

The Prior Period of Stability

It is widely recognized that incarceration in the United States has grown rapidly over the past 25 years, but it is not widely recognized outside the criminological community how much of a departure that has been from a prior period of striking stability. This transition is displayed in figure 3.1, the time series of the U.S. incarceration rate from 1925 to 2001. The incarceration rate was strikingly stable and trendless from 1925 to 1975. The rate adhered very closely to the mean of about 110 prisoners in state and federal prisons per 100,000 total U.S. population. For the

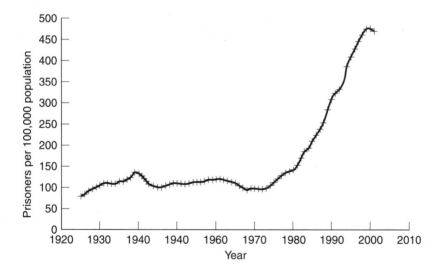

Fig. 3.1 Growth in U.S. incarceration rate.

Source: Cahalan and Beck et al., Bureau of Justice Statistics.

great majority of this period, the rate stayed closely within one standard deviation of 11, just 10 percent of the mean rate. The most significant deviation (after the early years of the series, which started in 1925 with a rate of 79 per 100,000) was in the late 1930s, when the Great Depression gave rise to a maximum deviation at 137 per 100,000 in 1939. This was followed by a rapid decline during World War II, when the nation had much better uses for its young men of prison age, and the incarceration rate dipped to a low of 100 (still well within one standard deviation of the mean rate) in 1945.

The only other deviation was in the late 1960s when the move to community-based treatment and "prison reform" led to a dip to a rate of 94 in 1968. This low rate could also be partly a consequence of the small cohort sizes in the prime imprisonment years at that time as a result of the low number of births in the later depression years and the wartime years.[1]

In the early 1970s, I was struck by the flatness of this curve, by its trendlessness, and by what I presumed were some sort of social homeostatic forces that kept this process in reasonable balance. The fact that a similar pattern was displayed in Norway over an even longer period (1880 to 1964) albeit at a lower rate (52.5 per 100,000 with a standard deviation of 8.2), and in other Scandinavian countries as well, strengthened the conviction that there must be some kind of stabilizing process at work and led to a search for explanation and interpretation. I explored these issues with Jacqueline Cohen in an essay entitled "A Theory of the Stability of Punishment" (Blumstein and Cohen 1973).

The homeostatic hypothesis, in short, recognizes the possibility that crime rates would be climbing and falling depending on a wide variety of social conditions that were far less amenable to control than would be the case with prison populations. The proposed mechanism was one of shifting thresholds. As crime rates went up, the threshold of the seriousness of the offense or of the offender's prior criminal history (or other attributes that might enter into sentencing decisions) would be raised in order to avoid imposing an excessive burden on the prison system. This recognized a degree of common interest that was shared by judges and prosecutors (who were generally far more subservient to judges in those days). With indeterminate sentences (one year to life was not uncommon in states like California), parole boards had a broad range of discretion over whom they released into the community. They, too, could shift thresholds on their readiness to tolerate risk in the released offenders if necessary to accelerate departures of inmates when admissions increased, and thus avoid overcrowding the state's prisons.

The process could also work similarly when crime rates were decreasing. If crime rates were to decline appreciably, then behaviors that were complained about but tolerated would become candidates for passing new laws or enforcing old laws more aggressively (e.g., laws prohibiting prostitution or drunk driving).

This is a variation on the Durkheim argument that *crime* (rather than punishment) is a natural—and even in some sense desirable—aspect of society, and that societies without crime will seek to redefine certain behaviors as crimes partly to reinforce the norms in that society (Durkheim 1966). This is an argument that was developed in rich detail by Kai Erikson (1966) in *The Wayward Puritans*.

With a variety of other collaborators,[2] I pursued the issue to provide a more elaborate structure of the dynamics of the process that maintains a homeostatic relationship. Some of that work explored the stability phenomenon within individual states and the similarity across neighboring states of the nature of their individual incarceration rate time series.

The Period of Dramatic Growth

It is difficult from figure 3.1 to pinpoint a precise year in which the dramatic growth of the right-hand portion of the graph began, but it does appear to be in the period 1973 to 1975, but with significant acceleration beginning in 1981. Even the simplest examination of that figure would challenge any presumption of stability after 1980. The period between 1974 and 1980 might be argued as being within a reasonable range of the prior stable rate. But that would be reasonable only if the rate had turned down after 1980 instead of accelerating upward.

Many who have looked at figure 3.1 must question whether that dramatic change does more harm than it does good; the trend over the last 25 years must raise considerable concern about the political forces that gave rise to this dramatic growth in incarceration that had over 1.4 million people in state or federal prisons by the end of 2001 for an incarceration rate of 470 per 100,000 population, more than four times the previous rate of 110 (see Harrison and Beck 2002). When the number in local jails (630,000) (see Beck, Karberg, and Harrison 2002) is added, the total number of incarcerated persons is around 2 million in the United States, which now has the world's largest incarceration rate of over 700 per 100,000, finally surpassing Russia, which had been the long-time champion with a current incarceration rate of 665. Two-thirds of nations have rates under 150, and most countries in Western Europe have rates under 100 (see Walmsley 2002).

It is clear that whatever forces maintained the homeostatic process from the 1920s through the mid-1970s had been fractured by the mid-1970s and totally abandoned by 1980. Several factors have contributed to those changes. One important feature was the internal control maintained by the criminal justice system, largely outside the attention of the political environment. That isolation from political forces may be hard to imagine in the current environment, given the intensity of the public's anxiety about crime over the past few decades: it has usually been the primary concern and it is rarely absent from the top three. Thus, the managers within the system could work without much external interference to maintain the homeostatic level. If prisons were getting crowded, the parole authorities could be counted on to ease up on the release processes. The political insularity of the criminal justice system was shattered by the challenges of "crime in the streets" raised by Barry Goldwater in the 1964 presidential campaign. This brought concern about crime directly into the political arena, and it has stayed there ever since with varying degrees of intensity.

It is ironic that most of the initial attacks on insularity appear to have come from the liberal Left, which is generally hostile to any increase in punishment. But the Left provided the openings that were exploited by the conservative Right, which seems to treat punishment as a free good. The initial assault on the control by parole boards followed a succession of findings through the 1960s that reported on various kinds of experimental and quasi-experimental evaluations of correctional treatment alternatives. Most of these found a "null effect," or no difference between the innovation being tested and any other approach.[3] The accumulation of these null-effect results led to a clamor that "nothing works." The initial response from the Left to these findings argued that, since the correctional system could not claim to rehabilitate (then the reigning ideology of "corrections"), then one ought to intervene less in the lives of those convicted. An exemplar of this stance was Robison and Smith (1971), who made this reduced-intervention argument with particular vigor.

Such an argument was clearly in conflict with the view of the Right, whose perspective was endorsed more broadly by the public. At that time, in the early 1970s, crime rates were soaring significantly from the low rates characteristic of the early 1960s to the values that prevailed from the mid-1970s through the mid-1990s. That growth was attributable to a mixture of the arrival of the baby-boom cohorts (starting with the 1947 cohort, which reached age 15 in 1962 and 19 in 1966) into the peak crime ages of 15 to 19. That demographic shift gave rise to the crime growth that brought political attention to "crime in the streets." That growth in crime continued with the increasing cohort sizes until the largest cohorts (those born around 1960) began to recede from the high-crime ages after 1980. At that point, crime began to decline until a reversal in the mid-1980s brought about by drug markets and their crime consequences.

Those demographic shifts were exacerbated by the disruptions and challenges to forces of authority that characterized the 1960s. The most salient challenges were associated with the civil rights struggles in the early 1960s and the protests against the Vietnam War in the late 1960s and early 1970s. The effects of the changing demographic composition (more people in the high-crime ages) were augmented also by the contextual effect of larger cohort sizes, which increased even the age-specific crime rates within the high-crime ages. Both the composition and the contextual effects contributed to higher aggregate crime rates.

With crime an increasing concern to the general public and with the traditional crime-control methods and prison populations maintained in a stable mode by the now discredited "corrections" functionaries, the policy issues were fully ripe for major reconsideration. There was little doubt that the arguments for punitiveness would prevail. An article entitled "Lock 'Em Up" by James Q. Wilson (1975) articulated the basic incapacitation argument that appealed to the general public—an offender in prison cannot be committing the crimes in the community that he might have committed if he were free.

The deterrence argument also has a natural appeal to legislatures and to the middle-class perception generally. With the growth of public concern about crime, there followed an intense battle among political figures to show who was being more "tough" on offenders and a corresponding scramble for political opportunities to label their opponents "soft" on crime. This battle emerged along with the growing use of the 30-second TV sound bite as a central feature of political campaigns. It was much easier to incorporate a slamming prison-cell door into one of those commercials than to discuss the complex trade-offs surrounding incarceration, its incapacitative effects, its opportunity costs, and its potentially criminogenic effects on the prisoner.

Aside from its symbolic nature, this battle to be the toughest candidate seems to be based largely on a presumption of the deterrent effectiveness of toughness. The underlying belief is that increasing the threat of criminal sanctions (usually articulated in terms of sentence severity) has a powerful influence in inhibiting criminal activity. While there is little doubt that deterrence works to some degree, there must be an important difference between its effectiveness in conventional middle-class populations—who have so much to lose from the condemnation and relative deprivation associated with a prison sentence—compared to the lower-class populations that comprise the great majority of offenders who engage in the

crimes that lead to imprisonment. The political effectiveness of the toughness stance results from the middle-class voters projecting their own
response to the deterrent threat onto the crime-committing population.
In the heat of a political campaign, it must be quite difficult to appre-
ciate that the potential offenders might not respond similarly. The voters
recognize that the threat of imprisonment would keep *them* from committing crimes, and so it should work comparably with others who are
much more likely to commit crimes. In their view, if current sanctions
are not working, then they should be increased in order to cross a response threshold. The threshold for people who do commit crimes would
probably be somewhat higher, but not necessarily out of reach. This
inevitably leads to a series of escalations of punitiveness: as each increment
fails to make a major dent in the crime rate, then that calls for a further
increment.

It does not seem to enter the public debate that the rational weighing
of costs and benefits—a salient characteristic of middle-class behavior—is
not necessarily characteristic of everyone's decision to engage in a criminal
offense. Or that actions that could lead to gaining "respect"[4] would have
great saliency to some people, enough to warrant risking their lives, let
alone risking imprisonment. Or that the loss in personal well-being (or
"disutility" in terms of the cost-benefit calculation) associated with imprisonment is considerably greater for a person who is employed and lives
with his family than it is for an unemployed or homeless person with no
such stable attachments. Indeed, for some, the opportunity for reasonable
room and board in prison may not be much worse than life on the streets,
especially if one has some protective affiliates in prison who will serve
as a shield against the predators that make prison life so threatening to
many.

The attempts to curry favor with the electorate also lead to efforts to
point with alarm to individual cases where an offender who committed
a serious crime was let out on probation or with a surprisingly small
sentence. Given the diversity of judges, their values, and the variety of
variables that they take into account, it is not surprising that such cases
can readily be found in any jurisdiction. Pointing to such errors of commission[5] usually leads to a further call for toughness in limiting the opportunity to release a prisoner. It also gives rise to a cry for "mandatory-
minimum" legislation that requires judges to sentence all offenders
convicted of a particular offense specified by the statute to at least the
specified minimum sentence, regardless of whatever mitigating circumstances might be present in the case.

Another means by which the conservative perspective has come to hold
greater sway in the development of punishment policy also derives from

the generally liberal concern about "disparity." Disparity occurs when two offenders equally placed (the idealized case where the two crimes are identical and the offenders' prior record and other relevant attributes are identical) receive different punishments, perhaps because they came from different jurisdictions (urban areas tend to be more lenient than rural areas for the same offense) or because they face judges who use different criteria. The pressure for reducing disparity gave rise in some places (most notably California) to determinate sentencing laws, which tried to specify by statute a sentence to be associated with each of the major offense categories. Of course, given the diversity of burglaries and the diversity of prior records and other relevant offender characteristics, this introduced its own form of disparity by bringing cases that were unlike into the same box. It also provided an opportunity for political pressure toward greater severity to ratchet up the prescribed sentence for any particular offense. This could happen, for example, when a particularly heinous version of the offense was reported in the newspaper headlines—or with much greater impact, on the evening television news. There would then follow a rush by legislators to get their bills into the hopper calling for an increase in the prescribed or mandatory-minimum sentence for that generic offense class. That would then apply also to even the most benign version of that offense class.

This introduction of determinate sentences was also usually associated with elimination of the parole release function and the parole release decision in particular. Parole boards, charged with making the release decision within the bounds of the indeterminate sentences prescribed by the judges, were branded as lenient evildoers fully as much as judges were. The public could always be reminded that they made a decision that in retrospect was wrong when a released prisoner recidivated by committing a serious felony.[6]

Along with the scapegoating of judges or parole boards as being too "lenient" came the legislative innovation of mandatory-minimum sentencing laws. If it could be shown that an offender put on probation (for a first offense with mitigating circumstances, say) committed a serious crime while on probation, then that was taken as proof of judges' leniency, and so the legislature would require that all such offenders would have to go to prison for at least the prescribed minimum sentence. This would then apply to all offenders convicted of the specified crime, regardless of the mitigating circumstances; only the prosecutor, with discretion over the charges filed, could make any accommodation. There may be good reason to suspect that people sentenced under mandatory-minimum sentencing laws do not have appreciably more serious prior records than others sent to prison for the same offense.

These mandatory-minimum sentences started as low as one year in the 1970s (or even 30 days for drunk-driving convictions) and have escalated since then to values as high as 10 years or more for individual convictions, most notoriously for drug offenses. The large majority of people sentenced to prison under mandatory-minimum laws are those sentenced for drug offenses. These are the offenses for which prison is least appropriate in terms of incapacitation (because someone else will replace that drug seller as long as the demand persists and as long as there is a willing queue of replacement candidates for the position) as well as from the viewpoint of deterrence (since those driven out of the business by the threat of extremely high sanctions will also be replaced by others whose disutility for prison may be lower or whose view of other forms of gainful economic activity is less attractive). [7]

If the intention is less utilitarian and more retributive, even then the hostility to the drug seller seems largely to have abated in the general public. The evil represented by the leading character in the film, *The Man with the Golden Arm,* no longer seems to represent the general public's view of a drug seller, especially at the retail level on the street. Rather, the public has come to view the seller as one more individual willing to take the risks in order to pursue that line of economic activity, either for inevitably small economic gain, merely for sustenance, or—most likely—because his own drug addiction prevents him from earning income in the legitimate economy.

It was undoubtedly recognition of the futility and the wastefulness of massive incarceration for drug offenses that caused California voters to endorse Proposition 36[8] in 2000 by a 61 percent majority. A similar initiative was passed in Arizona and a number of other states have passed or are considering similar policies. Despite all of the shortcomings of incarceration for drug offenses, by the end of 2001, 54 percent of federal prisoners and 21 percent of state prisoners were there on a drug charge.[9] Many of them are first-time offenders serving time under a mandatory-minimum sentence.

One particularly distressing example of a misplaced mandatory-minimum sentencing rule is the disparity in the federal sentencing guidelines (based on the mandatory-minimum provisions of the Anti-Drug Abuse Act of 1986) for crack compared to powder cocaine. A person gets a five-year mandatory-minimum sentence if convicted for dealing with 500 grams of powder and would receive the same sentence for only five grams of crack. What makes this 100:1 disparity particularly troublesome is that crack markets are operated predominantly by blacks and cocaine markets are operated primarily by whites and Hispanics. Thus, this stark difference conveys a strong sense of racial discrimination and represents a profound challenge to the legitimacy of the criminal justice system. The rationale for the original disparity may have been attributed to differences in the violence associated with the marketing of these respective drugs at the time of initial enactment in the mid-1980s, when crack was a relatively new illegal drug and had engendered vigorous competition in the street markets. Those differences, however, have largely diminished as a result of changes in the nature of the markets as the crack markets have matured and as the demand by new users has declined considerably. Certainly the nature of the markets has been much more relevant than any differences between the drugs in terms of their chemical composition or their pharmacological effects. The evolution of the crack markets has resulted in a significantly lower level of violence today than that which characterized their early years. Also, it seems much more rational to use sentencing enhancements to punish those individuals who use violence regardless of the drug they are dealing with than to base the sentencing difference on the chemical itself. Similarly, enhancements should be considered to account for an offender's role in the distribution hierarchy; if that were done, then federal crack offenders would be treated even more leniently than powder-cocaine offenders, since the former are far more often low-level street dealers than the "king pins" at whom federal legislation is ostensibly targeted.

The latest weapon in the armamentarium of those intent on greater use of incarceration is the "Three Strikes and You're Out" laws. The first of these was passed by public referendum in Washington State in 1993, subsequently in California and a large number of other states. A three-strikes provision was also included in the federal Violent Crime Control and Law Enforcement Act of 1994. Variants of this principle (mandatory life imprisonment without parole for conviction of a third "strike"—a third conviction for one of a set of specified serious offenses) somehow built on the presumption that this baseball metaphor was particularly appropriate for sentencing policy.

It is not clear to what extent the three-strikes laws are intended to achieve retribution or crime control. If the latter, it would be through deterrence and incapacitation. For either, this is a relatively inefficient means for achieving those effects. If focused on the most serious violent felonies, the offender with two prior violent convictions should already be facing a long sentence, and it is not clear how much more deterrent effect will be added by proposing that this be extended to a life sentence. In terms of incapacitation, the laws keep people in prison well after their active criminal careers have ended—very likely by age 50, almost certainly by age 60. If the choice arises about whom to release—a currently violent offender not under such a mandatory law and an aging one imprisoned under a three-strikes law—the system would have to release the currently serious offender, obviously a choice that contradicts any crime-control objective. Once such laws are passed, even when restricted to the most serious offenses, they then provide a platform for expanding the scope of offenses that can be counted as "strikes." Indeed, the federal law initially was confined to serious violent felonies, but ended up permitting drug convictions to be counted as one of the strikes.

Much of the growth in the prison populations since 1980 is attributable to the increase in drug offenders, who comprised only about 6 percent of prison populations in 1979. The adult incarceration rate for drugs increased by a factor of 10 from 1980 to 1996, far in excess of any of the other crime types contributing to prison population. Aside from drug offenses, there has been a general upward trend in the general sanction level for the five other crime types that are important for prison: murder, robbery, burglary, aggravated assault, and sexual assault.[10] This growth is displayed in figure 3.2, a graph of the incarceration rate for each of these six these offenses.

Blumstein and Beck (1999) analyzed the factors contributing to this incarceration growth. The candidate explanations they considered were

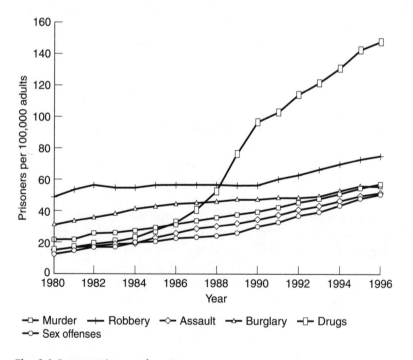

Fig. 3.2 Incarceration rate by crime type.

Source: Blumstein and Beck (1999).

(1) more crime, (2) more arrests per crime, (3) more commitments to prison per arrest, and (4) longer time served, including time served on parole recommitment. It turns out that none of the growth was attributable to more crime and there was no change over this period in arrests per crime. The growth was entirely attributable to a growth in punitiveness, about equally to growth in prison commitments per arrest (an indication of tougher prosecution or judicial sentencing) and to longer time served (an indication of longer sentences, elimination of parole or later parole release, or greater readiness to recommit parolees to prison for either technical violations or new crimes) (Blumstein and Beck 1999).

One of the most important recent sources of growth in prison population is the level of recommitment of parolees. Parole boards have received the same political message that they too ought to become tougher to keep up with the political tenor of the times. Indeed, they have been more aggressive in delaying release decisions where they still had that option, in performing urinalysis on parolees, and in making recommitments for parole violations.

Another significant contributor to the growth in prison populations through the 1980s was the same demographic shift that contributed to the growth of crimes in the 1960s and 1970s—the baby boomers. Since the peak age for crime occurs in the late teens, and the peak age for imprisonment is in the early thirties, the population bulge associated with that generation was expected to impact the prison population about a decade later than it impacted the crime rates.[11] The impact of that demographic shift on prison populations was relatively small, however, compared to the shift associated with the drug war, and in the same order of magnitude as the shifts in the punishment of the more common street crimes. In any event, those effects should have passed their peak by the early 1990s as the baby boomers passed out of the high imprisonment ages, and should already have begun working the other way, waiting for the arrival of the echo boom following the demographic trough associated with the 1976 cohort, the smallest cohort in the US population under age 50.

Some Indications That Rationality Is Being Restored

The growth of incarceration over the past 25 years has been a consequence of public concern about the widespread use of drugs, especially by children, the growing crime rate exacerbated by the growing attention to it by the media,[12] the political appeal of being tough on crime and the corresponding concern about being seen as "soft" on crime.[13] The steady decline of crime rates from a 1993 peak to a plateau in 2000, resulting in rates that had not been seen since the mid-1960s, certainly contributed to an easing of the pressure on politicians to do whatever they could, and increasing sentences always seemed to "work," not necessarily in reducing crime, but in alleviating the pressure and displaying responsiveness. There has also been an easing of the drug problem, particularly in the demand for crack, the drug whose markets have been most marked by violence in the past, so the insistence on incarceration for drug offenders has also diminished.

The result of the crime decline would probably not be very effective without some direct pressure to reduce corrections costs, which rose in direct proportion to prison population, augmented by inflation. That pressure has been provided by the serious revenue shortfalls seen in all the states in their 2002 budgets, with a reasonable prospect of things getting worse in the future. For example, California is projecting a $35 billion deficit in its $63 billion budget (Broder 2003). One estimate for the fiscal year 2004 is that all the states collectively will have deficits of between $61 and 85 billion, representing 13 to 18 percent of the total state budgets (Lav and Johnson 2002). Corrections costs, which have been growing without significant concern for fiscal implications, now find themselves on the list of reasonable candidates for reduction. States are proposing a variety of approaches for earlier release and treatment in the community of nonviolent offenders.

Perhaps one of the most striking approaches to introducing rationality is that embedded in California's Proposition 36, which requires treatment before incarceration for a defined group of drug offenders. This approach is being picked up by a number of other states. It represents not only a more rational response to the current drug problem, where the resilient market and its recruitment largely negate the incapacitative and deterrent effects of incarceration. Treatment efforts have been shown to reduce drug abuse, at least during the period of treatment. This approach also represents a significant potential for cost savings, since treatment costs are much less than incarceration costs.

The most direct indication of the approach to reconsidering the growth of incarceration is the fact that the incarceration rate in state prisons at the end of 2001 dropped for the first time in more than two decades—it dropped from 425 in 2000 to 422 in 2001(Harrison and Beck 2002) This was a consequence of prison-population reductions in 10 states, including some of the larger states like New York, New Jersey, and Texas. This reduction was not matched by the federal prison system, which continued its steady increase, with the incarceration rate in federal prisons increasing from 44 to 48. As a result, the total prison incarceration rate was essentially steady, with only a slight increase from 469 to 470.

Toward the Future

One approach that might be pursued to reverse the seemingly unbounded growth in punitiveness is to find means to enhance public education so that the naive belief that more punishment will lead to less crime, regardless of the social dynamics of the particular crime (e.g., the substitution in drug markets) or the offenders on whom the punishment is targeted (e.g., offenders with relatively low disutility for prison), becomes less prevalent. Somehow, the subtleties of those differences have not been able to get through the emotion and the rhetoric of sanction policy. It does appear that too much of the policy debate is from the perspectives of the ideological poles—arguing broadly for more incarceration at one extreme (with no concern for where it can be most effectively applied) or, at the other extreme, against incarceration as a broad generality rather than with a sharp focus on where it is least effective and most wasteful or even harmful.

In economic policy, in contrast, there still remain sharp ideological differences between the left and the right, but there has emerged a level of theoretical agreement and strong empirical observations that have brought the poles much closer together than has been the case in criminal justice policy. In part, this is attributable to the much more backward state of empirically grounded theory in criminology, which could force resolution on at least some aspects of the debate. A major rise in the level of support for research in the whole area of crime and crime control through the National Institute of Justice (whose annual discretionary budget has hovered at about $25 million for many years—in marked contrast to the $20 billion for the National Institutes of Health) could help move that process forward.[14]

In policy terms, one could argue for more widespread use of sentencing commissions as appropriate instruments for generating at least some degree of coherence in sentencing structures. Such commissions can represent an antidote to the passionate response to a particularly heinous crime or the mood of the moment and could sometimes serve as an inhibitor of the frequent legislative response of mandatory-minimum sentences. That approach is limited, however, because even sentencing commissions have to respond politically (in most cases, their guidelines must be approved by the legislature), but they have a degree of insulation from the political pressures compared to legislatures. Sentencing commissions that operate under capacity constraints (requiring their sentencing structure to be compatible with the available or committed prison capacity) make even more sense because the capacity constraint imposes an important discipline on the sentencing schedule; even the most conscientious sentencing commissions, however, are sometimes forced to ignore the constraint by the back pressure they get from the legislature, which must approve the guidelines. It is rare that a sentencing commission hears a demand for reduction of any sentences. Almost all the communications call for increased sentences, and so the capacity constraint provides a basis for asking for which offenses the sentence should be reduced in order to provide the capacity for the sentence to be increased. Alternatively, when appropriate, the capacity should be increased through the expenditure of public funds, and this budget constraint then becomes an operational constraint.

One might also require the development of prison impact statements to be provided to the legislature before any change in sentencing policy is enacted. This is done as a matter of course for other programs that have budgetary implications (and the Congressional Budget Office was established by the Congress for this purpose), but changes in sentencing policy are usually enacted first by a Judiciary Committee and then the legislature without consideration of their costs and prison population impacts. Changes in the legislative process here might force more responsible consideration of sentencing policy.

Probably the most likely prospect for change in consideration of sentencing will be through the emergence of a coalition between fiscal conservatives (as they become appalled at the costs of incarceration and the associated inefficiency, spurred on by the growing budget deficits) and liberals (who want to reduce sentences and use the funds for other social programs that might promise to reduce crime in the longer run). There are some glimmerings of the emergence of those coalitions, and one might hope to see them coalesce over the next decade.

One of the more helpful efforts at restoring rationality would be through reconsideration of the mandatory-minimum sentencing laws introduced over the past quarter century as acts of passion by legislatures. They epitomize the *politically* rational response to the pressure to "do something" about a particular societal problem, and their *functional* irrationality is best exemplified by the fact that they most often are targeted at drug offenses, where incarceration is least effective. One would hope that the crime decline of the 1990s would provide the political flexibility to enable the legislatures to rethink those laws (see Blumstein and Wallman 2000). It is impressive that the Michigan legislature has indeed done just that with the mandatory-minimum laws relating to drug offenses.[15] The new Michigan law also enhances the possibility for earlier parole release for current prisoners who were sentenced under the mandatory-minimum laws. Families Against Mandatory Minimums, which lobbied particularly effectively for the new law, reports that at least eight other states are already considering similar legislative change.

One might anticipate that many legislatures will be reluctant to consider such laws because of their lingering concern that such an act might be seen as "soft on crime." A strong alternative would be to pass a "sunset law" that terminates all mandatory-minimum sentencing laws five years after their passage or three years after the enactment of the sunset law. The sunset law recognizes that the mandatory-minimum laws were passed in response to immediate concerns that could well pass after some time. Typically, sunset laws call for an analysis of the effects of the sunsetted law—an assessment of its costs and its benefits—in the year before it is scheduled to be terminated. Thus, for those laws whose benefits are found to exceed their costs, the opportunity is preserved to reenact them. I doubt that there will be many cases where that occurs responsibly.

Thus, we do see some encouraging signs that rationality may be returning to the incarceration policy in the United States, particularly as the pressure of crime rates is diminished and the pressure of budget deficits increases. On the other hand, there has developed a significant political interest group with a stake in limiting any such reduction in prison populations. This could well include the prison guards unions. The California Correctional Peace Officers Association, representing prison guards, for example, has been reported to be a major political contributor to gubernatorial campaigns in California. They obviously have a strong economic interest in keeping prison levels high. Also, many communities that may formerly have eschewed a prison in their neighborhoods ("not in my backyard" or NIMBY) now see prisons as important economic development opportunities; those communities that have prisons are concerned about the economic impact of their prison being closed as the state reduces its total prison population.

Thus, it is entirely possible that prison populations may have reached a new homeostatic level, but at a rate four times that which prevailed for 50 years. The prospect for even that stability is limited as long as sentencing policy remains a salient aspect of the political process. And that is likely to continue as long as crime rates—even as low as they have become—are a troubling part of life in America. Maybe we need a new edition of *The Honest Politician's Guide to Crime Control*. That might be the next challenge for Norval Morris. He is certainly up to it, as I have seen over the past several years as he has served as the chair of the advisory committee for the National Consortium on Violence Research (NCOVR).

Notes

1. The denominator of the incarceration rate is the total national population. A more appropriate denominator would be a population weighted by some measure of the age-specific incarceration rate, which tends to peak in the late twenties or early thirties. To some limited extent, this would boost the rate during the 1960s and reduce it during the 1980s when the peak of the "baby boom" generation moved into the peak imprisonment ages.

2. See Blumstein, Cohen, and Nagin (1977), Blumstein and Moitra (1979), and Blumstein et al. (1981).

3. An essay by Robert Martinson (1974) attracted considerable attention to the null-effect findings. His essay was based on a more comprehensive survey in Lipton, Martinson, and Wilks (1975).

4. See Elijah Anderson's (1994) discussion of the importance of "respect" to the people he characterizes as "street people." Also see Anderson (1999).

5. The errors of omission—failure to release an offender who is a good risk and would not recidivate—are never seen.

6. Willie Horton, who was made infamous by the George H. W. Bush presidential campaign of 1988, was a notorious example of such a release that led to a heinous recidivist offense. That occurrence was eventually used to reach up to condemn the governor at the time, Michael Dukakis, who was the opposition Democratic candidate for president.

7. This was the essential point of Blumstein (1993). I was very pleased to see Norval Morris up front in the audience when I delivered the address and knew that he would agree with much of what I had to say.

8. Known officially as The Substance Abuse and Crime Prevention Act.

9. Based on data in Harrison and Beck (2002, pp. 13–14).

10. Together with drugs, these offenses account for about 80 percent of state prisoners.

11. These impacts of the demographic shifts on crime and on prison populations are examined in some detail in Blumstein, Cohen, and Miller (1980).

12. This attention is typified by the motto attributed to television producers, "If it bleeds, it leads." A recent study found that TV reports of violence doubled over a period when the violence rate actually decreased.

13. This was typified by news reports of the response of the Clinton White House opposing proposals by the U.S. Sentencing Commission to reduce the 100:1 crack – cocaine disparity in the federal sentencing guidelines. The reason for their objection was the concern that they would be seen as "soft on crime."

14. Joan Petersilia and I have argued for an annual doubling of the NIJ budget to a level of $1 billion per year. See Blumstein and Petersilia (1995).

15. "Michigan to Drop Minimum Sentence Rules for Drug Crimes," *New York Times*, December 2, 2002.

References

Anderson, Elijah. 1994. "The Code of the Streets." *Atlantic Monthly* 273 (May): 80–94.

———. 1999. *Code of the Street: Decency, Violence, and the Moral Life of the Inner City*. New York: Norton.

Beck, Allen J., Jennifer C. Karberg, and Paige M. Harrison. 2002. "Prison and Jail Inmates at Midyear 2001." Bureau of Justice Statistics Bulletin NCJ 191702. Washington, D.C.: U.S. Department of Justice.

Blumstein, Alfred. 1993. "Making Rationality Relevant—The American Society of Criminology Presidential Address." *Criminology* 31(1):1–16.

Blumstein, Alfred, and Allen J. Beck. 1999. "Population Growth in U.S. Prisons, 1980–1996." In *Prisons, Crime and Justice: A Review of Research*, vol. 26, ed. Michael Tonry and Joan Petersilia. Chicago: University of Chicago Press.

Blumstein, Alfred, and Jacqueline Cohen. 1973. "A Theory of the Stability of Punishment." *Journal of Criminal Law and Criminology, and Police Science* 63: 198–207.

Blumstein, Alfred, and Soumyo Moitra. 1979. "An Analysis of the Time Series of the Imprisonment Rate in the States of the United States: A Further Test of the Stability of Punishment Hypothesis." *Journal of Criminal Law and Criminology* 70(3):376–390.

Blumstein, Alfred, and Joan Petersilia. 1995. "Investing in Criminal Justice Research." In *Crime*, ed. Joan Petersilia and James Q. Wilson. San Francisco: ICS Press.

Blumstein, Alfred, and Joel Wallman, eds. 2000. *The Crime Drop in America*. Cambridge: Cambridge University Press.

Blumstein, Alfred, Jacqueline Cohen, and Harold Miller. 1980. "Demographically Disaggregated Projections of Prison Populations." *Journal of Criminal Justice* 8(1):1–26.

Blumstein, Alfred, Jacqueline Cohen, and Daniel Nagin. 1977. "The Dynamics of a Homeostatic Punishment Process." *Journal of Criminal Law and Criminology* 67(3):317–334.

Blumstein, Alfred, Jacqueline Cohen, Soumyo Moitra, and Daniel Nagin. 1981. "Testing the Stability of Punishment Hypothesis: A Reply." *Journal of Criminal Law and Criminology* 72(4):1799–1808.

Broder, John M. 2003. "Californians Hear Grim News on Budget." *New York Times*, January 11.

Durkheim, Émile. 1966. *The Rules of Sociological Method*. Trans. S. Solovay and J. J. Mueller. New York: Free Press.

Erikson, Kai. 1966. *The Wayward Puritans*. New York: Wiley.

Harrison, Paige M., and Allen J. Beck. 2002. "Prisoners in 2001." Bureau of Justice Statistics Bulletin NCJ 195189, July. Washington, D.C.: U.S. Department of Justice.

Lav, Iris J., and Nicholas Johnson. 2002 "State Budget Deficits for Fiscal Year 2004 are Huge and Growing." Center on Budget and Policy Priorities. Available: http:/www.cbpp.org/12–23-02sfp.htm.

Lipton, Douglas, Robert Martinson, and Judith Wilks. 1975. *The Effectiveness of Correctional Treatment: A Survey of Treatment Evaluation Studies.* New York: Praeger.

Martinson, Robert. 1974. "What Works? Questions and Answers about Prison Reform." *Public Interest* 35(2):22–54.

Morris, N., and G. Hawkins. 1970. *The Honest Politician's Guide to Crime Control.* Chicago: University of Chicago Press.

Morris, N., and M. Tonry. 1990. *Between Prison and Probation: Intermediate Punishments in a Rational Sentencing System.* New York: Oxford University Press.

Robison, James O., and Gerald Smith. 1971. "The Effectiveness of Correctional Programs." *Crime and Delinquency* 17(1):67–80.

Wilson, James Q. 1975. "Lock 'Em Up." *New York Times Magazine,* March 9, at 11.

Walmsley, Ray. 2002. "World Prison Population List, third edition." Home Office, *Findings,* no. 166.

PART II

Going In

4

Limiting Retributivism

Richard S. Frase

Norval Morris's theory of limiting retributivism provides one solution to the perennial problem of how to reconcile the often-conflicting purposes of punishment. Under Morris's theory, concepts of just deserts set upper and occasionally lower limits on sentencing severity. Within these outer limits, other purposes and principles provide the necessary fine-tuning of the sentence imposed in a particular case. Such other purposes and principles include not only traditional crime-control purposes such as deterrence, incapacitation, and rehabilitation but also considerations of equality (uniformity) and a concept Morris calls parsimony: a preference for the least severe alternative that will achieve the purposes of the particular sentence. Morris rejected coerced rehabilitation as a reason for imprisonment or for extending a prison term and also argued that the type or duration of the sentence should rarely if ever be based on individual predictions of dangerousness. His later writings expressed strong support for sentencing guidelines, provided they are flexible and incorporate intermediate sanctions as well as prison terms.

Many desert theorists reject Morris's model and would allow almost no role for nondesert sentencing goals in determining the severity of individual sentences. In their view such goals, as well as the concept of parsimony, should only be used to determine the overall severity of the punishment scale and the choice among different types of sanction that are deemed of equivalent severity. On the other hand, sentencing policy makers and practitioners seem to give just deserts an even smaller role than Morris does—most contemporary sentencing systems still follow some version of indeterminate sentencing, emphasizing judicial and parole discretion and crime-control purposes.

Can these differing views be reconciled? Is it possible to reach broad agreement on an overall sentencing model that has not only a principled basis but also some realistic prospect of being widely adopted or at least providing a suitable reform goal? In the absence of such a consensus model, can sentencing theorists, policy makers, and researchers even engage in useful dialogue, or settle on appropriate criteria and benchmarks to use in evaluating reform proposals and systems in practice?

Actually, there is already substantial agreement on two essential aspects of Morris's theory: concepts of just deserts must place limits on the pursuit of crime control and other consequentialist goals; and a pure desert approach is unlikely to ever be adopted in practice (indeed, even strong advocates of just deserts appear to concede the practical need for a hybrid theory, Robinson 1987, *passim*; von Hirsch 1988, p. 72). Thus, it is clear that some sort of limiting retributive (LR) theory is already the consensus model; the only real question is—what kind of LR? How can desert and nondesert goals be blended into a meaningfully specific, flexible, and widely adoptable hybrid theory?

This essay seeks to confirm the two points of general agreement noted earlier. As for the remaining question—what kind of LR?—I propose a formulation modeled after American state (not federal) sentencing guidelines. Although never actually put forth by Morris, this model is implicit in his later writings and those of his co-author Michael Tonry, and it has already been adopted in a diverse group of American states.

The first section of this essay summarizes Morris's LR theory and its evolution over time. The second section examines the broad support for LR that can be found among mainstream sentencing theorists and in model codes and standards. The third section surveys the many examples of sentencing regimes embodying a hybrid LR theory that can be found in foreign nations as well as in U.S. jurisdictions. Particular attention is given to the Minnesota Sentencing Guidelines. Although the Guidelines are widely believed to be based on a just deserts model, they also give substantial weight to all nondesert sentencing purposes, within retributive limits, producing an LR system very similar to what Morris proposed.

The fourth section addresses what is perhaps the greatest weakness of LR, as well as its greatest strength: as revealed in the writings of Morris and other theoreticians, the provisions of model codes and standards, and the many examples of LR systems in practice, LR can mean many different things and has been implemented in many different ways. This diversity shows that LR can be adopted in a wide range of legal, social, and political contexts. But LR must, itself, be kept within some limits or it ceases to have any real meaning or utility, even as a consensus model. This section of the essay proposes a suitably limited formulation of LR, modeled on Minnesota-style guidelines, which nevertheless retains the balance and flexibility of Morris's version. The proposed consensus model includes a few sentencing principles, found in state guidelines, which Morris did not advocate, but also includes some important Morrisonian LR features that have not yet been incorporated into most state guidelines systems.

The fifth section compares the delimited LR model with other theories and argues that this model is superior to any realistic alternative. The final section of the essay notes the various practical advantages of recognizing a consensus model of punishment and concludes that Morris's LR theory, with appropriate limitations on its scope and application, is the best choice. The model is theoretically sound and has proven to be practically viable over the long term in a number of American states.

Norval Morris's Theory of Punishment

Throughout his career, Norval Morris has been concerned with the inter-related problems of sentencing disparity and the conflicting purposes of, and at, sentencing.[1] His earliest works also show his strong belief in the importance of relating sentencing theory to sentencing practice (Morris 1951, p. 16). Morris is an empiricist and a realist; he believes that sentencing theory should reflect the accumulated wisdom of the past and avoid imposing highly unpopular rules that will only be circumvented in practice. Morris was one of the first mainstream writers to suggest the empirical and moral defects of the "rehabilitative ideal" of coerced, prison-based treatment linked to the timing of parole release ("Penal Sanctions and Human Rights," in Morris and Howard 1964, p. 175). He explicitly linked retributive sentencing goals to the human rights of defendants and implied that such rights place firm upper limits on the severity of punishments imposed to achieve crime-control purposes (Bottoms 1995, pp. 19, 22–23). He argued strongly in favor of community-based sentencing and treatment, much broader use of fines in lieu of short custodial terms, and elimination of mandatory-minimum statutes and other arbitrary limitations on probation eligibility (Morris and Hawkins 1970, pp. 112–113, 115–124, and 141–143; see also Morris 1977a, p. 150; 1977b, pp. 279–280; Morris and Hawkins 1977, pp. 60–61; Morris 1993, p. 310).

The Emergence of Morris's Limiting
Retributive Theory

A more comprehensive statement of Morris's LR theory was first presented in his 1974 book, *The Future of Imprisonment*, and was further developed in later lectures and writings. Morris's upper limits of desert are strict and explicit: "No sanction should be imposed greater than that which is 'deserved' for the last crime, or series of crimes" being sentenced (Morris 1974, pp. 60, 73–77). However, Morris strongly emphasized that courts are not obligated to impose the maximum that the offender deserves (ibid.,

p. 75). In later writings, Morris extended the concept of maximum desert to include the defendant's prior record of convictions (Morris 1982, pp. 151–152, 162–163, 184–186; 1992, p. 145).

In Morris's view, "desert also sometimes dictates the minimum sanction a community will tolerate" (Morris 1974, p. 78), thus, the sentence must not "depreciate the seriousness" of the current offense (ibid., p. 60). This language was taken from the Model Penal Code (see further discussion in the section "LR Concepts Recognized by Other Writers and in Model Codes and Standards"). Although Morris often refers to this as a retributive concept, he also saw it as consistent with a norm-reinforcement theory: such minimum severity limits are needed because "[t]he criminal law has general behavioral standard-setting functions; it acts as a moral teacher" (Morris 1974, p. 78). However, Morris has consistently opposed mandatory-minimum statutes.

Within the upper and lower limits of desert, Morris envisioned a range of "not undeserved" penalties. In some writings he characterizes these ranges as "overlapping and quite broad" (Morris 1982, p. 151). He also explicitly differentiated his own views from other desert-based theories by distinguishing between purposes of punishment which are "defining," those which are "limiting," and those which are only "guiding" principles (Morris 1977a, pp. 140–142; 1982, pp. 182–187). Morris suggested that deterrent purposes could precisely define the proper punishment, but only if we knew much more than we now do about the deterrent effects of punishment. As for desert, however, he argued that this concept is inherently too imprecise (and perhaps also too lacking in political and philosophical consensus, Morris and Tonry 1990, pp. 86–89) to precisely define the sentence; it can only establish rough outer limits, an allowable sentencing range, beyond which penalties would be widely seen as clearly undeserved (i.e., either excessively severe or excessively lenient) (Morris 1977a, pp. 158–159; 1982, pp. 198–199; Morris and Tonry 1990, pp. 104–105). Within those broad ranges of desert, other punishment goals, acting as "guiding principles," will interact to "fine-tune" the sentence. A guiding principle is "a general value which should be respected unless other values sufficiently strongly justify its rejection in any given case" (Morris 1977a, p. 142).

What, then, are Morris's "guiding principles" and what precise role does each play? Morris was an early critic of the rehabilitative ideal. In later writings he argued that post-prison risk cannot reliably be predicted based on in-prison behavior; that coerced in-prison treatment programs waste resources on unamenable subjects, while encouraging feigned cooperation which may actually preclude genuine reform; and that such coercive treatment would be morally wrong even if it were effective (Morris and Hawkins 1970, ch. 5; Morris 1974, pp. 12–27; 1977a, p. 139; Morris and Hawkins 1977, ch. 6). Thus, Morris concluded that rehabilitation is not a reason either to impose or to extend a prison sentence, and that all in-prison treatment programs must be voluntary and not linked to the timing of release. However, Morris strongly advocates community-based treatment and apparently does not object to requiring a person on probation or parole to participate in an appropriate community-based treatment program closely related to the conviction offense (Morris and Hawkins 1970, pp. 112–113, 118–124; Morris 1974, pp. 34, 42–43; Morris and Tonry 1990, pp. 186–203, 206–212).

Morris's views on the goal of incapacitation were similarly in conflict with the traditional theory and practices of indeterminate sentencing—he opposed basing prison commitment, duration, and release decisions on individualized assessments of the defendant's degree of "dangerousness" (Morris 1974, pp. 62–73; 1977b, pp. 276–277). Again, Morris argued that we lack the ability to accurately predict future behavior and are very likely to err on the side of massive overprediction and overincarceration. However, he would permit parole release decisions to be based on actuarial predictions of parole success, for various offender categories (Morris 1977a, p. 148), as well as predictions based on the defendant's past behavior (Morris 1974, p. 34). In later writings, Morris—always the realist— recognized that individualized predictions of dangerousness will be made, whether they are formally permitted or not (Morris 1992, p. 139). He therefore sought to define the narrow conditions under which such predictions might be a fair and effective basis for prison commitment and duration decisions. In particular, he argued that sentencing severity may be increased (up to the retributive maximum) if "reliable actuarial data" indicates that the defendant's risk of assaultive behavior is "substantially" higher than that of other offenders with very similar prior record and current offense (Morris 1982, pp. 166–172; 1992, pp. 138–147; see also Morris and Miller 1985 and Miller and Morris 1986). However, Morris felt that these conditions would rarely be met.

Morris would also allow increased severity (up to the retributive maximum) for recidivists, when "other less restrictive sanctions have been frequently or recently applied to this offender" (Morris 1974, pp. 60, 79–80). He seemed to base such increases on retributive grounds (Morris 1974, pp. 79–80), but they can also be justified on a theory of special deterrence or incapacitation of high-risk defendants. Although Morris rejected most individual assessments of risk, he approved of parole release decisions based on actuarial predictions—"[t]he best predictor of future criminality is past criminality" (Morris 1982, pp. 162–163). He would also permit sentencing severity to be increased (up to the retributive maximum) if such an increase "is necessary to achieve socially justified [general] deterrent purposes, and the punishment of this offender is an appropriate vehicle to this end" (Morris 1974, pp. 60, 79).

In Morris's view, the goal of equality in punishment is important "but it is by no means a categorical imperative . . . the principle of equality— that like cases should be treated alike—is . . . only a guiding principle which will enjoin equality of punishment unless there are other substantial utilitarian reasons to the contrary" (Morris 1982, pp. 160, 198; see also Morris 1977a, pp. 137, 142). Morris acknowledges "the long tradition of justice as equality" (Morris 1982, p. 204) and also recognizes that equality is an especially important value in the American context (Morris 1982, p. 180). Nevertheless, he argues that, within the range of "not undeserved" penalties, punishment can be unequal—and even, in some sense, "unfair"—and yet still be "just" (Morris 1977a, pp. 151–163; 1982, pp. 187–192). He noted that numerous traditional law enforcement and sentencing practices (e.g., giving leniency to defendants who turn state's evidence; pardon and amnesty; granting of early parole release to avoid prison overcrowding) are inconsistent with a very restrictive requirement of equality. In light of such substantial (and, perhaps, inevitable) system-wide inequality, the sentencing process cannot, and should not, attempt to observe strict equality constraints (Morris 1982, pp. 206–208). This conclusion also follows from his strong belief in the concept of parsimony (discussed later on), which "overcomes the principle of equality" (Morris 1982, p. 191; 1977a, p. 154).

Parsimony is one of Morris's most important guiding principles—"[t]he least restrictive (punitive) sanction necessary to achieve defined social purposes should be imposed" (Morris 1974, p. 59). Morris found direct support for this principle in the ABA's Sentencing Standards, the Model Penal Code, and Eighth Amendment principles (see the section on "LR Concepts Recognized by Other Writers and in Model Codes and Standards"), as well as in mental health and juvenile justice dispositional standards (Morris 1974, pp. 60–62). For Morris, the principle of parsimony "is both utilitarian and humanitarian" (Morris 1974, p. 61). Parsimony in the use of custodial sentences also permits the preservation of the defendant's social ties (Morris 1974, pp. 8, 75) and the avoidance of needless suffering and expense (Morris 1977a, p. 154). In any event, Morris argued, the ability to grant case-level mitigation of punishment, without strict desert or equality constraints, is a necessary and inevitable feature of our chronically overloaded and underfunded criminal justice system (Morris 1977a, pp 156–158; 1982, p. 190).

To summarize, Morris believed that judges should use the lower end of the range of deserved punishments as a starting point and should increase that penalty only to the extent that one or more of his other guiding factors requires increased severity. Thus, the specific sentence would be determined by whichever factor required the greatest severity. Of course, the guiding principles of equality and parsimony will often be in conflict. But if the presumption in favor of the least severe sentence is a *strong* one, and if judges thus usually sentence near the bottom of the "not-undeserved" range, then sentences will tend to be fairly uniform among offenders whose cases fall in the same range. Morris probably did expect that sentences would cluster near the bottom of the desert range—if only for lack of sufficient utilitarian justification for raising them higher; he has often argued that criminal laws and punishments have very little effect on crime rates (Morris 1977b, pp. 267–269; 1993, p. 309).

As everyone familiar with American criminal courts knows, another important "guiding" factor in sentencing is the defendant's plea. Morris expressed dislike for the exchange of "concessions" for guilty pleas (Morris 1974, p. 52), and the resulting coercion, overcharging, and distortion of the sentencing process (Morris 1977a, p. 147; Morris and Hawkins 1977, pp. 57–58). But Morris is a realist and recognizes the practical reasons that underlie the grant of leniency to defendants who cooperate. He proposed the use of a pretrial settlement conference attended by the judge, all parties, and the victim (Morris 1974, pp. 50–57), but charge or sentence mitigation would still be permitted. For similar practical reasons, Morris recognized the need to grant good-conduct reductions of prison terms to encourage cooperation and maintain order (Morris 1974, p. 49; 1977b, p. 277).

Morris on Sentencing Guidelines and Other Determinate Sentencing Reforms

Morris has long advocated two reforms that became essential features of most sentencing guidelines systems: the requirement that trial judges state reasons for their sentences and appellate review of sentences (Morris 1953, p. 200; 1977a, pp. 149–150, 164–165; 1977b, pp. 275–276; Morris and Hawkins 1977, pp. 59–60). Morris hoped that these reforms would facilitate the gradual evolution of binding precedents on frequently occurring issues—what he termed a "Common Law of Sentencing."

Morris gave qualified support to the earliest federal bills calling for the creation of a sentencing commission to promulgate guidelines—provided that such guidelines retained sufficient judicial discretion and incorporated requirements of trial court reasons and appellate review (Morris 1977a, pp. 149–150, 165; 1977b, pp. 276, 281–285). In his later writings, Morris gave much stronger support to the new, commission-based sentencing guidelines movement (Morris 1982, pp. 172–176; Morris and Tonry 1990, pp. 48–49; Morris 1993, pp. 307, 309), but he criticized state and federal guidelines for putting too much emphasis on prison sentences, without enough attention to the wide variety of noncustodial sanctions more restrictive than straight probation (Morris and Tonry 1990, pp. 37–42; Morris 1993, pp. 307–308, 310).

Although some state guidelines systems have retained parole release discretion (Frase 1999), Morris was quite willing to abolish it. He felt that such discretion could not be justified by the need to make individualized assessments of reform or dangerousness (which he rejected) and was not needed to maintain prison discipline, maximize deterrence, avoid prison overcrowding, or rectify unjust disparities; each of the latter functions could be better served by other means or were not being effectively served by parole discretion in any case (Morris 1977b, pp. 276–279).

Summary

Norval Morris's theory of punishment is both principled and pragmatic. Some features are based on strong normative arguments. However, he also very deliberately tried to fashion a theory that is congruent with the widely held values and practices of judges and other system actors. In opting for a hybrid theory, seeking to balance conflicting punishment goals, case-specific factors, and practical realities, Morris recognized (quoting H. L. A. Hart) that "the pursuit of one aim may be qualified by the pursuit of others." In the end, he concluded, "there is no universal formula . . . penal policy always represents a choice among a plurality of aims and objectives and every decision we reach may be attended by some disadvantages" (Morris and Hawkins 1970, p. 123).

LR Concepts Recognized by Other Writers and in Model Codes and Standards

Although Morris coined the term "limiting retributivism" and provided by far the most detailed exposition of its rationale and features, the basic elements of LR have been proposed by numerous other writers and model code drafters. The broad agreement on these principles among academics and practitioners (as well as the many examples of LR in American and foreign sentencing laws, see the section "Examples of LR in Practice") demonstrate that LR is already the consensus model of punishment. However, LR concepts have been applied in several different ways, and it is important to distinguish among them.

One LR principle that is not directly relevant to sentencing should be mentioned at the outset because it shows the breadth of support for LR concepts. Almost all writers agree that only those who are morally culpable, and who have violated a prohibition clearly announced in advance, are eligible for criminal punishment of any type or degree. Several writers have referred to this concept as "retribution in distribution" (Hart 1968, pp. 9–13; Walker 1969, pp. 15–19; see also Honderich 1969, pp. 14, 134; Longford 1961, p. 33; Packer 1968, *passim*). These limits also find expression in the Model Penal Code (American Law Institute 1985), Sections 1.02(1)(c) and (d); in due process limitations on vague criminal statutes; in the ban on ex post facto laws; and in the general criminal law concept of "legality" (LaFave 2000, § 3.1). Similar principles prohibit retroactive increases in offense grading or severity of punishment (Model Penal Code, Section 1.02(2)(d)).

Weak Requirements of Proportionality and Uniformity

Other writers have, like Morris, viewed desert and equality principles as only loose constraints. H. L. A. Hart gave these principles a "subordinate role" (Hart 1968, p. 233); he acknowledged "the somewhat hazy requirement that 'like cases be treated alike'" (p. 24) and argued that only "broad judgments" and "rough distinctions" of moral desert can be made (p. 25). Lord Longford (1961, p. 33) would only avoid penalties "conspicuously out of proportion"; Ted Honderich (1969, p. 168) objected only to "gross" inequalities; Herbert Packer (1968, p. 140) advocated punishments that are "individualized but within limits" set by the need for general deterrence and "judgments about comparative morality"; Michael Tonry (1994) similarly prefers weak proportionality constraints.

On the other hand, even strongly utilitarian writers have recognized the importance of maintaining proportionality between offense and punishment severity, both to give offenders an incentive to "stop at the lesser" crime and to match punishment costs with crime-control benefits (Bentham (1748–1832), p. 326). Hart suggested an educative or norm-reinforcing reason to preserve at least rough proportionality; if "the relative severity of penalties diverges sharply from this rough scale, there is a risk of either confusing common morality or flouting it and bringing the law into contempt" (p. 25).

Retributive Limits on Maximum Allowable Sanction Severity

Several writers besides Morris have recognized the particular importance of placing desert limits on maximum sanction severity (Hart 1968, p. 237; Longford 1961, pp. 61–62; Honderich 1969, p. 139). This principle is also made explicit in Model Penal Section 1.02(2)(c) (no "excessive, disproportionate or arbitrary punishment"). According to the Code's revised commentary, section 1.02, in combination with other Code provisions setting "relatively modest" maximum terms and regulating extended terms, provides "a kind of retributive limit on utilitarian objectives . . . as a general matter, people should not be punished more severely than they deserve even if such punishment would have beneficial social consequences" (American Law Institute 1985, Pt. I, vol. 3, Introduction to Articles 6 and 7, pp. 3–4).[2] An even stronger role for LR, based explicitly on Morris's writings, can be found in the early drafts of the revised MPC sentencing provisions (American Law Institute 2002, Section 1.02(2)(a) through (c) at p. 6, and comment at pp. 14–20).

Maximum severity LR is also explicit or implicit in the two most recent editions of the American Bar Association (ABA) sentencing standards. The second edition, adopted in 1979, explicitly stated that the sentence must never "exceed a ceiling equal to that level justly deserved by the offender for the instant offense" (ABA 1979b, Standard 18–3.2(a)(i)). The third edition dropped this limitation from the black letter, but the commentary urged legislatures to consider adopting Morris's LR theory, with emphasis on limiting maximum sanction severity (ABA 1993, Standard 18–2.1, commentary, at 13–14).

All three editions of the ABA's guilty plea standards incorporate a form of maximum severity LR (ABA 1968a, 1979a, 1997). These standards allow defendants who plead guilty to receive charge and sentence concessions for various reasons, some of which do not relate closely or at all to blame (ABA 1997, Standard 14–1.8(a)). But a defendant who refuses to plead guilty may not receive a sentence "in excess of that which would be justified by any of the protective, deterrent, or other purposes of the criminal law" (Standard 14–1.8(b)). The commentary explains that "there is an essential difference between [giving such a defendant] the greatest punishment justifiable under accepted principles of penology [while a similar defendant who pleads guilty] receives something less" (ABA 1979a, p. 21).

Looser Requirements of Minimum Sanction Severity

Although he rejected mandatory-minimum statutes, Morris agreed that some minimum degree of sanction severity is necessary, at least in serious cases, for retributive reasons or deterrence and norm reinforcement. The Model Penal Code drafters, like Morris, rejected mandatory minimums, and the Code's only expression of a minimum severity concept is the provision, in Section 7.01(1)(c), calling for a custody sentence when "necessary for the protection of the public" because a lesser penalty would "depreciate the seriousness" of the offense. However, the commentary makes clear that this limitation is based on crime prevention, not retributive grounds; the Institute "wholly rejected the idea" that desert might require imprisonment even if public protection did not (American Law Institute 1985, Pt. 1, vol. 3, pp. 227, 231, 233–234).

The ABA sentencing standards contain no explicit minimum severity requirements, although such a requirement is weakly implied in the second edition's appeals to equality goals (see later discussion). The ABA Guilty Plea standards, discussed earlier, which allow undeserved concessions to defendants who plead guilty, place no lower limits on sanction severity. Several writers (Tonry 1994, p. 80; Crocker 1992, *passim*) have argued explicitly that minimum severity requirements should be deemed more flexible than maximum severity limits.

Can such an asymmetrical, "softer down than up" (von Hirsch 1994, p. 45) conception of desert be justified? I believe that it can, and in any event, such asymmetry is unavoidable in practice. As a matter of principle, the upper and lower limits of desert raise different questions (a similar "bias" in favor of leniency underlies the requirement of proof beyond a reasonable doubt). Maximum allowable desert is a human rights issue; it is about fairness to the defendant and the limits of governmental power. Minimum required desert is about fairness to victims, fairness to law-abiding persons who refrained from similar conduct, and perhaps especially, fairness to other, similarly situated defendants. If fairness in the minimum-desert context is primarily a question of uniformity (fairness to other defendants), not proportionality (fairness to victims and the law-abiding), then this focus, as well as the absence of governmental power, human rights concerns here, would help to explain why Morris viewed lower limits as less confining. In Morris's view, equality is only a guiding principle that should be followed "unless there are other substantial utilitarian reasons to the contrary" (Morris 1982, pp. 160, 198). Although Morris's later support for sentencing guidelines suggests an increased concern for uniformity, he still would require only "roughly equivalent" sanctions for comparable offenders, and a "weak version" of the equality goal (Morris and Tonry 1990, p. 89).

In any event, strict requirements of minimum sanction severity are unenforceable in practice, for the same reason that mandatory-minimum prison terms are widely evaded (Tonry 1996, ch. 5). Defendants can be counted on to object to the sentencing court and to file an appeal if necessary, whenever the sentence exceeds the maximum allowed, or even the presumptive (guidelines) maximum. But prosecutors will rarely object or appeal sentences below the minimum (and no one else has standing to raise this issue) because in many cases the prosecution will have agreed to the sentence as part of a plea bargain; even if the sentence was not agreed to, prosecutors tend to be very selective in filing appeals (Frase 1991, pp. 752–753; 1993a, pp. 316–319; MSGC 2003, p. 23).

Parsimony

This concept has long been a central tenet of utilitarian philosophy. Jeremy Bentham argued that "punishment itself is an evil and should be used as sparingly as possible . . . 'it ought only to be admitted in as far as it promises to exclude some greater evil'" (Tonry 1994, p. 63, quoting Bentham). Cesare Beccaria (1738–1794, pp. 2–3), citing Montesquieu, argued that "every punishment which does not arise from absolute necessity" is tyrannical and unjust. Parsimony is also perhaps a necessary (or at least a natural) corollary of a theory of limiting retributivism; if judges are permitted broad rather than narrow ranges of "just" punishment, some overarching principle such as parsimony is needed to give them more guidance or at least a more precise starting point.

The Model Penal Code and all three editions of the ABA sentencing standards explicitly or implicitly recognized the principle of parsimony. Model Penal Code Section 7.01(1)states a presumption in favor of probation,[3] and Section 305.9 contains a presumption in favor of granting parole as soon as the offender becomes eligible.

The first edition of the ABA sentencing standards stated that offenders should receive "the minimum amount of custody" consistent with public protection, the gravity of the offense, and rehabilitative needs (ABA 1968c, Standard 2.2; see also ABA 1968b, Standard 1.3 (presumption in favor of probation)). The second edition contained similar language (ABA 1979b, Standard 18–2.2(a) (citing Morris and numerous other authors and standards) and Standard 18–3.2(a)(iii)), albeit qualified by strong appeals for sentencing equality.[4] The third edition specified that sentences authorized, as well as sentences imposed, "should be no more severe than necessary" to achieve their societal purposes, while taking into account the gravity of the offense (ABA 1993, Standards 18–2.4 and 18–6.1(a)). This edition, influenced by a perception of excessive uniformity under the federal sentencing guidelines and mandatory-minimum laws, called for sentencing courts to exercise "substantial discretion" (Standard 18–2.6(a)). Sentencing uniformity was given much less emphasis and seemed to be deemed important as much for its value in permitting accurate forecasts of correctional resource needs as for reasons of equal justice (compare Standard 18–2.5(a) (value of accurate forecasts) with Standard 18–2.5(b) (need for "guide[d]" discretion to avoid "unwarranted and inequitable disparities").

A concept akin to parsimony, limiting intrusive governmental measures to what is needed to achieve the asserted government needs, can be found in many other areas of American law, including regulation of speech; equal protection analysis; state regulations burdening interstate commerce; federal legislation under Section 5 of the Fourteenth Amendment; government "takings" of private property; and Eighth Amendment excessive bail standards (Frase 2002, p. 389, n. 300).

Examples of LR in Practice

Sentencing theories and the recommendations of model codes and standards are of little value if they cannot gain acceptance and prove their worth in practice. Morris's theory was, itself, inspired by practical experience; so it is not surprising to find many examples of LR theories in traditional and contemporary sentencing laws and practices. Indeed, such examples can be found not just in the common law systems with which Morris was familiar but also in a wider sampling of nations, providing strong evidence of the universality and fundamental wisdom of his theory.

Traditional American Sentencing Systems

Indeterminate systems, which are still the most common sentencing regime in the United States (Reitz 2001), reflect a very loose version of LR. The statutory maximum sentence, and occasional mandatory-minimum requirements, set upper and lower limits on sanction severity based solely on the offense of conviction (and, in the case of habitual offender laws, prior convictions). Within these wide ranges, judges and parole boards may tailor the sentence to reflect crime-control purposes.

Traditional indeterminate sentencing systems differ from Morris's LR model in several important respects. These systems allow prison commitment and duration decisions to be based on case-specific assessments of the offender's treatment needs and dangerousness. Furthermore, these systems lack an explicit desert rationale for the statutory maxima and minima or for the choice of sentence within the statutory range. They also lack any theoretical or procedural commitment (e.g., via required reasons or appellate review) to sentencing uniformity, and they do not recognize the principle of parsimony. These features of traditional systems were originally attributable to the emphasis in almost all jurisdictions on rehabilitation goals, which were seen as requiring the maximum degree of judicial and parole discretion.

The survival of so many indeterminate sentencing regimes, despite the widespread loss of faith in the rehabilitative ideal (Allen 1981), is probably due both to institutional inertia and vested interest, and to the current popularity of incapacitation and other risk management theories (which, like rehabilitation, are assumed to require substantial case-level discretion). But at least part of the durability of these regimes, despite decades of sustained attack by sentencing theorists and reformers, may be due to the widespread support for a hybrid, LR-type approach—one that recognizes outer, offense-based limits on sanction severity, within which all sentencing purposes may play a substantial role.

International Examples of LR in Practice

Most other Western countries, including those in the civil law as well as common law legal families, also employ an indeterminate sentencing system within statutory ranges (Tonry and Frase 2001)—and thus, a loose version of LR. There is broad agreement on the overarching importance of the principles of proportionality and parsimony[5], within which these countries apply sentencing purposes and criteria, both utilitarian and nonutilitarian, which are similar to those recognized in the United States.

A number of foreign nations have devised sentencing schemes that explicitly seek to reconcile desert and nondesert purposes within an LR framework. For example, in Germany, Sweden, Finland, and the Netherlands the overall severity ("penal value") of the punishment is based on the retributive value assigned to that particular crime (which courts may adjust, to take account of case-specific variations in culpability and harm) (Albrecht 1995; Jareborg 1995; Lappi-Seppälä 2001; Tak 2001; Weigend 2001). Within each range of penal values, certain forms of punishment (e.g., custody, community service, or fines) are allowed. In choosing among these forms, courts may consider offender characteristics, crime-control goals, and other nonretributive factors, to arrive at the form or forms of punishment most appropriate for that case. In Sweden, Finland, and the Netherlands, this two-step approach places a high priority on avoiding disproportionately severe sentences, while granting courts greater flexibility in mitigating penalties and choosing among sanction types of roughly equal severity (Jareborg 1995; Lappi-Seppälä 2001; Tak 2001). However, the sanction equivalencies used in these systems suggest very loose standards of "equality," similar to those Morris advocated. For example, an hour of community service in Finland is deemed equivalent to one day in custody, which is admittedly "more lenient than prima facie required" by penal value assessments (Lappi-Seppälä 2001).

Australia, France, and Germany likewise place greater emphasis on avoiding sentences that are too severe than on avoiding sentences that are too lenient or on achieving sentencing uniformity (Freiberg 2001; Tomlinson 2000, pp. 8–14; Weigend 2001). The frequent use of suspended or conditional prison sentences in many Western countries (Albrecht 2001; Frase 1995; Kelk, Koffman, and Silvis 1993; Weigend 2001) is also consistent with LR—the defendant is spared the full measure of his court-ordered but suspended prison sentence, provided that he complies with the court's conditions.

A flexible, limiting-retributive theory also appears to be more consistent with evolving worldviews on the priority of sentencing goals and values. Whereas disparity and just deserts were central issues in the comparative sentencing literature of the early 1990s (Kelk, Koffman, and Silvis 1993; Morgan and Clarkson 1995; Tonry and Hatlestad 1997 (collecting articles published through 1995)), these considerations received less emphasis in literature of the late 1990s (Tonry and Frase 2001). In most Western countries, there continues to be broad acceptance of official discretion and a willingness to trust judges and releasing authorities to make wise use of that discretion.

American Sentencing Guidelines Systems

A minority of American jurisdictions have at least partially replaced the indeterminate model with sentencing guidelines, usually limited to felonies (Frase 1999). State and federal guidelines systems vary dramatically, but they all involve recommended, LR-type sentencing ranges—sometimes substantially narrower than the previous statutory ranges—based on the offender's conviction offense and prior record. The least ambitious versions address only judicial sentencing decisions (retaining parole release discretion) or provide no appeal rights or other enforcement mechanism. Several state guidelines systems explicitly base the recommended sentences on principles of desert, but even these systems leave substantial room for the application of nondesert sentencing principles, both within the guidelines range and as a basis for departure. Plea bargaining concessions are not regulated in any of these systems, which introduces further scope for mitigation on practical and other nondesert grounds. Some guidelines systems explicitly recognize the principle of parsimony.

Minnesota's Successful Guidelines-based LR System

The Minnesota Sentencing Guidelines, in effect since 1980, provide a particularly strong example of a successful guidelines-based LR system in operation. Indeed, the sentencing regime that has evolved under the Guidelines bears a strong resemblance to Morris's LR model (Frase 1997). Minnesota's experience demonstrates the practical viability of LR and illustrates how guidelines concepts can be used to make Morris's LR theory more specific.

1. Overview of the Minnesota Guidelines. The Minnesota Sentencing Guidelines Commission adopted just deserts (uniformity and proportionality) as its primary sentencing principle, but also made clear that its overall approach was one of "modified just deserts" (MSGC 1980, p. 9; 1984, p. v, 10–14). The Guidelines give substantial emphasis to utilitarian goals, which continue to have strong legislative support. Consistent with Morris's views, desert defines the maximum sentence severity in almost all cases. For the most serious cases (about one-quarter of the annual caseload), desert also specifies relatively flexible standards of minimum severity; for the remaining three-quarters of the cases, there are no minimum severity requirements.

The 1978 guidelines enabling statute (Minn. Stat., chap. 244) abolished parole release discretion and substituted a limited reduction (up to one-third off the pronounced sentence) for good behavior in prison. This earned "good time" reduction then constitutes a period of parole-type post-release supervision (later statutes have provided longer periods of supervision for certain offenders, see, e.g., Minn. Stat., § 609.108, subd. 6). The enabling statute also provided that in-prison treatment programs were to become voluntary; thus, consistent with Morris's views, prison release could be delayed only for disciplinary violations (this was changed in 1993, see later discussion). Finally, the statute requires sentencing judges to provide written reasons when they depart from the Guidelines, and both defendants and the prosecution are given the right to appeal any sentence (whether or not it is a departure).

The new Commission was directed to develop guidelines regulating both the decision to impose a state prison term and the duration of such a term, while taking into "substantial consideration" two factors: "current sentencing and releasing practices" and "correctional resources, including but not limited to the capacities of local and state correctional facilities." The Commission was also permitted (but was not required) to develop guidelines regulating the conditions of nonprison sentences. The Commission chose not to include such probation condition guidelines in the original version of the Guidelines; over the years, this issue has been considered several times, but no such guidelines have been implemented.

The Commission promulgated a set of guidelines (MSGC 2002) regulating prison commitment and duration decisions, using the two-dimensional "grid" of offense severity by offender criminal history, which has subsequently been employed in almost all guidelines systems. Offense severity (the vertical axis of the grid) was based on the Commission's own rank-order assessments; the defendant's criminal history score (horizontal axis) consisted primarily of previous felony convictions; prior felonies originally counted one point each, but they are now weighted by their severity levels (from one-half to two points each). The Guidelines specify the sentence that is presumed to be correct for each combination of offense severity and criminal history. Offenders convicted of lower severity offenses, with low to medium criminal history scores, presumptively receive a stayed (suspended) prison term of a specified number of months (e.g., 18 months for residential burglary with no criminal history points). For more serious offenses or criminal history scores, the presumptive sentence is an executed prison term within a narrow specified range (e.g., 44–52 months for armed robbery with no criminal history points; 54–62 months, with one point). The Guidelines were expressly designed to send more violent offenders to state prison and fewer property offenders, and this goal has been achieved.

Judges may depart from the presumptive sentence only if they cite "substantial and compelling circumstances." Guidelines rules specify permissible and impermissible bases for departure from the presumptive disposition (stayed or executed prison term) and the presumptive prison duration. A large body of appellate case law has emerged, interpreting and expanding these departure criteria (and amply fulfilling Morris's ideal of an evolving "common law of sentencing"). For example, although most of the listed grounds for departure are desert-based, the Minnesota Supreme Court almost immediately ruled that the offender's exceptional amenability or unamenability to probation, or his vulnerability in prison, could constitute valid grounds for dispositional (but not durational) departure (Frase 1997).

For offenders placed on probation, the Guidelines list a wide variety of possible conditions of stayed prison sentences, which judges may select in their discretion—up to one year of confinement in a local jail or workhouse; treatment (residential or outpatient); home detention (with or without electronic monitoring); probation (with "intensive," regular, or no supervision); fines; restitution; victim – offender mediation; and community service.

The Commission took very seriously the statutory directive to consider resource limits and adopted a goal of never exceeding 95 percent of prison capacity. It then developed a computerized model to predict the future prison populations that would result from proposed guidelines and tailored the latter to stay within expected capacity. The Commission's prison-impact model has also been applied to all proposals for Guidelines amendments and changes in criminal or sentencing statutes, and many severe proposals have been rejected or scaled back because of the projected fiscal impact. As a result, Minnesota has not experienced serious prison overcrowding, with its attendant problems of reduced security and court intervention. Prison populations have grown substantially since 1980, but at a slower rate than the average of other states (Reitz, chapter 8 in this volume)—and Minnesota already had one of the lowest per capita prison rates in the nation. Minnesota was the first jurisdiction to base its sentencing policies on "resource-matching," but most other guidelines states have now adopted this approach (Frase 1999).

2. The LR features of Minnesota sentencing theory and practice. Minnesota recognizes fairly strict, desert-based limits on maximum sanction severity, with relatively weak limits on minimum severity (or none at all). The Guidelines' presumptive prison durations define the ordinary range of desert, based on the offender's current conviction offense and prior record; of these two factors, offense severity has a far greater impact on prison duration.[6] Departures above or below these durational ranges must be based on case-specific desert. Only in exceptionally aggravated cases may a desert-based upward durational departure exceed twice the presumptive duration (in which case, the statutory maximum becomes the upper limit). Offender dangerousness, need for treatment, and general deterrence are not valid grounds for an upward durational departure, with one exception: beginning in 1989, several "dangerous offender" statutes were enacted, permitting or even requiring increased prison terms for certain offenders, without regard to the offender's desert (Frase 1993c, pp. 356–357, 360–363). However, these statutes are narrowly drafted and thus infrequently used.

Under the Guidelines, presumptive stayed prison terms may be revoked if the defendant violates probation and, very exceptionally, may be executed from the start if the offender is found unamenable to probation. Such probation revocations and "upward" dispositional departures do not require a case-specific finding of increased desert. However, these practices are still consistent with a recognition of strict upper desert limits, provided one views a prison term equal in length to the presumptive stayed term as the offender's actual desert (or, as Morris would put it, the upper limit of his "not un-deserved" punishment) (Frase 1991, pp. 742–747). Such offenders are recommended to initially receive less than their maximum desert for reasons of parsimony and to permit judges to consider a variety of nondesert purposes. Support for the latter view is found in the structure and language of the Guidelines, as well as in Guidelines case law (Frase 1997).

In Minnesota, as under Morris's theory, lower desert limits are often not present and, when present, are much more flexible than the upper limits described earlier. In presumptive-stay cases (constituting 70–75 percent of the caseload), there are almost no requirements of minimum sanction severity.[7] In presumptive-prison-commit cases, the Guidelines do prescribe minimum severity limits (i.e., the low end of the range of presumptive prison terms in each grid cell). However, these formal limits are often avoided by means of departures and charging mitigations. Since 1990 the mitigated dispositional departure rate for these cases has varied between 30 and 35 percent (MSGC 2003, p. 25). If de facto departures achieved by charging leniency are included, the mitigated dispositional departure rate is over 40 percent (Frase 1993a, p. 302). As for prison durations, the mitigated departure rate for executed sentences has varied between 20 and 30 percent (ibid., p. 28). (Aggravated dispositional and durational departure rates are much lower, averaging about 4 and 11 percent, respectively (ibid., pp. 25, 28).) Minnesota statutes impose relatively few mandatory prison terms, and the most frequently applicable "mandatory" statutes actually allow probation under certain circumstances (Minn. Stat. Annot., § 609.11, subd. 8 and. §609.342, subd. 2). In practice, probation is frequently granted in these cases (Frase 1993a, p. 309).

From the perspective of Morris's LR theory, the allowable ranges in Minnesota's Guidelines grid cells might be seen as either too narrow or too broad. For presumptive-commit defendants, the range of presumptive prison terms is quite narrow (2 months, at the lowest offense severity level; 14 months, at the highest level), allowing too little scope for "fine-tuning" of desert and application of utilitarian sentencing purposes. But in practice, this may not be a serious problem given the frequently used power to adjust sentence durations via departure or charge reduction.

For presumptive-stay defendants, the "desert range" is quite broad. Judges may, but need not, impose a year in jail as a condition of probation, so the effective custody range without a departure is 0–12 months; factoring in the option of invoking the stayed prison term (by finding the offender unamenable to probation at the outset or by later revoking probation), the upper limit of desert is between 13 and 48 months, depending on the grid cell. Such wide custody ranges (and the court's power to impose other onerous probation conditions such as treatment, intensive supervision, community service, and fines) clearly create a potential for disparate treatment and violation of ordinal proportionality. In practice, however, probation revocation rates have been quite modest in most years (Frase 1993b, p. 10), and upward dispositional departures, particularly those based on unamenability, are very rare (Frase 1993a, p. 326). The imposition of excessively onerous probation conditions is limited by the defendant's right to refuse probation and demand execution of the (ordinally scaled) presumptive prison term.

As for the role of various factors serving to "fine-tune" the sentence within desert limits, Minnesota's approach is similar to Morris's. Minnesota judges may consider all traditional purposes of punishment in selecting a prison term within the cell range or when deciding on conditions of probation. As Morris specified, a defendant's need for treatment in prison is not a sufficient reason to impose a prison term (i.e., it is not a basis for an upward dispositional departure), and prison release does not depend on an assessment of the inmate's progress in treatment; however, since 1993 the timing of release may be influenced, via denial of good time credit, by the offender's "refusal to participate in treatment or other rehabilitative programs" (Minn. Stat., § 244.05, subd. 1b(b)).[8] Like Morris, Minnesota also permits rehabilitative and risk assessments to determine conditions of probation and of post-prison supervised release, as well as decisions to revoke probation or release.

Morris might be troubled by the concepts of "amenability" and "unamenability" to probation, which Minnesota cases recognize as a basis for mitigated and aggravated dispositional departure based on individualized assessments of treatment needs and risk. However, these departures operate within desert limits and are only granted on an exceptional basis. Although amenability mitigations are fairly common, they are consistent with Morris's more flexible approach to minimum sanction severity, and they help to achieve several goals he espoused: preservation of the offender's social and community ties, and the principle of parsimony (avoiding suffering and expense, which provide no social benefit). Morris is also very much a realist and might very well conclude that, in a heavily treatment-oriented state like Minnesota ("the land of 10,000 treatment centers" as well as 10,000 lakes), it is wiser to permit and then seek to regulate amenability departures, rather than attempt to prohibit them, which would only invite subterfuge and evasion (Morris 1982, p. 158; Morris and Hawkins 1977, p. 21).

The Minnesota Guidelines only expressly adopt the principle of parsimony with respect to the use of custodial sanctions (MSGC 2002, § I(3)), but sentencing practices suggest that judges and other practitioners apply this concept to other issues as well. Seventy to 75 percent of presumptive sentences under the Guidelines are for probation, and probation constitutes an even higher proportion of sentences imposed; furthermore, mitigating departures far outnumber aggravated departures under the Guidelines, and the difference is even greater when de facto mitigating departures (achieved by charging discretion) are included (Frase 1993a, pp. 299–303, 317–318). Although the Guidelines grid cells with presumptive prison terms suggest a "starting point" at the mid-point (not the bottom) of the cell range, judges seem to prefer to use the lower half of the range (Frase 1997, p. 419). Overall, Minnesota sentencing remains closer to Morris's model of "parsimony" than almost all other American jurisdictions; Minnesota's per capita prison rate was the lowest or second lowest of any state from 1983 to 2001, and its jail rate is also far lower than the national average (Bureau of Justice Statistics 2002, pp. 3, 13).

However, Minnesota has become steadily *less* parsimonious in its use of jail terms; two-thirds of convicted felons now receive a local jail sentence, and the frequency of such sentences has grown considerably since Guidelines sentencing began (in 1978 only 35 percent of felons received a jail sentence, MSGC 2003, p. 16). Still, Minnesota's heavy use of jail terms occurs in cases where many other states impose prison (Frase 1993a, p. 332, n. 120). Moreover, jail sentences are much shorter, are served closer to the defendant's home community, and can more easily accommodate work and other temporary releases. Even when jail inmates are counted, Minnesota's per capita incarceration rate remains the second lowest in the nation (Bureau of Justice Statistics 2002, p. 13).

Morris thought that the use of intermediate sanctions could be encouraged, and useful additional guidance could be provided to trial courts, by the use of multiple presumptions or "bands" on the sentencing grid. He expressed approval of a four-band grid: (1) never prison; (2) presume no prison, absent departure; (3) permit either prison or community-based sanctions; and (4) always prison (Morris and Tonry 1990, pp. 60, 77).

Minnesota's grid still only has two formal "bands": presumed prison and presumed probation (stayed prison). However, in practice, the pattern of prison use across the Guidelines grid reveals four bands or zones similar to what Morris proposed (Frase 1997, p. 422).

Like Morris, Minnesota permits "good-time" credits, in recognition of the need to maintain order in prison without parole release discretion. It also appears that plea bargained concessions continued unabated, under the Guidelines, by means of formal mitigating departures or charging leniency (Frase 1993a, pp. 310, 316–319).

The Need for a More Precise Formulation of the LR Model

As the previous survey of LR theories and systems in practice shows, LR can mean, and has meant, very different things. Indeed, several formulations of this concept can be found even in Morris's own writings. His earlier work suggested very broad, overlapping ranges of "not undeserved" punishment, perhaps not much more confining than the broad statutory ranges provided in most indeterminate sentencing codes of the time. In later writings, Morris's desert ranges seemed to become narrower. He approved of state sentencing guidelines reforms under which the range of presumptively deserved punishment for many offenses is much narrower than typical statutory ranges. He also proposed using interchangeable punishments, and exchange rates between different sanction types, to maintain rough equivalency of sanction severity for equally culpable offenders while allowing sanctions to be tailored to the particular needs of the offender (Morris and Tonry 1990). Morris probably still intended to allow a wider range of sanction severity than pure desert theorists would allow,[9] but how much wider?

The flexibility of the LR concept is part of its strength—it can be accepted and adopted in a wide range of legal, social, and political contexts. But LR must, itself, be kept within some limits or it ceases to have any real meaning or utility. Much of the criticism of Morris's theory is based on his earlier, wider range version (von Hirsch 1981, 1984, 1985, 1992, 1993). Such critics may have sometimes unfairly characterized Morris's theory and ignored its evolution over time, but one can legitimately object that his theory seems to contain no principles that prevent adherents from adopting an extremely loose version or a very strict one. Without further specification, LR could conceivably include anything between a traditional indeterminate sentencing scheme and the strictest form of determinate sentencing.[10]

State guidelines such as those in Minnesota provide a useful model for a more delimited formulation of LR. Such guidelines narrow the available sentencing range for most cases, thus substantially constraining case-level discretion, while still leaving considerable room for individualization and the parsimonious application of utilitarian sentencing goals. The departure option provides further flexibility, subject to the outer limits of sentence type and severity specified by statute.[11] This structure seeks to reconcile the universal conflict between the values of uniformity (equality, proportionality, predictability) and the advantages of flexibility (efficiency, parsimony, case-specific justice, and crime-control measures). Within a narrow range, comparable to the Minnesota presumptive-prison cell ranges, judges have almost complete discretion,[12] and flexibility is given priority. Within a broader severity range, up to the statutory maximum and down to the statutory minimum, if any, flexibility is tempered by uniformity goals—judges have limited discretion to sentence in this broader range provided they state reasons, based on desert and subject to appellate review. Judges may not, in any case, exceed the absolute outer limits of authorized sentences for the conviction offense, specified by statute; here, uniformity values are preferred.

Critics of Morris have questioned not only how broad his desert ranges are, but also how the particular sentence ranges—or, in the example discussed earlier, the presumptive guidelines cell ranges and outer statutory limits—would be chosen and justified (von Hirsch 1992, p. 90). Morris has implied that this is ultimately a political decision, which could be made in a variety of ways, including public or judicial surveys, and legislative or sentencing commission deliberation and consensus-building (Morris and Tonry 1990, p. 85). It would also seem that the legislature or commission could look to the methods that pure desert theorists have proposed for generating ordinal ranking and spacing, and use these same methods to produce one series of proportioned upper limits (Tonry 1994, p. 80), tied to appropriate desert-based categories of conviction offense and prior record, and a second series of proportioned lower limits (at least for those offenses deemed serious enough to require minimum desert standards).

As for the question, how are the precise sentences within these ranges (the grid cell and the wider, departure zone) determined, Morris's parsimony principle provides considerable guidance: judges should start at the bottom of the range and increase severity only to the extent needed to meet all appropriate utilitarian and case-specific desert needs.

Like many other state guidelines, the Minnesota Guidelines contain broad sanction severity ranges for offenders with recommended probation sentences—zero to 12 months in jail, and/or other onerous probation conditions and the possibility that the longer stayed prison term will be executed. These wide, overlapping ranges maximize flexibility and—if practitioners are willing—also maximize parsimony. In a state like Minnesota this is not a major problem, since practitioners tend to use the lower part of these wide ranges (thus achieving both parsimony and a substantial degree of uniformity and ordinal proportionality). But even in Minnesota, some defendants may be unfairly sentenced near the upper end of these broad ranges. And there are undoubtedly other jurisdictions where practitioners, given this broad a choice, would tend to use the upper part of the range, or spread their sentences across the entire range, thus sacrificing uniformity, proportionality, and parsimony values.

One option would be to define a narrower range of sanction severity (punishment units) for each presumptive-probation cell, scaled to maintain ordinal proportionality, and create a system of exchange rates between different sanction types. Using these exchange rates, judges would be allowed to impose any combination of sanction types (jail, day-fines, community service, intensive probation, etc.) provided that the overall punitiveness of the sentence falls within the permissible severity range (for a looser version of this approach, see Morris and Tonry 1990, pp. 56–108; a stricter version has been proposed by pure desert theorists, see the section "A Desert Model with Interchangeable Sanction Types"). In previous writings, I have argued that narrow severity ranges for nonprison sentences are problematic (Frase 1997, pp. 423–425). It is very difficult to develop consensus on precise exchange rates for all types of sanctions, and minimum severity requirements would be very difficult to consistently enforce when practitioners feel that such severity serves no practical purpose. To the extent that such minimum requirements could be enforced, this would make the sentencing system much more complex, greatly increase the frequency of probation violations and revocations (by increasing the number of probation conditions), risk overloading local resources, and violate legitimate local value choices—including a preference for restorative justice measures that rely on consensus to depart substantially from ordinal desert. Moreover, no state has yet adopted such a restrictive regime for presumptive probation cases.[13]

However, upper presumptive limits on the use of the most severe nonprison sanctions seem to be workable and desirable. Such an "asymmetric" limitation is also consistent with the view, expressed by Morris and other writers, and clearly evident in the Minnesota system and in many other Western nations, that it is especially important to prevent disproportionately severe punishments. A suitable model of this probation-severity-capping approach can be found in Oregon; for each grid cell with a presumptive nonprison sentence, the Oregon guidelines specify a presumptive upper limit on the maximum number of "sanction units" (including jail, residential treatment, home detention, and community service), and also a presumptive maximum number of jail days that may be imposed.[14]

The modified LR model proposed here is consistent with Morris's later writings (especially Morris and Tonry 1990) and is quite similar to the system that actually exists in Minnesota, but it is not identical to either the Morris or the Minnesota model. One necessary and very important addition to Morris's theory is the concept of resource-matching, by which the sentencing commission, in drafting and amending the guidelines ranges and prison-commitment rules, uses the greater uniformity of presumptive guidelines sentencing to predict and stay within available prison capacity and other resources. Without this mechanism, it is doubtful that states such as Minnesota would have been able to actually achieve parsimonious use of prison sentences (Frase 1997, p. 429). Another small but important modification to Morris's theory, consistent with Minnesota's approach, would permit prison commitment decisions to be based on assessments of offender amenability to prison or probation—but only in exceptional (departure) cases. Morris was not unsympathetic to the concerns underlying such departures (ibid., pp. 416–417), and most other LR systems, including many with presumptive guidelines, have not forbidden all prison commitment decisions based on treatment and dangerousness assessments. Minnesota's limited acceptance of such assessments (along with its abolition of parole release discretion, which many U.S. jurisdictions have also done, see Reitz, chapter 8 in this volume) seems like the most restrictive approach that can be widely accepted and implemented.

In several other respects, the modified LR model seeks to go modestly beyond what Minnesota has done, based on Morris's theory and experience in several other states. As noted already, roughly proportionate probation severity caps can and should be specified for each presumptive-probation cell. In addition, the parsimony principle should be stated more generally than Minnesota did (Frase 1997, p. 419). Finally, the ordinal proportionality provided by statutory maxima and any mandatory minima would be greatly improved by a comprehensive reexamination of all criminal statutes (Tonry 1988), many of which were enacted at differing times and in no coherent pattern.

The Modified LR Model Compared with Other Sentencing Theories

The delimited, state-guidelines-inspired form of LR proposed in the previous section would properly balance all legitimate values of and practical needs in sentencing. This LR model is also superior to alternative approaches.

There are only three real alternatives.[15] Neither a purely retributive nor a purely utilitarian theory is a realistic option; such regimes have never to my knowledge been implemented, they would be strongly opposed by practitioners, and they are unacceptable in principle because they fail to give appropriate roles to all major punishment purposes.[16] The most likely alternative to be adopted is the one already in place in a majority of jurisdictions in the United States and other Western countries—indeterminate sentencing, with generous upper and occasionally lower statutory limits. At the other extreme are highly determinate systems such as the one that now exists in U.S. courts under the federal guidelines. Finally, several desert theorists have proposed a plausible (but as yet, never adopted) model incorporating strong ordinal proportionality requirements, but permitting considerable choice among different sanction types of equal severity.

Indeterminate Sentencing

The steady spread of LR-compatible guidelines systems in the United States, and the strong support for less far-reaching limits on sentencing and prison release discretion in many other jurisdictions within the United States and abroad, suggests a widespread consensus that predictability (truth in sentencing), uniformity, and proportionality (especially maximum severity proportionality) are very important values. Such values have been and must continue to be incorporated into all sentencing systems as a matter of fundamental fairness (to defendants, victims, and the law-abiding), to maintain public respect for the criminal law and its commands, and to permit the criminal law to play its important role as teacher and reinforcer of the moral values underlying those commands (these utilitarian arguments for just deserts scaling are discussed more fully in the section "A Desert Model with Interchangeable Sanction Types"). Finally, a substantial degree of uniformity and predictability of sentences is needed in order to permit sentencing policy to reflect available correctional resources, avoid prison and jail overcrowding, and set priorities in the use of these limited resources.

Several recent variants of indeterminate sentencing are Restorative and Community Justice (Kurki 1999), and what might be called the Risk Management model (see, e.g., Smith and Dickey 1999). The former emphasizes the needs and participation of crime victims and communities, while the latter focuses on evaluating and managing each offender's risk. Each of these approaches features highly case-specific decision making and gives little weight to predictability, uniformity, and proportionality. Given the broad and growing support for the latter values, it seems unlikely that any of these approaches will replace LR as the consensus model. However, risk management and restorative or community justice can be pursued within an LR model, and this has been done in several state guidelines systems (Frase 1999, pp. 79–80).

Highly Determinate Sentencing

At the other extreme of the flexibility continuum are existing systems that allow much less case-level flexibility than exists under Minnesota and similar state guidelines. The paradigm of this approach is the sentencing system created by the U.S. Sentencing Commission's guidelines (combined with numerous, severe federal mandatory-minimum statutes). The widespread opposition to this approach among federal judges, defense attorneys, scholars, and even some prosecutors (Tonry 1996, ch. 3) suggests that this approach is too extreme to gain consensus support and widespread adoption. Indeed, state sentencing reforms have often begun with a consensus *not* to adopt the federal model (ibid., p. 73).

A Desert Model with Interchangeable Sanction Types

Some desert theorists have argued that LR is not needed in order to reconcile utilitarian and just deserts values, and preserve substantial case-level sentencing discretion. Sentencing severity can be precisely scaled to desert by means of sanction equivalency scales and interchangeable sanctions. This would allow equally culpable offenders to receive very different forms of punishment that are deemed to have equivalent punitive bite but which can be tailored to the particular crime control, restorative justice, or other needs of the particular case (Robinson 1987; von Hirsch, Wasik, and Greene 1989; von Hirsch 1992).[17] These theorists argue that a looser, Morris-style LR approach fails to give sufficient weight to the values of uniformity and proportionality. Paul Robinson has also argued that punishment severity must be directly proportional to desert in order to effectively control crime. The direct crime-control effects of criminal punishments are minimal, given low detection and conviction rates, but punishments based on community perceptions of desert can control crime both by reinforcing specific social norms violated by the offender's actions and by maintaining public respect and support for criminal laws generally (Robinson and Darley 1997; see also Hart 1968, p. 25). Robinson argues that this is especially true in modern heterogeneous and secular societies such as the United States, where many criminal prohibitions are morally neutral mala prohibita.

There is much truth to Robinson's arguments, but they do not prove that sanction severity must be precisely scaled to desert. What is the evidence that the public's views on desert scaling are so exacting? Given the widespread adoption of various forms of LR sentencing, a more likely assumption is that the public accepts mitigating deviations from desert, provided they are not too large and are based on good reasons—including conserving scarce resources and not making offenders worse than they were before. (Conversely, the public is probably least willing to accept deviations from desert when the latter result from clearly illegitimate reasons such as favoritism or corruption.)

It is also probably true that people obey the law more readily if they view the law as procedurally and substantively fair (Tyler 1990). However, the earlier review of LR concepts suggests that some aspects of perceived fairness are more important than others. Punishment of the innocent, conviction by unfair procedures, and excessive punishment probably undermine legitimacy and respect for the law much more than failures to punish enough. Everyone knows that the law cannot punish all violators. Most people are also familiar with the use of probation and parole, and thus know that many offenders receive conditional remission of their just deserts. The informed public understands the normative premise underlying the requirement of proof beyond a reasonable doubt—that protection of the innocent is more important than conviction of the guilty.

In other words, the public is well accustomed to and seems to accept the essential features of the LR model—unfair conviction and excessive punishment are greater evils than underconviction and underpunishment (or, in Morris's terms, imposition of less than the maximum "not undeserved" penalty). Barring specific research data about the public's tolerance for various types of deviation from desert, the best evidence is the continued existence, in every jurisdiction in every Western nation, of sentencing systems that reject strong proportionality constraints; the majority of systems still use an indeterminate model, and even the most desert-based regimes such as Minnesota's have adopted LR. As Michael Tonry (1994) has argued, there may be substantial support for a "weak form" of proportionality, similar to LR, but very little support for a strong version.

There is also much truth to the argument that the relative severity with which different criminal acts are punished is an important "communication," influencing public views about the wrongness of conduct and reinforcing moral values and inhibitions. But the public knows that sentences imposed on individual offenders must reflect practical as well as theoretical concerns. Moreover, the modified LR model proposed here provides considerable norm reinforcement by means of the ordinal scaling embedded in statutory sentence maxima, in the presumptive guidelines ranges, and in the prison and jail sentences imposed by courts—even if many of those sentences are initially stayed.

There is also serious doubt whether consensus can be reached on precise exchange rates for all types of sanctions; indeed, desert theorists have conceded this (von Hirsch, Wasik, and Greene 1989, p. 603). In addition, strong punitive equivalency requirements raise many of the previously noted problems associated with minimum severity requirements for probation conditions (lack of enforceability, complexity, etc.).

In any case, such precise scaling of sanction severity to desert has never been achieved in practice and probably never will be. One fundamental practical barrier to any proposal to closely link every offender's punishment to his deserts is the pervasive need to reward guilty pleas and other forms of defendant cooperation. All modern adjudication and sentencing schemes depend to a great extent on such cooperation. Before and at trial, defendants must be promised leniency to induce and reward guilty pleas, jury trial waivers, testimony against other defendants, and so forth. At sentencing, the court must initially give defendants less than they deserve (or less than the maximum "not-undeserved" penalty)—not only to reward the defendant's cooperation up to that point, but also to induce further cooperation (in obtaining and holding employment, supporting dependents, making restitution, accepting treatment and supervision, etc.) and to leave room for subsequent tightening of sanctions (e.g., by revocation of probation) if the defendant fails to cooperate. Desert theorists recognize this need for "backup sanctions" (von Hirsch 1992, n. 12; von Hirsch, Wasik, and Greene 1989, pp. 609–610), but have not explained how it can be reconciled with a pure desert model. Although some forms of cooperation might be seen as reducing the defendant's "deserts" (at least under a broad definition of that term), many forms do not; society often needs and must reward cooperation whether or not mitigation is deserved. Thus, in practice, modern systems of law enforcement and punishment always function according to an LR model. In the real world of law enforcement and sentencing, a pure, "defining" retributive model is unworkable.

Conclusion

Developing consensus on punishment goals, limitations, and other normative issues is a high priority (von Hirsch 2001; Ashworth 1995, pp. 256–258). Without this, researchers, reformers, and sentencing policy makers cannot even agree on what is "relevant" and "important" (i.e., what to study and what to change) about different systems or proposed systems. Norval Morris's theory of limiting retributivism provides the best starting point for developing such a consensus model of punishment. Some version of LR is already the overwhelming choice among practitioners and law-makers. However, many LR systems give too little weight to the important values of uniformity and proportionality, while some give too much. The LR concept must be made specific enough to rule out such unacceptable extremes.

The delimited, state-guidelines-inspired LR model proposed in this essay provides the best choice for a consensus model. This approach is theoretically sound and has proven to be practically viable over the long term in a number of American states. It accommodates retributive values (especially the importance of limiting maximum sanction severity), makes sentences predictable enough to permit sentencing policy to be coordinated with available resources, and gives appropriate weight to all traditional nonretributive sentencing purposes, including deterrence, incapacitation, rehabilitation, and denunciation. Like Morris's original version, the modified LR model also promotes parsimony and provides sufficient flexibility to incorporate victim and community participation, local values and resource limitations, and restorative justice programs.

The proposed consensus model will strike some readers as an immediate non-starter—"sentencing guidelines" are so unpopular in some quarters that proponents of structured sentencing reforms have had to studiously avoid use of the "G word" (Frase 1999, p. 81). But Minnesota-style guidelines are the essence of LR—they strike a workable and principled balance between retributive and nonretributive values, and between uniformity and flexibility. The balance struck need not be exactly the same in all jurisdictions. More flexible guidelines are suitable for naturally parsimonious jurisdictions, like Minnesota and most European nations, where sentences naturally cluster at the bottom of the applicable ranges. More restrictive guidelines may be needed in jurisdictions with more punitive traditions; in such a context, broad ranges would result in too many sentences at the top of the range or scattered widely across the range.

In the past, guidelines may not have been needed in most jurisdictions outside the United States; the lenient sentencing scales in these systems left few possibilities for major disparities (Tonry 1995, pp. 279–281). But rising populist punitivism and unmanageable prison growth are growing risks in every Western nation (Frase 2001); LR principles, made specific via a Minnesota-style sentencing guidelines regime, can help to reduce these risks.

Notes

1. For a fuller description of the evolution and major features of Morris's theory, see Frase (1997).

2. The commentary goes on to state that proportionality limits can also be supported "on enlightened utilitarian grounds" (given the risks of mistake and abuse, of weakening the link between sanctions and social condemnation, and of undermining citizens' sense of security and control over their lives).

3. See also U.S. National Advisory Commission (1973), Standard 5.2(2) (sentencing criteria should include provision "against the use of confinement . . . unless affirmative justification is shown on the record").

4. Under Standard 18–2.2(a), sentencers should "give serious consideration to the goal of sentencing equality and the need to avoid unwarranted disparities." Standard 18–3.2(a)(ii) urges sentencers to "treat like cases alike" except where "compelling reasons" require inequality.

5. See also Council of Europe 1993, Arts. A4, B2, B5a, and D2 (disproportionality between offense and penalty seriousness should be avoided; sentence ranges should guide courts as to crime seriousness, but minimum penalties should not prevent courts from considering individual circumstances; custodial sentences should be the sanction of last resort; sentences may take into account prior convictions, but should be kept in proportion to the current offense).

6. Within offense levels (grid rows), the presumptive prison duration for the highest criminal history category is on average two times the duration for the lowest criminal history score; within criminal history categories (grid columns), the presumptive duration for the highest offense level is on average 26 times the duration for the lowest offense level (MSGC 2002). Nevertheless, some desert theorists have claimed that the impact of prior record in Minnesota is far greater than can be justified under a true just deserts model (von Hirsch 1994, pp. 39–40).

7. There are, however, a few statutory provisions imposing minimum jail terms, see, e.g., Minn. Stat. Annot., § 609.583 (presumptive sentence for first-offense residential burglary is a 90-day jail term, restitution, or community service).

8. Morris accepted a more limited form of "encouragement" to enter prison programs: the inmate may be compelled to participate in such a treatment program long enough to "know what it is about" (1974, pp. 18–19).

9. Morris and Tonry (1990) probably intended to authorize but not require judges to impose up to full equivalent severity, when switching between sanction types. They recognized the political reality that in most jurisdictions in 1990 the public and its officials would not agree to move offenders from custody to intermediate sanctions unless the latter could be seen to be "roughly" as punitive (pp. 83, 90). Also, to the extent that such sanctions are used to replace straight probation, equivalency rates serve to ensure that the aggregate severity of these sanctions (including eventual revocation to prison or jail) stays within upper desert limits.

10. The Halliday Report, a British sentencing policy paper released in 2001, purported to adopt an "LR" approach, but in an extremely weak form, especially regarding parsimony (Tonry and Rex 2002, pp. 5–9).

11. Tonry (1994, p. 80). The guidelines systems in some states (e.g., North Carolina) have eliminated separate statutory maxima; the guidelines themselves contain an "aggravated" sentencing range, use of which constitutes a departure.

12. Minnesota appellate courts will almost never reverse a sentence within the presumptive range. *State v. Kindem*, 313 N.W. 2d 6 (Minn. 1981).

13. Several guidelines states have attempted to structure probation conditions by placing sanction types in three or more groups (custody; restrictive intermediate, RI; and less restrictive intermediate, LRI) and specifying, for each grid cell, which types may be used. However, these systems are not very confining. For instance, North Carolina permits a non-custody sentence in 34 of its 54 felony grid cells, but precludes custody in only three of these cells (one of which requires LRI) (North Carolina Sentencing and Policy Advisory Commission 2003). Pennsylvania permits a non-custody sentence in only 19 of its 104 grid cells (including misdemeanors) and precludes custody in only two of these cells (both of which require LRI) (Pennsylvania Commission on Sentencing 2003).

14. One day spent in any of these sanctions counts as one unit except for community service (16 hours per unit) (Oregon Criminal Justice Commission 2003, § 213–005-0012). Minnesota maintains these upper limits more crudely, under case law permitting defendants to refuse probation and demand execution of the stayed prison term (Frase 1997, p. 399).

15. For a fuller discussion of these and other alternatives, see Frase (1999, pp. 78–80).

16. A variant of retributivism would require penalties scaled to ordinal proportionality, subject to exceptional upward departures needed to prevent an "intolerable level of crime" (Robinson 1987). However, this approach has been questioned by other desert theorists (von Hirsch 1992) and still provides much too small a role for non-desert purposes.

17. Norval Morris seemed to adopt a looser version of this approach, requiring only "rough" equivalency of punitive bite for comparable offenders (Morris and Tonry 1990, pp. 97–104). Robinson does not specify the degree of precision; von Hirsch has said such equivalence should be "approximate" (von Hirsch, Wasik, and Greene 1989, p. 600; von Hirsch 1992, p. 80).

References

ABA, see American Bar Association

Albrecht, Hans-Jörg. 1995. "Sentencing in the Federal Republic of Germany." *Federal Sentencing Reporter* 7:305–307.

———. 2001. "Post-Adjudication Dispositions in Comparative Perspective." In *Sentencing and Sanctions in Western Countries*, ed. Michael Tonry and Richard S. Frase. New York: Oxford University Press.

Allen, Francis A. 1981. *The Decline of the Rehabilitative Ideal: Penal Policy and Social Purpose.* New Haven: Yale University Press.

American Bar Association ["ABA"]. 1968a. *Standards Relating to the Administration of Criminal Justice: Pleas of Guilty.* Chicago: American Bar Association.

————. 1968b. *Standards Relating to the Administration of Criminal Justice: Probation.* Chicago: American Bar Association.

————. 1968c. *Standards Relating to the Administration of Criminal Justice: Sentencing Alternatives and Procedures.* Chicago: American Bar Association.

————. 1979a. *Standards Relating to the Administration of Criminal Justice: Pleas of Guilty.* 2d ed. Chicago: American Bar Association.

————. 1979b. *Standards Relating to the Administration of Criminal Justice: Sentencing Alternatives and Procedures.* 2d ed. Washington, D.C.: American Bar Association.

————. 1993. *ABA Standards for Criminal Justice: Sentencing.* 3d ed. Washington, D.C.: American Bar Association.

————. 1997. *Standards for Criminal Justice: Pleas of Guilty.* 3d ed. Chicago: American Bar Association.

American Law Institute. 1985. *Model Penal Code and Commentaries, Official Draft and Revised Comments,* Part I, vols. 1–3; Part II, vols. 1–3. Philadelphia: American Law Institute.

————. 2002. *Model Penal Code: Sentencing, Preliminary Draft No. 1.* Philadelphia: American Law Institute.

Ashworth, Andrew J. 1995. "Reflections on the Role of the Sentencing Scholar." In *The Politics of Punishment and Sentencing,* ed. Chris Clarkson and Rod Morgan. Oxford: Oxford University Press.

Beccaria, Cesare (1738–1794). 1983. *An Essay on Crimes and Punishments.* 4th ed. Brookline Village, Mass.: International Pocket Library, Branden Press, Inc.

Bentham, Jeremy (1748–1832). 1931. *The Theory of Legislation,* ed. C. K. Ogden. New York: Harcourt, Brace & Co.

Bottoms, Anthony. 1995. "The Philosophy and Politics of Punishment and Sentencing." In *The Politics of Punishment and Sentencing,* ed. Chris Clarkson and Rod Morgan. Oxford: Oxford University Press.

Bureau of Justice Statistics. 2002. *Prison and Jail Inmates at Midyear 2001.* Washington, D.C.: U.S. Department of Justice.

Council of Europe. 1993. *Consistency in Sentencing,* Recommendation no. R (92) 17. Strasbourg: Council of Europe.

Crocker, Lawrence. 1992. "The Upper Limits of Just Punishment." *Emory Law Journal* 41:1059–1110.

Frase, Richard S. 1991. "Sentencing Reform in Minnesota, Ten Years After: Reflections on Dale G. Parent's *Structuring Criminal Sentences: The Evolution of Minnesota's Sentencing Guidelines.*" *Minnesota Law Review* 75:727–754.

————. 1993a. "Implementing Commission-based Sentencing Guidelines: The Lessons of the First Ten Years in Minnesota." *Cornell Journal of Law and Public Policy* 2:279–337.

————. 1993b. "Prison Population Growing under Minnesota Sentencing Guidelines." *Overcrowded Times* 4(1):10–12.

————. 1993c. "The Role of the Legislature, the Sentencing Commission, and Other Officials under the Minnesota Sentencing Guidelines." *Wake Forest Law Review* 28:345–379.

————. 1995. "Sentencing Laws and Practices in France." *Federal Sentencing Reporter* 7:275–280.

————. 1997. "Sentencing Principles in Theory and Practice." In *Crime and Justice: A Review of Research*, vol. 22, ed. Michael Tonry. Chicago: University of Chicago Press.

————. 1999. "Sentencing Guidelines in Minnesota, Other States, and the Federal Courts: A Twenty-Year Retrospective." *Federal Sentencing Reporter* 12:69–82.

————. 2001. "Comparative Perspectives on Sentencing Policy and Research." In *Sentencing and Sanctions in Western Countries*, ed. Michael Tonry and Richard S. Frase. New York: Oxford University Press.

————. 2002. "What Were They Thinking? Fourth Amendment Unreasonableness in *Atwater v. City of Lago Vista*." *Fordham Law Review* 71:329–421.

Freiberg, Arie. 2001. "Three Strikes and You're Out—It's Not Cricket: Colonization and Resistance in Australian Sentencing." In *Sentencing and Sanctions in Western Countries*, ed. Michael Tonry and Richard S. Frase. New York: Oxford University Press.

Hart, H. L. A. 1968. *Punishment and Responsibility: Essays in the Philosophy of Law*. New York: Oxford University Press.

Honderich, Ted. 1969. *Punishment: The Supposed Justifications*. London: Hutchinson & Co.

Jareborg, Nils. 1995. "The Swedish Sentencing Reform." In *The Politics of Punishment and Sentencing*, ed. Chris Clarkson and Rod Morgan. Oxford: Oxford University Press.

Kelk, Constantijn, Lawrence Koffman, and Jos Silvis. 1993. "Sentencing Practice, Policy, and Discretion." In *Criminal Justice in Europe: A Comparative Study*, ed. Phil Fennel, Christopher Harding, Nico Jörg, and Bert Swart. Oxford: Clarendon Press.

Kurki, Leena. 1999. "Incorporating Restorative and Community Justice into American Sentencing and Corrections." Washington, D.C.: U.S. Dept. of Justice, Office of Justice Programs.

LaFave, Wayne R. 2000. *Criminal Law*. 3d ed. St. Paul, Minn.: West Group.

Lappi-Seppälä, Tapio. 2001. "Sentencing and Punishment in Finland: The Decline of the Repressive Ideal." In *Sentencing and Sanctions in Western Countries*, ed. Michael Tonry and Richard S. Frase. New York: Oxford University Press.

Longford, Frank Pakenham (Lord). 1961. *The Idea of Punishment*. London: Geoffrey Chapman.

Miller, Marc, and Norval Morris. 1986. "Predictions of Dangerousness: Ethical Concerns and Proposed Limits." *Notre Dame Journal of Law, Ethics, and Public Policy* 2:393–444.

Minnesota Sentencing Guidelines Commission ["MSGC"]. 1980. *Report to the Legislature*. St. Paul, Minn.: Minnesota Sentencing Guidelines Commission.

———. 1984. *The Impact of the Minnesota Sentencing Guidelines: Three-Year Evaluation*. St. Paul, Minn.: Minnesota Sentencing Guidelines Commission.

———. 2002. *Sentencing Guidelines and Commentary*. Available: http://www.msgc.state.mn.us/.

———. 2003. *Sentencing Practices: Annual Summary Statistics for Felony Offenders Sentenced in 2001*. Available: http://www.msgc.state.mn.us/.

Morgan, Rod, and Chris Clarkson. 1995. "The Politics of Sentencing Reform." In *The Politics of Punishment and Sentencing*, ed. Chris Clarkson and Rod Morgan. Oxford: Oxford University Press.

Morris, Norval. 1951. *The Habitual Criminal*. New York: Longmans, Green.

———. 1953. "Sentencing Convicted Criminals." *Australian Law Journal* 27: 186–200.

———. 1974. *The Future of Imprisonment*. Chicago: University of Chicago Press.

———. 1977a. "Punishment, Desert and Rehabilitation." In *Equal Justice under Law* (U.S. Dept. of Justice, Bicentennial Lecture Series), pp. 137–167. Washington, D.C.: U.S. Government Printing Office.

———. 1977b. "Towards Principled Sentencing." *Md. Law Review* 37:267–285.

———. 1982. *Madness and the Criminal Law*. Chicago: University of Chicago Press.

———. 1992. "Incapacitation within Limits." In *Principled Sentencing*, ed. Andrew von Hirsch and Andrew Ashworth. Boston: Northeastern University Press.

———. 1993. "The Honest Politician's Guide to Sentencing Reform." In *The Socio-economics of Crime and Justice*, ed. Brian Forst. Armonk, N.Y.: M. E. Sharpe, Inc.

Morris, Norval, and Gordon Hawkins. 1970. *The Honest Politician's Guide to Crime Control*. Chicago: University of Chicago Press.

———. 1977. *Letter to the President on Crime Control*. Chicago: University of Chicago Press.

Morris, Norval, and Colin Howard. 1964. *Studies in Criminal Law*. Oxford: Clarendon Press.

Morris, Norval, and Marc Miller. 1985. "Predictions of Dangerousness." In *Crime and Justice: A Review of Research*, vol. 6, ed. Michael Tonry and Norval Morris. Chicago: University of Chicago Press.

Morris, Norval, and Michael Tonry. 1990. *Between Prison and Probation: Intermediate Punishments in a Rational Sentencing System*. New York: Oxford University Press.

MSGC, see Minnesota Sentencing Guidelines Commission

North Carolina Sentencing and Policy Advisory Commission. 2003. *Felony Punishment Chart*. Available: http://www.nccourts.org/Courts/CRS/Councils/spac/Default.asp

Oregon Criminal Justice Commission. 2003. *Oregon Sentencing Guidelines*. Available: http://www.ocjc.state.or.us/.

Packer, Herbert. 1968. *The Limits of the Criminal Sanction*. Stanford, Calif.: Stanford University Press.

Pennsylvania Commission on Sentencing. 2003. *Basic Sentencing Matrix*. Available: http://pcs.la.psu.edu/.

Reitz, Kevin. 2001, "The Disassembly and Reassembly of U.S. Sentencing Practices." In *Sentencing and Sanctions in Western Countries*, ed. Michael Tonry and Richard S. Frase. New York: Oxford University Press.

Robinson, Paul. 1987. "Hybrid Principles for the Distribution of Criminal Sanctions." *Northwestern University Law Review* 82:19–42.

Robinson, Paul, and John M. Darley. 1997. "The Utility of Desert." *Northwestern University Law Review* 91:453–499.

Smith, Michael E., and Walter J. Dickey. 1999. "Reforming Sentencing and Corrections for Just Punishment and Public Safety." Washington, D.C.: U.S. Dept. of Justice, Office of Justice Programs.

Tak, Peter. 2001. "Sentencing and Punishment in the Netherlands." In *Sentencing and Sanctions in Western Countries*, ed. Michael Tonry and Richard S. Frase. New York: Oxford University Press.

Tomlinson, Edward A. 2000. "Translator's Preface." In *The French Penal Code Revised Edition*. Littleton, Colo.: Rothman & Co.

Tonry, Michael. 1988. "Sentencing Guidelines and the Model Penal Code." *Rutgers Law Journal* 19:823–848.

———. 1994. "Proportionality, Parsimony, and Interchangeability of Punishments." In *Penal Theory and Penal Practice: Tradition and Innovation in Criminal Justice*, ed. Antony Duff et al. Manchester: Manchester University Press.

———. 1995. "Sentencing Reform across National Boundaries." In *The Politics of Punishment and Sentencing*, ed. Chris Clarkson and Rod Morgan. Oxford: Oxford University Press.

———. 1996. *Sentencing Matters*. New York: Oxford University Press.

Tonry, Michael, and Richard S. Frase, eds. 2001. *Sentencing and Sanctions in Western Countries*. New York: Oxford University Press.

Tonry, Michael, and Kathleen Hatlestad. 1997. *Sentencing Reform in Overcrowded Times: A Comparative Perspective*. New York: Oxford University Press.

Tonry, Michael, and Sue Rex. 2002. "Reconsidering Sentencing and Punishment in England and Wales." In *Reform and Punishment: The Future of Sentencing*, ed. Sue Rex and Michael Tonry. Cullompton, Devon: Willan Publishing.

Tyler, Tom R. 1990. *Why People Obey the Law*. New Haven: Yale University Press.

U.S. National Advisory Commission on Criminal Justice Standards and Goals. 1973. *Corrections*. Washington, D.C.: U.S. Government Printing Office.

von Hirsch, Andrew. 1981. "Utilitarian Sentencing Resuscitated: The American Bar Association's Second Report on Criminal Sentencing." *Rutgers Law Review* 33:772–789.

———. 1984. "Equality, 'Anisonomy,' and Justice: A Review of *Madness and the Criminal Law*." *Michigan Law Review* 82:1093–1112.

———. 1985. *Past or Future Crimes: Deservedness and Dangerousness in the Sentencing of Criminals*. New Brunswick, N.J.: Rutgers University Press.

———. 1988. "Hybrid Principles in Allocation of Sanctions: A Response to Professor Robinson." *Northwestern University Law Review* 82:64–72.

———. 1992. "Proportionality in the Philosophy of Punishment." In *Crime and Justice: A Review of Research*, vol. 16, ed. Michael Tonry. Chicago: University of Chicago Press.

———. 1993. *Censure and Sanctions*. Oxford: Clarendon Press.

———. 1994. "Sentencing Guidelines and Penal Aims in Minnesota." *Criminal Justice Ethics* 13:39–49.

———. 2001. "The Project of Sentencing Reform." In *Sentencing and Sanctions in Western Countries*, ed. Michael Tonry and Richard S. Frase. New York: Oxford University Press.

von Hirsch, Andrew, Martin Wasik, and Judith Greene. 1989. "Punishments in the Community and the Principles of Desert." *Rutgers Law Journal* 20:595–618.

Walker, Nigel. 1969. *Sentencing in a Rational Society*. New York: Basic Books, Inc.

Weigend, Thomas. 2001. "Sentencing and Punishment in Germany." In *Sentencing and Sanctions in Western Countries*, ed. Michael Tonry and Richard S. Frase. New York: Oxford University Press.

5

Sentencing Reform "Reform" through Sentencing Information Systems

Marc L. Miller

Norval Morris often quotes an eminent nineteenth-century English politician who, when asked about proposals for parliamentary reform, responded, "Reform, reform. Don't talk to me about reform. We are in enough trouble already."

Sentencing has undergone more reform over the past several decades than any other area of criminal justice, and perhaps as much reform as any area of the law. Indeed, one way to describe sentencing reform over the past half century is that law came to sentencing—an idea framed in the title of Marvin Frankel's famous speech and book, *Criminal Sentences: Law Without Order* (Frankel 1973).

About half of the U.S. states and the U.S. federal system have adopted "guideline" sentencing reforms over the past 30 years. These reforms vary substantially (Frase 1997, 2000; Reitz 1997) and have succeeded in varying degrees in both popular and professional assessment (Frase 1997, 2000; Miller 1995; Wright 2002). Guideline reforms typically involve the legislative creation of a sentencing commission, often a permanent commission, to promulgate sentencing rules and conduct sentencing research (Tonry 1996). The "commission and guideline" reform movement is now sufficiently advanced that the American Law Institute has begun the process of developing a model sentencing code based on the best practices from among these reforms (Reitz 2002).

Despite the high visibility of guideline sentencing reforms in legal, popular, and scholarly discourse, about half the U.S. states still use systems primarily modeled on an indeterminate sentencing model (Reitz 2001). In many of these states some common aspects of guideline systems other than the core elements of commissions and guidelines have been adopted, including various kinds of mandatory-minimum sentences, three-strikes provisions, and restrictions on parole (Wright 1998; Reitz, chapter 8 in this volume). Just over half the states, lured in large part by federal funding enticements, have adopted "truth in sentencing policies" requiring violent felony offenders to serve at least 85 percent of the sentence imposed. But even with the significant overlay of changes in parole or mandatory penalties, states without guidelines still sit on a foundation of broad legislative sentencing ranges, substantial and largely unregulated judicial discretion, and, except in those states that have eliminated parole, executive sentencing review that ultimately determines the actual sentence offenders serve.

Very little is known about sentencing in these still-indeterminate states. Indeterminate systems with their lack of rules and opinions and multiple overlapping discretionary decision making are inherently difficult to study, and scholars and policy makers have focused their attention on the federal system and the guideline states. It is hard to believe that the guideline reforms swirling in the air from other jurisdictions have not influenced the law and practice in these states. And it is possible that within an indeterminate framework some portion of the modern reforms have occurred, though more hidden from view. Modern reform concepts may have come to the still-indeterminate systems in the discussions about sentencing between lawyers, judges, and probation officers, and in the increasing structure and regulation of release decisions (a trend visible in the federal system and many guideline states before the shift to guideline sentencing).

It is not apparent why so many states have resisted such a powerful reform movement. Perhaps some states have obtained an unduly negative impression because one of the most widely discussed guideline reforms (the federal system) is one of the worst and atypical in many key respects (Reitz 1997). States may find the highly structured, rule-intensive nature of the federal guideline system and some states unattractive (Miller 1992b; Wright 1992), or be skeptical of independent agencies, or believe judges should be central to sentencing and perceive that guidelines (again, perhaps, overly attuned to the troubled federal system) have tended to remove too much judicial discretion (Freed 1992; Stith and Cabranes 1998). Perhaps the surprise should be how quickly guideline reforms have spread, and the reasonable expectation should be that most of all of the remaining states will adopt some version of sentencing guidelines in the near future.

An important reform issue for the U.S. states and other jurisdictions that have not been convinced about the virtues of guideline systems is whether there are other reform options that answer the critique of indeterminate systems. In addition, 30 years into modern guideline reforms in practice, it is useful even for the most successful state guideline systems to see whether the hopes and aspirations for better sentencing systems have been fulfilled.

This essay considers a model of sentencing reform different from the "commission and guidelines" model that might nonetheless address the goals of modern sentencing reform. It begins with a quick review of a powerful essay by Norval Morris, written in 1953, in which he sketched the foundation for the structured sentencing reform movement that would emerge over the next two decades. In addition, Morris hinted at the possibility of providing feedback to judges about the sentencing decisions made by other judges in similar cases and about whether prior sentences had achieved the sentencing purposes sought by the court.

In the 1980s and 1990s, several countries began to experiment with Sentencing Information Systems (SIS). These experiments have received limited evaluation and only modest recognition in the sentencing literature. The second section suggests why Sentencing Information Systems have become more plausible in the context of the developing "language" of sentencing and in light of modern information technology, and describes several of these experiments, with a focus on ongoing reform efforts in Scotland and New South Wales, Australia. No SIS has yet demonstrated the capacity to achieve the central goals of modern sentencing reform, and substantial questions exist about whether and how "bottom up" information systems might integrate reform goals such as efficient resource allocation. Nonetheless, this section offers reasons to think that SIS may be a viable sentencing reform alternative and therefore encourages continued experimentation with SIS.

While SIS may offer an alternative approach for jurisdictions that have been unwilling to pursue the commission and guidelines model, information systems might also be used in conjunction with such systems. Indeed, information systems may have their greatest role to play in testing, nurturing, and nudging guideline systems. The third section asks whether a feedback system might produce less "trouble" in systems such as the federal system and, even in successful state guideline systems, whether the addition of an SIS might produce more justice.

Morris's 1953 Sentencing Prolegomenon

In 1953, before he moved to the United States, Norval Morris wrote an important critique of sentencing, "Sentencing Convicted Criminals" (Morris 1953). This essay, based on a speech at the Eighth Australian Legal Convention, and therefore aimed, in good part, at judges, set the stage for the many individual and institutional challenges to indeterminate sentencing that would follow over the next several decades. It also contained suggestions about the possibility of a judge-centered, information-driven sentencing system very different from the commission and guidelines model that has become the dominant mode of sentencing reform.

Morris observed, in language that Marvin Frankel (1973) would later mirror, that

> within the wide discretion left to courts to determine the appropriate punishments for crime they have failed to develop any agreed principles or practices and that consequently judicial sentencing lacks uniformity and equality of application, is considerably capricious, and can be shown to fit neither the crime nor the criminal. . . . The individual personality of the judge or magistrate plays too large a part in the assessment of the punishment. . . . There is . . . too great an illogical and fortuitous variation between sentences. (Morris 1953, p. 186)

The 50 years since that essay was published have shown continued concern with disparity, but less attention to the judge's role in sentencing or to the purposes of sentencing. With a dramatic shift away from the central role of rehabilitation and greater skepticism about the role of the sentencing judge, the hope that judges and magistrates would become trained in criminology and the social sciences no longer speaks to reformers (Morris 1953, p. 197). Morris was concerned about the possible removal of sentencing discretion from judges, including the idea that all sentencing discretion might be shifted to administrative "Treatment Tribunals" made up of experts (Morris 1953, pp. 198–199). Yet he did not foresee the possibility that the expert panels might be established not to sentence offenders but to establish sentencing "principles" and "practices" to guide sentencing courts. Thus, Morris did not address the idea of the modern sentencing commission, which is often composed not of experts in a technical or substantive sense but instead in a political or experiential sense, with judges, prosecutors, citizens, and sometimes defense lawyers as representatives and with technical experts present in staff roles.

But while some of Morris's comments seem antiquated in light of subsequent theory and practice, much of his commentary and suggestions remain visionary. For example, Morris pointed to the importance of "alternative" sanctions to a wise and purpose-driven system, emphasizing that "judges can sentence only within the penal facilities available to them" (1953, p. 187). This is an idea that Morris and Michael Tonry would nicely capture and develop in their book *Between Prison and Probation* (Tonry and Morris 1990).

An important example of insights both antiquated and visionary comes with Morris's extended discussion of the purposes of sentencing and the role of purposes in individual sentencing decisions. Morris's comments assume the centrality of utilitarian purposes, with a special concern for rehabilitation, as both a general justifying aim of criminal sanctions and to decide on particular sentences. The common current themes of retribution and just deserts play a decidedly lesser role.

Morris's own theory of the general justifying aims of punishment evolved considerably, and his later theory of limiting retributivism gives a secondary role to rehabilitation and other utilitarian aims (Frase, chapter 4 in this volume). But even in 1953 Morris revealed an understanding of the multiple levels and varying roles of purposes in a way that seems fresher and more subtle than much policy or writing on purposes since that time:

> No one theory explains the different punitive measures to be found in our criminal law. . . . *All too often the purposes of punishment are discussed as if they could be treated as a single problem. . . . Surely the truth is that we have a series of related problems rather than a single problem.* . . . Surely, at the present level of our knowledge, we aim at a whole congeries of various purposes in respect not only of various types of crime but various types of criminals. . . .
>
> [B]ecause we do not seek any single purpose or set of purposes through our penal sanctions, we must not suppose we are facing an academic and impractical problem. . . .
>
> Prevention, reformation, deterrence, retribution, expiation, vindication of the law, and the Kantian argument that punishment is an end in itself all mingle in the wild dialectic confusion which constitutes most discussions of the purposes of punishment. (pp. 188–189, emphasis added)

Morris introduced the very important idea of articulating "purposes *at* sentencing" for individual offenders in contrast to the more abstract debate over purposes *of* sentencing for an entire system (Miller 1992a).

> *When a court decides what sentence to impose on a criminal . . . it must do so with reference to some purpose or purposes, conscious or unconscious, articulate or inarticulate. . . . [A] compass is desirable . . . even if only for a short distance and over a particular part of the journey. . . .* [F]or certain types of criminals reformation is one important aim. None will dispute that our hope of deterring the criminal from repeating his crime by the punishment we inflict and by that same punishment deterring others who are like-minded also plays a considerable part. Few will deny that there is in the community a deep-rooted hatred of the criminal . . . and that in our penal sanctions we must take into account these

emotional demands of the community. The extent to which these aims of reformation, deterrence and community satisfaction blend in relation to any particular offender will vary considerably. (1953, p. 189, emphasis added)

The emergence of the guideline and commission model of sentencing mediates the force of some aspects of this critique. Sentencing judges in the federal guideline system sidestep the issue of purposes either for the system as a whole or "at sentencing" (for the particular offender) by assuming, if they consider the issue at all, that the Congress has accounted for sentencing purposes by statute and the sentencing commission has accounted for sentencing purposes in its rules. Federal judges under the guidelines rarely make reference to any primary or theoretical purpose or purposes for sentencing a particular offender, but refer more frequently to the secondary or functional purposes of producing reasonable uniformity across cases. State judges often note a concern in guideline systems for limiting the total impact on prisons and state budgets. It is difficult to find published decisions in federal or state guideline systems discussing primary purposes at all. In some guideline system cases, the conceptual structure provided by guidelines and an authorizing statute make it possible for judges to discuss primary purposes of punishment in the context of resolving specific questions such as "in/out" decisions, or the use of nonprison sanctions, or interpretation of difficult statutory or guideline concepts such as the relevance of an offender's criminal history.

One of the great puzzles of modern sentencing reform in practice is the absence of explicit discussion of sentencing purposes concerning many guideline systems, either in the authorizing legislation or in the sentencing rules. One notable exception is Minnesota in the early 1980s where the sentencing commission discussed and articulated purposes, and then used those discussions to shape the guidelines (Frase, chapter 4 in this volume; Parent 1988). But where statements of purpose exist, they are often so general as to be meaningless or are meaningless in practice—both of which are true, for example, of the federal sentencing guidelines system (Miller 1992a; Rappaport 2003a, 2003b; Hofer and Allenbaugh 2003).

The primacy of functional or secondary purposes—largely concerns about wise resource allocation, reduction in sentencing disparity, and various kinds of transparency and certainty (sometimes labeled "truth in sentencing")—has shifted the deeper, primary issues of why we sentence offenders to the interstices of sentencing reform practice. Where resource limitations force commissions to make choices, primary purposes sometimes reappear at this later stage of policy and rule making. The societal shift toward retribution (or "just deserts") as a general justifying and limiting principle may also have encouraged this trend, since the proper scale of retribution is hard to precisely state, and the "effectiveness" of retribution a difficult idea to state at all. Morris's own theory of limiting retributivism leaves room for the play of utilitarian and perhaps secondary purposes in sentencing decisions (Frase, chapter 4 in this volume; Reitz, chapter 8 in this volume).

In his 1953 essay, Morris offered a suggestion that might be easily lost after so many insights and because the suggestion may have been unworkable at the time. Morris suggested as "immediate steps" on the path to a more principled, purpose-driven system that judges be provided with far greater information about the sentencing practices of their fellow judges and the impact of sentences actually imposed.

> *More information on current sentencing practice and the effects of different punishments is essential, and this should be of two kinds: statistics in each state regarding the sentences to be imposed by different courts (related at least to the crimes committed, to the ages of the criminals sentenced and to their criminal records), so that individual judges and magistrates may see where they stand in relation to their brethren;* and follow-up studies of the later histories of samples of convicted criminals, so that the effectiveness of different punishments for different types of criminals may be gauged and enlightened rather than fortuitous individualization of punishment become possible.
>
> It would be neither difficult nor relatively expensive to obtain these kinds of information. (p. 200, emphasis added)

Was he right? Could the availability of information on sentences imposed, and perhaps on their success at achieving utilitarian aims, be the basis for a modern sentencing system? Could such a system provide an alternative to the dominant guideline and commission model? Could it be integrated with a guideline system?

Sentencing Offenders in Light of Systemic Knowledge

Morris suggested that a system of providing information about sentences imposed by other judges would be a good step towards further reform and that the relevant information would be "neither difficult nor relatively expensive to obtain." This section considers whether such a "sentencing information system" (SIS) was possible in the early 1950s, and, more importantly, assesses whether such a system is possible now.

Sentencing Law Requires
a Sentencing Language

A functional and substantial sentencing information system would have been difficult in 1953. U.S. criminal codes in the middle of the century were hardly models of conceptual or functional purity. In the United States, the Model Penal Code effort to bring greater coherence to American codes had just begun. But the problem was not limited to the U.S. codes: a coherent and functional sentencing information system requires specification of a reasonable number of reasonably well-defined offense, offender, and other categories, and mechanisms for recording information about each case in a reasonably consistent fashion. While an experiment might have begun to create this conceptual framework, no such list of categories existed at the time. The problem is not just one of categories—of creating terms and concepts—but of developing a social language among sentencers to understand, apply, and challenge those categories.

Structured sentencing reforms have produced a language sufficient to make sentencing information systems a reality. One of the greatest successes of the structured sentencing movement has been to create a language of familiar terms and concepts, and to have that language become part of modern legal discourse through the creation and application of guidelines in many systems. Ideas including more nuanced assessment of harms, "relevant conduct," "role in the offense," "substantial assistance" to government authorities, "vulnerable victims," and the like are now part of sentencing discourse across jurisdictions (even where the terms vary).

Moreover, any system complex enough to provide detailed, dynamic information would require substantial and ongoing computation. That kind of computation, which is everyday in a world of personal computers and information systems, would have been too expensive and incomplete to make it worth the effort in the 1950s. While not trivial as a matter of cost or organization today, it is not difficult to design or establish information systems that can provide complex and varied analysis and rapid feedback (Doob 1989).

What would a sentencing information system look like? What is the theory in support of such a system in contrast to the guidelines and commission model? What are the necessary elements for such a system? Is a commission or some kind of administrative body necessary for sentencing information systems? What role might legislatures, sentencing courts, appellate courts, or sentencing commissions serve in designing and operating a sentencing information system?

Fortunately, judges in Canada, Scotland, and in New South Wales, Australia have been experimenting with such systems, as have some courts in other jurisdictions. The next section considers the justification for and structure of those systems, and the relevance of these early experiments to other jurisdictions.

Sentencing Information System (SIS) Experiments

The central idea of a sentencing information system is fairly simple: judges should be provided with sufficient information to place an offender into a larger context, and the most useful context for judges is how other offenders like that offender have been sentenced before—by the same judge, by other judges in the same courthouse, or by other judges in the same state or country. A separate question is what judges then do with that information—whether and how it might constrain their authority beyond general statutory sentencing limits.

Despite the existence of several SIS experiments over the past 20 years, only a modest amount is known about sentencing under sentencing information systems. The three most widely reported efforts are in Canada, Scotland, and New South Wales, Australia. An early and ultimately failed experiment in several Canadian provinces suggests some of the difficulties in creating and more importantly in using an SIS (Doob and Park 1987; Doob 1989, 1990). In Scotland, a five-year experiment was only adopted for all 32 judges on the high court in late 2002. An SIS has been operating in New South Wales, Australia, since 1988, and the Scottish judge who took the lead in developing the Scottish SIS learned about the concept from New South Wales. The Israeli system has also been described as an SIS (Schild 2000), and there is fragmentary information about an SIS in Holland (van der Vinne, van Zwol, and Karnekamp 1998). Recently, there has been a call by English senior appeal court judge Robin Auld for development of an SIS in England in a major report, and work has begun on an SIS for magistrates' courts (Auld 2001).

There do not appear to have been many substantial U.S. experiments with sentencing information systems: computerized sentencing "application" software that leads users through guideline systems does not provide information about the actual operation of the system or decisions of judges, and therefore is of a fundamentally different (and less interesting) character than any SIS (Simon, Gaes, and Rhodes 1991; Fino 1987). The most interesting effort in the United States to develop a sentencing information system has been a county-level system spurred by a Portland,

Oregon (Multnomah County) state judge, Michael Marcus, and focuses not on inputs but on information about available sanctions and recidivism (Marcus forthcoming; see http://www.smartsentencing.com).

The Canadian experiment operated for six years in the late 1980s in four provinces. The Canadian system emerged as part of the same efforts and discussions that led to early guideline systems. In 1978, before the implementation of the first modern guideline system in Minnesota and a decade before the implementation of the U.S. federal system, Anthony Doob of the Centre of Criminology at the University of Toronto spent a sabbatical at the Institute of Criminology at Cambridge, where he developed the idea that sentencing reform to address sentencing disparities might come from the judges in Canada, if they knew more about what their fellow judges were doing in similar cases (Doob 1990). Doob found Canadian judges in several provinces interested and willing to participate in the experiment, and found public and private funding (Doob 1990; Doob and Park 1987; Hogarth 1971).

Doob worked with judges to develop the relevant categories of sentencing information and ultimately developed a "workable" system where judges first selected an offense (from among 34 offenses), and then added information about six other "dimensions," including criminal record, involvement of the offender in the offense, seriousness of the offense, impact on the victim, and prevalence of the offense in the community (Doob 1989). A judge would then be given a distribution of sentences from "like" cases. Contrary to initial expectations by Doob and from judges, judges did not find the system helpful, and the experiment ceased in the early 1990s. The Canadian experiment failed according to Doob because most judges in most cases turned out not to be interested in knowing about the practices of other judges (Doob 1989; Hutton, Tata, and Wilson 1994).

> [I]t is clear that the *kind* and *amount* of information that decision makers want about sentencing *in the current climate* is quite different from what we had originally thought. . . . Judges do not, as a rule, care to know what sentences other judges are handing down in comparable cases. . . .
>
> [J]udges do not appear to feel a need to seek out information . . . about sentences in "normal" cases. . . . [J]udges . . . tend to have a lot of experience sentencing a small number of common offences. For these offences, there may be a lot of inter-judge disparity. But, when judges are reasonably confident, rightly or wrongly, about their own sentences, why would they want to examine others' decisions, *especially*

if they knew (or thought) that these other judges have different approaches? (Doob 1989, pp. 4–6, 10)

Doob has also suggested that the Canadian experiment failed because of a lack of institutional authority (Doob 1989). Doob noted that if judges were required by the Parliament of Canada to assess "guideline ranges," then the response might have been different (Doob 1989). The failure of the voluntary exchange of sentencing information in Canada, and the corresponding absence of any indication (or expectation) that the information actually shaped sentencing decisions, offers lessons and hypotheses for other SIS efforts, but, given the further development of sentencing reform demands and experiences, may not be entirely predictive of even similar efforts today.

The Scottish SIS has been described in a series of published and government publications, most written by Neil Hutton and Cyrus Tata. The Scottish SIS was born in the shadow of two modern reform movements, the use of sentencing guidelines, mostly in the United States, and the development of a tradition of appellate court sentencing guidelines in England. In the early 1990s, the Scottish judges—led by one senior judge in particular—wanted to respond to the reform sentiments pushing many systems towards greater regulation and guidance of sentencing decisions, while at the same time maintaining substantial judicial independence. The main motivation was not so much to introduce reform for its own sake as a desirable rationalization of sentencing but rather to head off what was seen as potential political intervention in the form of sentencing guidelines that would restrict discretion. The Scottish SIS, therefore, emerged from the courts. The Scottish experiment includes no additional restrictions on what judges must do with the information they receive. There is no appellate review of a sentencing judge's use of the SIS (though appeals remain on other grounds, including occasional appeals of sentencing decisions).

Judges participated in the design of the Scottish system, including specification of the relevant offense and offender categories (Hutton, Paterson, Tata, and Wilson 1996; Hutton, Tata, and Wilson 1994). The explicit goal of the Scottish system was to assist judges at sentencing: "The aim of [the SIS] project was . . . to provide judges with a form of support which they thought would assist them in their sentencing work. [T]he SIS was conceived as a practical tool for sentencers" (Hutton and Tata 2000b). The Scottish SIS was developed for the High Court, which hears about 1,000 cases a year, including the most serious matters, and covering about 1 percent of all caes brought before the criminal courts. Before the development of the Scottish SIS high court judges received little sentencing guidance. Most Scottish criminal offenses are common law offenses for which no legislative maximum penalty has been specified (Hutton and Tata 2000a).

The system was designed starting in 1993, with a prototype in 1995, and a first stage of implementation, to about half of the 32 judges on the high court, in 1997. As of the end of 2002, the Scottish SIS has been extended to all judges, and is now operating with a database of 13 years and 13,000 cases.

A judge faced with a new case can specify various offense and offender characteristics. Information is entered through a simple set of forms with drop-down lists for each type of information. For any combination of factors, the system will depict the range of sentences imposed. Because Scotland has a uniform system, results are portrayed for all cases in the system. By adding or removing facts, or making different hypothetical determinations, a judge can compare the outcomes for a set of case scenarios. Hutton and Tata describe the operation of the system as follows:

> The easiest way to describe how the SIS works is to imagine a sentencer faced with a sentencing decision in a particular case who wishes to use the system to see the range of penalties passed by the High Court for similar cases. For example let us take a case where a 19 year old male offender, with no previous convictions, has been convicted of a robbery from a shop using a knife where there was no injury to the shopkeeper. What counts as a "similar" case in this instance? Is it all robberies using a weapon or just a knife? Does the sentencer only want to look at sentences passed for 19 year old offenders or should older offenders be included? Is the absence of injury important or should the sentencer also look at cases where there was slight injury? There could be many more questions. The point here is that it is impossible to construct an objectively settled definition of similarity. The system is flexible and allows users to vary the set of specified characteristics. . . .
>
> [T]he system can be used to show penalty distributions for bundles of cases which are similar to the one at hand although each definition of similarity is different. . . . The flexibility of the system is a strength: it permits the sentencer to gain a subtle picture of the previous sentencing practices of the courts for broadly similar cases. (Hutton and Tata 2000a, p. 44)

In other words, judges can add or subtract facts and see the results. Generally, fewer factors will portray a wider range of outcomes, based on a larger number of cases. A system could easily include defaults or options for different time periods and different jurisdictional subunits, including prior sentences by the individual judge. A sentencing information system is also not necessarily limited to information that can be quantified (Tait 1998). Indeed, judges who participated in the initial implementation of the Scottish SIS requested more case-specific information (Hutton and Tata 2000b). The system was modified by allowing judges to enter narrative information about each case. This development had a parallel in the Canadian experiment, where Doob and Park noted the importance of including textual case summaries and access to trial or appellate decisions (Doob and Park 1987, p. 68).

Although the New South Wales system has been in operation for almost 15 years, there is no published evaluation of the system (Hutton and Tata 2000a). Indeed, it appears that none of the current sentencing information systems have been "subject to rigorous analysis and evaluation" (Lovegrove 1999). The system has been said to be the product of public reports on wide sentencing variation for drug offenders (Chan 1991). The New South Wales SIS was designed "to show a sentencer the range of penalties imposed in past cases *which are similar along the main legal dimensions of interest*" (Chan 1991, p. 139).

In contrast to the Scottish system, the New South Wales system was the product of both executive and judicial calls for reform, and the particular reform was the product of legislation. Like the Scottish system, the New South Wales legislation specified that "[n]othing in this section limits any discretion that a court has in determining a sentence" (Chan 1991, p. 138). The variables in the New South Wales system were developed from prior appellate decisions, research, and a survey of all judges and magistrates in New South Wales. The designers favored factors that were more objective over those that were more subjective or harder to measure. As in the Scottish high court, the New South Wales system displays the range of prior sentences for judge-specific combinations of offense and offender facts.

Experts at the Judicial Commission of New South Wales, created to develop the SIS, claim it is "one of the most sophisticated yet unobtrusive systems of its kind in the world" (Potas et al. 1998, p. 100; Auld 2001). The New South Wales system combines sentencing statistics, full text opinions (3,500 cases) and factual case summaries (an additional 2,500 cases), a database structured around sentencing "principles" (including multiple logical entry points, such as offenses and offender characteristics, and including sentencing trends and changes over time), available punishment facilities (resources), current and proposed legislation, and access to various publications (Potas et al. 1998, pp. 106–111; see http://www. judcom.nsw.gov.au/). Notably the New South Wales system includes appellate review for reasonableness and proportionality (Potas et. al 1998).

The initial experiences with sentencing information systems confirm several important points. First, sentencing information systems are by no means simply a technical matter, nor are they value neutral. Doob and Park put it this way in describing the Canadian experience:

> The absence of clear [sentencing] principles creates a distinct difficulty for anyone interested in providing information to judges about sentencing. [O]ne does not know what information should be provided. No information system on sentencing can be completely neutral with respect to principles of sentencing. (Doob and Park 1987, pp. 55–56)

A related problem was the difficulty of getting more factors like criminal history to capture more subjective information relevant to judges such as whether prior offenses were "minor" or "serious" or whether the offender had a "long but non-violent" criminal history (Doob and Park 1987, pp. 62–63).

If information systems are not neutral, who should define the relevant categories and principles? The experiences in Canada, Scotland, and Australia suggest that sentencing information systems are more likely to succeed if judges are actively involved in their creation and implementation (Tata 1998). Since none of these systems have evaluated the ability of information systems to shape sentencing behavior, the claim here is modest: judicial involvement may be essential in shaping categories if the system is to work at all. But the larger point may hold as well: judges will be more likely to have their decisions guided by the patterns of decisions by other judges if the information fits with the way that judges assess offenders and offenses.

It is clear that an SIS alone is not the "answer" to all sentencing problems. To the extent that an SIS is intended to be an alternative to guidelines, it should be combined with some process or tradition of decision making. At the least this should include narrative explanations by sentencing judges of their decisions (Miller 1989). An SIS that encouraged a practice of narrative sentencing decisions would also encourage reflection on the relationship between quantitative data and sentencing narratives. Narrative descriptions might be used to test or question the adequacy of the data categories. An SIS that included both sentencing decisions and appellate sentencing decisions might provide the foundation for the common law of sentencing that Morris and others have hoped for over the years, but which has yet to emerge (Sweet, Van Hook, and Di Lello 1996, p. 946; Miller 1989).

The current systems in Scotland and New South Wales, the earlier experiment in Canada, and the occasional references to sentencing information systems elsewhere have yet to prove the viability of the SIS approach alone at meeting the modern goals of sentencing reform. Perhaps in the absence of underlying agreement about purposes and other foundational principles, sentencing information systems might perpetuate a "false justice" (Lovegrove 1999, p. 71). At the very least, however, the early experiments suggest the practicability of such systems and offer a source of expertise and a place for further study by judges, reformers, and scholars.

Sentencing Information Systems and the Purposes of Sentencing Reform

How does providing information on sentencing patterns respond to concerns about unjustified disparity, resource allocation, "truth in sentencing" or reveal the basis for sentencing in each case?

Sentencing information systems have some hope of addressing disparity concerns, but it is harder to see how an SIS alone would be likely to account for resource concerns. Indeed, the difficulty if not impossibility of accounting for system-wide resource constraints in a "bottom up" fashion is one of the greatest weaknesses in the idea of an SIS alone as a substitute or full competitor to the commission and guidelines model.

Any explanation, including one built around statistical norms, may provide more transparency than a traditional indeterminate system, but an SIS, like some guideline systems, runs the risk of appearing to provide more information while not revealing enough of the judge's thought process to allow observers (defendants, lawyers, scholars, and other judges) to really understand the judge's thought process in each case.

One of the modern reforms that probably can be joined to information systems is the abolition or severe restriction on parole—often referred to as the goal of "truth in sentencing" (this phrase has also been co-opted and abused by the U.S. Congress, which has required a particular and severe form of "truth in sentencing" from states that wish to receive certain federal monies).

The Canadian, Scottish, and New South Wales systems did not try to respond to the full range of modern sentencing reform goals, but focused on the aim of reducing unwarranted disparity (Lovegrove 1999, p. 32). In theory, the Scottish judges believe that if judges saw the range of sentences imposed by other judges, it would lead them to sentence the next offender in a more reasoned fashion, in line with prior sentences. The New South Wales approach did not intend "to curtail discretion, but to better inform it" (Potas et al. 1998, p. 99).

In theory, the availability alone of sentencing information might produce both more consistent and more principled and visible sentences. However, the literature on non-binding or voluntary guidelines raises questions about the necessary and sufficient conditions for non-binding systems to "work" in the sense that they actually shape judicial decisions (Tonry 1996; Berman 2000, p. 28). Twenty years ago scholars and reformers would probably claim that non-binding or voluntary guidelines could not work. The last several decades of experience in a range of guideline systems, however, suggests that the language of "binding" and "voluntary" are too crude, and that many finer gradations of guidance have emerged in practice and turn on such things as the kinds of social norms and degree of acceptance among judges (Miller and Wright 1999).

Perhaps the availability of information would have a more powerful shaping power than the availability of rules: the information is the product of the actual decisions of judges, while rules are typically (though not necessarily) the product of a panel or commission. There does not appear to be any direct evidence on the impact of the Scottish SIS, even though the fact that some judges used the system while others did not would offer an unusual opportunity to test the impact of the system.

Although the literature is modest, with the current adoption of the SIS across all Scottish high court judges, it is reasonable to expect more attention and analysis in the future. During the five years the prototype system has been in place, the judges have not allowed external access to the available data by lawyers or scholars. As Hutton and Tata note, the underlying information comes from public records, and it is reasonable to hope that greater confidence on the part of judges and public expectations will encourage greater access to this information over time (Hutton and Tata 2000a).

The options for making a voluntary or non-binding SIS into one that could more plausibly match the shaping power of commission-bred guidelines—assuming that changing sentencing patterns to produce greater consistency and responsiveness to resource constraints are in fact goals— include developing or requiring sentencing explanations or opinions, perhaps backed up by some appellate review. Resource management is a question that requires some source of external information for judges to add into the sentencing calculus in each case and across cases. Another possibility would be to join presumptive rules to the sentencing range— rules that might be set wholly internally to the judiciary or with external input, for example accounting for prison space and other resources—but to allow the SIS to define the available size of the range for a mix of factors.

If judges are allowed to pick and choose which factors apply to each case without any standards or principles for identifying which factors should be relevant, it is hard to see how such an SIS would lead to more consistent and principled sentencing. However, there are many options for structuring sentencing within sentencing information systems. Judges might be told that they had to identify four basic kinds of information (offense, harm, prior record, and mode of adjudication). More likely, judges would be required to specify a sufficient number of categories or factors, including a time factor, that would produce a meaningful number of cases (e.g., 30, 50, or 100 cases). The system might include even more formal tests of confidence in the meaning and reliability of the information (its significance).

One very attractive option, after a proper "pool" of sufficiently "like" cases had been identified, would be to allow judges to sentence within one standard deviation above or below the mean without exceptional justification, but to require such justification, perhaps subject to more sweeping appellate review, beyond that range. Note that in such a system the size of the presumptive range would vary. Where sentences clumped for a particular kind of offense and offender, judges would have less discretion. For other combinations of offense and offender, the range would be wide as many additional factors (the proper subject of judicial discretion) would guide the actual sentence.

Among the many questions that do not appear to have been faced by the early SIS experiments is the relevance of geographic variation. A judge might want to know what his or her courthouse neighbors did, even if there was no formal jurisdictional line at stake. The jurisdictions that have experimented with SIS are relatively small and cohesive. But sentencing information systems also offer the possibility of illuminating sentencing variation beyond jurisdictional boundaries and in both directions—California judges might find what Washington State or North Carolina judges do of interest, U.S. judges might find Canadian and English sentences of interest, and judges on the new International Criminal Court might find the sentences of many countries of interest. The question is whether systems should allow factors and distinctions that should not have any binding weight, but which might nonetheless inform a judge or a system. A sentencing information system that created some procedures and presumptions about how the information should be used could more easily distinguish between shaping, informing, and irrelevant information.

Another puzzle for information systems is how to encourage the use of similar definitions within each information category. One familiar and serious problem is whether judges restrict themselves to offenses that have been proven beyond a reasonable doubt, or also look at various kinds of "real offense" information, which may include unproven aspects of a conviction offense, or facts proven at sentencing by lesser standards of proof, and in some systems information about uncharged, dismissed, and even (shockingly, and not in most guideline systems) information underlying acquittals (Reitz 1993; Yellen 1993; Tonry 1997).

It is interesting to contrast a sentencing information system with a commission-produced guidelines model. For example, some guideline systems, including the federal system, are developed based on statistical models of prior sentencing decisions (Breyer 1988). How different would sentences look when they are modeled at one time or constantly remodeled over time?

A set of rules modeled on prior sentencing practice and a statistical portrait of prior sentencing practice might at first glance seem similar. But on closer examination they are distinct conceptually and practically. A critical factor for any structured system is its language and grammar—the operative concepts involving the offense and offender and their relationships that shape final sentencing choices. Systems, such as the federal system, that allegedly model their rules retrospectively, based on prior practice, must take records designed for one purpose (such as pre-sentence investigation reports prepared by probation officers in the pre-guidelines federal system) and superimpose (or try to superimpose) the categories the rule-designers later choose. An SIS can and should be designed prospectively, with careful thought to the sentencing categories, and then fact-finding and record keeping should be done in accordance with those categories.

In practice, the retrospective modeling of available sentencing information is ripe for manipulation, as the U.S. federal experience shows (Miller and Wright 1999). A prospective system is less susceptible to such manipulation. Retrospective modeling can be more or less sophisticated, but the U.S. federal experience suggests a tendency to opt for the medians and means of prior sentences, given various (available) offender and offense facts. The goal of drafting sentencing "guidelines" may contribute to this excessive tendency to average almost everything, at least if the presumptively available sentences are restricted to some fairly narrow range.

In contrast, sentencing information systems should portray the full range of sentences applicable to a given set of factors. Moreover an SIS can continue gradually to take account of changing social norms. Guideline systems can also take account of changing social norms through the promulgation of revised guidelines.

Changing norms could come in the form of new legislation or popular movements such as recent efforts in several states to change presumptive punishments for low-level nonviolent drug offenders. Another source of variation and change over time could be "local conditions" (Sifton 1993; Raggi 1993; Braniff 1993; Broderick 1993). Sentencing information systems might be slower than commission-driven guidelines systems to respond to legislative changes such as changing the maxima or minima for particular offenses. But an SIS could take account of local variation and variation over time more easily than top-down guidelines.

Guideline systems, at least in the United States, do not seem to produce standard narratives about offenses and offenders. (The appellate guideline practice in England may do a much better job at laying out what makes a set of cases more or less serious for the same general type of offense.) Instead, some U.S. guideline systems (and notably the federal system) focus courts, participants, and critics on particular factors, isolated from a picture of the offender and offense as a whole—for example, was the offender an "organizer," what quantity of drugs were involved, or was a gun used in the offense. Sentencing information systems offer the possibility of suggesting different narratives that vary by key facts, and that may in theory span a range of seriousness as reflected in the distribution of sentences actually imposed. Neil Hutton and Cyrus Tata explained that the SIS was designed on the assumption that judges sentenced with narratives in their mind.

> Cases are necessarily simplified, standardized, interpreted and reinterpreted to conform to typified and familiarized patterns of behavior and character. [Judges] are aware that there are other judges making decisions about similar cases, and there is a history of these decisions and that such decisions will be made in the future. . . . Judges are also aware that . . . their decisions are unavoidably part of the continuing public debate about punishment and, more broadly, about law and order. . . . Sentencers do not view each case . . . as if it were a completely distinctive and fresh set of circumstances. They experience cases as more or less familiar and predictable narratives or "Typical Whole Case Stories," and their sentencing decisions need to be made against this background. (Hutton and Tata, 2000b, p. 309)

Potential virtues of a complete SIS compared to the U.S. federal sentencing guidelines include the capacity to identify offense and offender mixes requiring a wider range of sanctions to satisfy sentencing purposes, the possibility of gradual explicit and implicit evolution in severity and choice of sanction, and the possibility of constructing relatively coherent sentencing narratives and variations.

One substantial puzzle of modern commission and guideline sentencing reforms is the proper role for the sentencing judge. Most guideline systems include statements retaining a central role for the sentencing judge. But in the federal system, the judicial role seems largely to be one of either fact-finding (including calculation of sentences, often with the aid of a probation officer) or of validating bargains (often including fact bargains) reached by the parties. Judges have been forced to this more limited role by narrow sentencing ranges and restrictive departure standards, with many cases especially in the dominant drug category governed by mandatory sentences or by sentences sufficiently severe that the de facto federal system is one of specific sentences, not sentencing ranges.

Honoring the role of the sentencing judge both as decision maker in individual cases and in shaping guideline systems has been one of the greatest weaknesses of the federal commission. Most legislatures and commissions have asserted that the opinions and suggestions of judges (formal and informal) will be used as feedback to improve the system, and some states seem to have done a much better job at living up to this goal (Reitz 1997; Wright 2002).

Sentencing information systems offer a dramatically different way of depicting the sentencing judge's role and could perhaps help to achieve the promise of more principled sentencing while maintaining a central role for sentencing judges. In the spirit of Morris's 1953 essay, judges would be provided with much more information about the decisions of their fellow judges. Sentencing information systems respond to the actual decisions of judges rather than directing judges how to sentence. Even with stronger rules and presumptions than in the SIS in Scotland or New South Wales, judges should retain a much stronger individual and collective role in such systems than in current commission and guideline systems. Sentencing information systems would not rely on the input of judge members of commissions to capture systematic judicial insights about sentencing.

Sentencing information systems might echo traditional common law systems in some ways: indeed an SIS might help to nurture the common law development of sentencing principles. But the common law rides the crest of precedent, while an SIS with some "bite" (one that is not wholly voluntary or where judicial social norms create strong pressures to match sentences to prior sentencing patterns) should ride the crest of group action, but with no strong binding force to the act of any one prior court.

The appeal of an SIS and principles that allow for expanding and contracting presumptive ranges based on combinations of factors has some similarities to the appeal of markets more generally. A well-designed SIS would allow in effect for market pricing of sanctions (albeit a market constrained—as other markets are often constrained—by some degree of legislative superstructure, and perhaps constrained as well by some resource pressures on the default rules). The contrast with the dominant commission and guidelines model is revealing: in comparison, the dominant model has the character not of a market for proper principles and punishments but of an economy designed by "command and control." Sentencing information systems need not be solely "ground up"; as with the varying degrees of authority and constraint in different guideline systems, different mixes of ground-up and top-down rules and case-level decision making are possible.

While an SIS, at least with some process or principles beyond the mere provision of information, may offer an alternative path to the reduction of unwarranted disparity and might offer a major alternative to sentencing guidelines, it is not clear, in the absence of some addition rule or process, how an SIS that merely provides information can answer the critique of indeterminate sentencing that called for more legal principle and regulation to guide each sentencing decision. Nor is it clear how SIS can respond to important resource allocation concerns, at least in the absence of some "top down" or centralized guidance, whether from a legislature, the executive branch, or a sentencing commission.

Sources and Uses of SIS

This essay has suggested that sentencing information systems may offer a plausible alternative to commission-driven guidelines yet still respond to the basic demands of modern sentencing reform. One interesting feature of sentencing information systems is that they might plausibly be developed by (or under the leadership of) the judicial branch, as they were in Scotland. The first section considers the advantages and disadvantages of legislative versus judicial origins for sentencing information systems. The second section asks whether sentencing information systems are not only a plausible alternative to guideline systems, but also a plausible supplement. Could an SIS rehabilitate a guideline system like the federal system that has been unsuccessful in achieving the purposes of sentencing reform? Could an SIS add a useful dimension to even successful guideline systems without undue costs? The third section asks whether government agencies are needed at all for sentencing information systems to work their reformative powers.

Legislative versus Judicial Sentencing Information Systems

Judges, acting through a judicial conference or court administrative office, can establish an SIS to provide sentencing judges with information and a context for their sentencing decision. An SIS would probably be considerably more complicated and more expensive than the type of administrative processes and rules of procedure typically developed by courts. Such a system would likely require resources that would lead the judiciary to ask for additional support from the legislature. But so long as the SIS did not include binding rules about how judges must sentence that conflicted with statutes defining crimes and penalties, such a system, if challenged or questioned, would be likely to be considered an appropriate and acceptable (if not exactly traditional) part of the judicial function. This is especially true for sentencing rules, given the long-standing view in courts and in the scholarly literature—perhaps as a fading echo of the indeterminate sentencing systems—that sentencing is predominately a judicial function.

A closer constitutional and policy question might arise if judges tried to include sentencing rules (like guidelines) or strong presumptions to bind sentencing judges as part of an SIS. The problem would become especially acute, and the likelihood increase of finding that the judiciary had usurped the legislative function, if judicial sentencing rules, whether enacted as part of a judicial administrative sentencing reform or by a trial or appellate court in a particular case, precluded the use of some sentence authorized by statute.

To the extent that sentencing information systems will not help to achieve the modern goals of sentencing absent some additional guidance with some binding weight, and to the extent that judges will either be hesitant or lack the authority to impose such additional limitations, the argument becomes stronger for some legislative role in creating an SIS. But the legislative role can range from a fully-specified system to one where the legislature authorizes a judicial conference or "agency within the judicial branch" to set up a data system and specify presumptions and preferences. Judges who see sentencing information systems as a plausible and preferable alternative to commission-generated guideline systems could go to legislatures with a request for such general funding and authority.

Data collection and analysis are not part of the training or experience of most judges, court clerks, or court administrators. Even in a system that rejects the dominant commission and guidelines model, it may be preferable or necessary to have some body or office that designs, implements, updates, and runs the SIS. This body might be a purely technical arm of the judiciary or it might be a commission differently constituted than most modern sentencing commissions. Perhaps the term "sentencing commission" bears too much negative weight for those U.S. states that have so far resisted this reform, and so the office might be called the "SIS Office." But imagining that judges with current resources in most systems could operate such a system on their own is implausible.

Sentencing Information Systems
as a Supplement to Guidelines

Guideline and sentencing information systems could be combined. An SIS might offer judges the kind of confidence in sentencing guidelines that has been lacking in some U.S. systems or help to reveal the extent to which guideline systems were failing. In systems with a sentencing commission, the commission itself may have sufficient data to establish an SIS: indeed, such data may be used by commissions already for their own purposes, as in the U.S. federal guidelines system. In those systems— and in the federal system in particular—it is time to share.

Would an SIS be of any use in a commission and guideline system? What relevance would data have to judges obligated to follow specific sentencing rules?

An SIS would tell judges very useful things. An SIS would let judges know the distribution of actual sentences in similar cases, including whether other judges were sentencing at high or low ends of available ranges, or making use of available nonprison sanctions. Judges could see the impact of specific sentencing facts on the distribution of sentences. They could look at sentences in similar cases that they alone had decided, that their immediate fellow judges had decided, perhaps limited to the same courthouse, and how judges from the entire jurisdiction sentence similar offenders. An especially rich system could include information on how similar offenders are sentenced in other jurisdictions in the same country and abroad. Judges, armed with all of this information, could sentence more thoughtfully in each case. Judges, armed with that information, could better work with sentencing commissions and legislatures to improve sentencing guidelines.

An SIS would also tell litigants and researchers information that would help them shape sentencing arguments to the court in each case. Such information could become a powerful basis for arguments for further reforms, including development of sentencing rules and sentencing ranges.

Other than the moderate cost and complexity of setting up an SIS, there are no downsides apparent from initial SIS experiments to providing such information. Administrative costs will depend in part on the size of the system and the caseload, though in either case, as the experience in Canada suggests, the cost of developing and implementing a system may be much greater than the cost of administering it. Administrative burdens can be lightened through the use of automation (e.g., a well-designed interface with check boxes or drop-down lists that records at least the ultimate election of relevant factors by the judge) or by placing the administrative burden on those actors attuned to record keeping, such as the court clerk or probation officer (of course the judge must reveal his or her thought process to the record keeper). Inputting basic information is not that hard or time-consuming, even with the expectation (or perhaps just invitation) to add a narrative description, and processing of individual offenders (including removing the case from the judge's docket) could be held up until the relevant information has been entered and submitted.

The availability of the World Wide Web and increasingly robust database technology have lowered the cost of information collection, evaluation, and access. The Web and a highly standardized data interface is used in the current New South Wales system, and Judicial Commission staff noted that "the entire development and implementation" of the web-based system "cost less than the annual hardware and software maintenance budget of the [original] SIS" (Potas et al. 1998, p. 105).

In indeterminate systems that desire sentencing reform but not sentencing guidelines, an initial and critical challenge will be to specify relevant categories of sentencing information. But in current guideline systems, the task is considerably easier: the guidelines have specified a presumptive list of relevant factors.

Of course no SIS should be set up simply to mirror guideline categories. Systems set up only around the categories defined by current guidelines will test whether those rules are being followed more than what sentences are in fact (and should be) imposed (Tonry 1992). But fortunately there is no reason to limit sentencing information systems to the categories defined by existing guidelines, nor even necessarily to limit information to that specified or found by judges. Information systems might keep track of additional information, such as offender information not captured within the current guidelines, but the basic conceptual sentencing framework would already be in place. Indeed, in most systems, much of the information that would serve as the basis for an SIS is already collected and analyzed; it just is not shared, or if shared, is not shared in a form that judges and others without highly technical backgrounds can use to answer the most obvious and basic questions (How did I sentence in similar cases? How have other judges sentenced in similar cases?).

One current substantial barrier to a complete SIS in most guideline systems, including the federal system, is the refusal to release judge identifiers as part of available data. Judge identifiers are necessary to answer two of the most basic questions raised by modern sentencing reforms: first, what is the variation in sentences for similar offenders across different judges, and second, what is the variation in sentences for similar offenders with the same judge. Remember Morris's first criticism of sentencing systems in the 1950s: "The individual personality of the judge or magistrate plays too large a part in the assessment of the punishment.

... There is ... too great an illogical and fortuitous variation between sentences" (1953, p. 186).Or consider similar language from Marvin Frankel:

> [W]e place no burden of explanation upon the judge who decides that the defendant before him must be locked up for ten years rather than five or one or none. The judge thus loosed may be one of the world's most virtuous people. Or he may not. . . . He may be propelled toward a stern sentence by high moral values or by private quirks of a less elegant nature or by a perceived affront to his dignity in the courtroom. . . . It is certain beyond question that a power this wild will spawn at least some results that are bizarre and would be promptly condemned as unlawful if the unspoken grounds of decision were known. [E]very criminal lawyer knows cases in which sentencing judges have done crazy and horrible things. (1973, p. 41)

If interjudge variation was one of the critical problems that led to sentencing reform, then sentencing information systems should allow interjudge variation to be examined. That can only happen when judge identifiers are provided.

Oddly, judge identifiers have been almost absent from the sentencing literature as a topic of concern, although the availability of judge identifiers is relevant to critical questions about the success or failure of modern sentencing reform even in current guideline systems (without SIS supplementation). Preliminary research in the federal system using hand-collected data—the name of the sentencing judge is, after all, public information—suggests just how important such information would be to robust sentencing debates (Waldfogel 1991, 1998). This information is collected by and available to the U.S. Sentencing Commission—and some federal judges assert in private that the Commission has used the information to badger them about their own sentencing practices. In April 2003, new federal legislation required judge identifiers to be made available to the U.S. Department of Justice and Congress but not to judges, defendants and their lawyers, or scholars. Judges, scholars, and everyone interested in open government and wise sentencing should call for judge identifiers to be made public.

In theory, if only the abstract question of the amount of interjudge variation was at issue, judge identifiers could be anonymous. But anonymous identifiers dramatically limit the kinds of information that an SIS can provide. Anonymous identifiers are probably unworkable except at very high levels of aggregation—in a courthouse or district with one, two, or three judges, it will not be hard to figure out which judge is identified by an assigned number.

Most importantly, anonymous identifiers are unprincipled. Sentencing is an awesome power; it is a public power. The identity of the judge in all systems is public information. Judges have no principled reason to obscure that information from public view and to hide from the sentences they impose. And in the federal system, with life tenure, even the unprincipled position that judges are in part "political" actors who must stand for reelection disappears.

To the extent that sentencing information systems might provide judges with greater discretion than in a guideline model (though that is not a logically necessary result), judges should be willing, in turn, to make sentencing information including identifiers available. Early SIS experiments have been motivated by judges, yet judges in Scotland, for example, have been stingy with the information.

Judges have many reasons for desiring less transparency, including a concern that the public (and media) will push for more severe sentences, and that in systems where judges are elected, those pressures will be hard to resist (this reason carries little weight for federal judges with life tenure). Perhaps judge identifiers will lead to individual judges carrying too much influence, for example, with newer judges deferring to senior or especially well-known jurists (after all, it was *Judge* Frankel).

But none of these reasons carry the day, and in any case are at best hypotheses about judicial behavior, and even if true, can be answered. Sentencing should be among the most transparent of judicial acts. Among U.S. systems, only Pennsylvania has made judge identifiers public, and that decision is quite recent, applies only to sentences after 1998, and the judge is informed about the source of each such request. The Minnesota sentencing commission also shares some information about specific judges in response to requests from reporters.

The Democratic, Participatory, Transparent Sentencing Option

An organization outside of government could design and publish guidelines or sentencing rules, but it is hard to imagine such "independent" guidelines having much impact on actual sentencing decisions. Brilliant and compelling rules proposed by the most august organizations might encourage legislatures to adopt their suggestions. But individual judges in specific cases would be unlikely to do more than at best cite to the "model" rules, since they would carry no binding weight, and any persuasive weight they might carry would have to operate within the bounds of existing guidelines.

Independent sentencing information systems present a different story. Unlike guidelines developed by a commission (or, for that matter, guidelines developed by courts), an independent group might construct an SIS that would help to inform judges and advocates in actual cases. Even in guideline systems, an external and independent SIS could help to shine light on actual practices under those rules, and in the context of factors not considered by the existing rules. Indeed, competing sentencing information systems could each try best to capture the interplay between rules, social norms, and philosophical ideals. The system that best revealed the nature of sentencing decisions—what matters to judges, what might matter, what *ought* to matter—would come to be used by advocates in their arguments, by judges in their sentences, and by reformers in turn to critique and then improve upon the applicable rules.

This happy, democratic vision of sentencing practice and reform need not be a chimera (Tait 1998, p. 175). To come to life it requires only one thing: full access to current and accurate sentencing information, including "guideline" information (in guideline systems), judge identifiers, and narrative or other records that would allow outsiders to code additional potentially relevant sentencing facts (perhaps from presentence investigation reports).

Far from being an academic fantasy, systems like this are already beginning to emerge in one of the most inhospitable places—the federal sentencing system. The U.S. Sentencing Commission already makes huge sentencing data files available, albeit in large chunks, late, and with some substantial questions about the quality of the data (Alexander, Arlen, and Cohen 2000). Some of the sentencing commission data has been combined with information from other federal agencies and organized in much more accessible, interactive fashion by the Federal Justice Statistics Resource Center, an arm of the Bureau of Justice Statistics in the U.S. Department of Justice (see http://fjsrc.urban.orghttp://fjsrc.urban.org/). An even more impressive private effort to organize vast quantities of data about the operation of the federal government, including prosecutorial and sentencing information, is being conducted by the Transactional Records Access Clearinghouse (TRAC) under the name of TRACFED (http://trac.syr.edu; http://tracfed.syr.edu). While neither of these systems yet offers a full federal sentencing information system, they suggest how useful even the restricted current federal sentencing information can be if restructured and made available through a relatively straightforward (if not exactly intuitive) interface.

The idea of providing far better, more complete, faster information to lawyers, judges, scholars, and reformers may be the most attractive sentencing reform model of all, as it is one that does not ultimately rely on government agencies alone to develop wise sentencing rules and practices. The barriers to good public data are not trivial. But they are also not insurmountable, and wide availability of sentencing data including judge identifiers and detailed offense and offender information offer great promise for further improving the law and practice of what Norval Morris and Herbert Wechsler have both called "the strongest force that we permit official agencies to bring to bear on individuals" (Morris 1953, p. 187 (quoting Wechsler); Morris 1977, p. 268).

Conclusion

The last 30 years have seen the emergence of a dominant model of sentencing reform. In pursuit of greater uniformity, greater control over resources, and a more legalized sentencing process, this model has led legislatures to create sentencing commissions, and to authorize those commissions to develop sentencing guidelines. Some of the commission and guideline experiments appear to be working, both in achieving the goals of reform, and in rawer functional terms (e.g., do sentences seem "fair" and "consistent" to the actors in the system or to legislators who provide oversight); others are widely perceived by actors in the systems and observers largely to have failed, most especially the U.S. federal sentencing guidelines.

For reasons that are not apparent from the sentencing literature, about half of the U.S. states have so far chosen not to follow the commission and guidelines path. They retain indeterminate systems whose actual function remains largely a mystery, in part because of the nature of indeterminate systems, and in part because scholars have focused their energies on systems that have opted for guideline reforms.

Perhaps states have been misled by the judicial and scholarly criticism of the prominent federal guidelines system. If so, then the current Model Penal Code—Sentencing effort led by Professor Kevin Reitz may convince the remaining states that commissions and guidelines, done right, are the proper way to go.

But states may also reject the commission and guidelines model because they are skeptical of independent regulatory bodies or of the idea that sentencing should be the product of rules produced by experts. Or perhaps they are more protective of a substantial judicial role in sentencing and have not seen guidelines that allowed or honored a primary judicial role.

If states have rejected the commission and guideline model for these reasons, Norval Morris 50 years ago pointed to another path. Sentencing information systems may provide a different means to achieve the same ends of modern sentencing reform and a means that allows for greater prominence for the judicial role and for more principled and justified flexibility in sentencing, where appropriate for a class of offenses or offenders.

The first experiments with sentencing information systems have come from judges, with the most notable and current examples in Scotland and New South Wales. Judicially motivated reforms have their own appeal, especially to judges, but for sentencing information systems to achieve the multiple reform goals of reasonable uniformity, resource allocation, transparency, and "truth in sentencing" some legislative and administrative guidance, principles, processes, or presumptions may be necessary. Perhaps one of the remaining indeterminate states will be inclined to experiment with the SIS alternative. Judges in these states should follow the lead of their Scottish colleagues and encourage such an experiment. Sentencing information systems offer the possibility of honoring judicial sentencing authority, discretion, and the need for individualization with the virtues of some additional transparency, information, and principled decision making that comes with the best of modern sentencing practice.

Sentencing information systems are not simply an alternative to guidelines; they may be the salvation of failed guidelines and a boon even to the most successful guideline systems. Where guideline systems have met resistance and suspicion, sentencing information systems may provide judges, and ideally prosecutors, defenders, and scholars, with a different window on the sentencing process—a way to assess, critique, and reform guidelines. In particular, the U.S. Sentencing Commission should add an SIS component to the federal guidelines, and if it does not, Congress should consider mandating such a system, or at the very least directing that Commission to release judge identifiers and other information sufficient for nongovernmental entities to build their own SIS. Liberals (concerned with continuing bias) and conservatives (concerned with continuing softness) should both celebrate this cause, as should judges (who will gain power with knowledge) and scholars.

In the general direction Norval Morris suggested, and very much in the spirit he offered, it may now be time for more creative sentencing reform, even if we are in "enough trouble already."

Notes

I am grateful to Doug Berman, Steve Chanenson, Nora Demleitner, Anthony Doob, Richard Frase, Dan Freed, Terry Gordon, Sara Harrop, Neil Hutton, Kevin Reitz, Robert Street, Michael Tonry, and Ronald Wright for advice, and to Norval

Morris, who started my career as a scholar by inviting me, when I was a second-year law student, to coauthor an article, Marc Miller and Norval Morris, "Predictions of Dangerousness," *Crime and Justice* 6:1 (1985). Indeed, I began my public career as a more-than-raw scholar when, on the day of law school graduation, I was sent to Boston to appear at a Law and Society Conference panel on predictions of dangerousness as a substitute for Norval (a demonstrable impossibility) after Norval told the organizers he had a conflict (which turned out to be a good meal at home).

References

Alexander, C., J. Arlen, and M. Cohen. 2000. "Evaluating Data on Corporate Sentencing: How Reliable Are the U.S. Sentencing Commission's Data?" *Federal Sentencing Reporter* 13:108–113.

Auld, R. 2001. *Report of the Review of the Criminal Courts of England and Wales.* London: HMSO.

Berman, D. 2000. "Balanced and Purposeful Departures: Fixing a Jurisprudence That Undermines the Federal Sentencing Guidelines." *Notre Dame Law Review* 76:21–108.

Braniff, W. 1993. "Local Discretion, Prosecutorial Choices and the Sentencing Guidelines." *Federal Sentencing Reporter* 5:309–313.

Breyer, S. 1988. "The Federal Sentencing Guidelines and the Key Compromises Upon Which They Rest." *Hofstra Law Review* 17:1–50.

Broderick, V. 1993. "Local Factors in Sentencing." *Federal Sentencing Reporter* 5: 314–316.

Chan, J. 1991. "A Computerized Sentencing Information System for New South Wales Courts." *Computer Law and Practice* 7:137–150.

Doob, A. 1989. "Sentencing Aids: Final Report." Unpublished report, December 1989.

———. 1990. "Computerized Sentencing Information for Judges: An Overview of Progress Reports on the Sentencing Aids Project." Unpublished report, January 16, 1990. Toronto: University of Toronto, Department of Criminology.

Doob, A., and N. Park. 1987. "Computerized Sentencing Information for Judges: An Aid to the Sentencing Process." *Criminal Law Quarterly* 30(1):54–72.

Fino, S. 1987. "Microcomputers and Criminal Sentencing: Michigan as a Case Study." *Rutgers Computer and Technology Law Journal* 12:407–432.

Frankel, M. 1973. *Criminal Sentences: Law Without Order.* New York: Hill and Wang.

Frase, R. 1997. "Sentencing Principles in Theory and Practice." In *Crime and Justice: A Review of Research*, vol. 22, ed. Michael Tonry. Chicago: University of Chicago Press.

———. 2000. "Sentencing Guidelines in Minnesota, Other States, and the Federal Courts: A Twenty-Year Retrospective." *Federal Sentencing Reporter* 12:69–82.

Freed, D. 1992. "Federal Sentencing in the Wake of the Guidelines: Unacceptable Limits on the Discretion of Sentencers." *Yale Law Journal* 101:1681–1754.

Hofer, P., and M. Allenbaugh. 2003. "The Reason behind the Rules: Finding and Using the Philosophy of the Federal Sentencing Guidelines." *American Criminal Law Review* 40(1):20–26.

Hogarth, J. 1971. *Sentencing as a Human Process*. Toronto: University of Toronto Press.

Hutton, N., A. Paterson, C. Tata, and J. Wilson. 1996. "A Sentencing Information System for the Scottish High Court of Justiciary: Report of the Study of Feasibility." Central Research Unit, Scottish Office, Edinburgh.

Hutton, N., and C. Tata. 2000a. "Sentencing Reform by Self-Regulation: Present and Future Prospects of the Sentencing Information System for Scotland's High Court Justiciary." *Scottish Journal of Criminology* 6:37–51.

———. 2000b. "The 'Balance' between Two Visions of Justice in Sentencing." In *The Judicial Role in Criminal Proceedings,* ed. S. Doran and J. Jackson. Oxford: Hart Publishing.

Hutton, N., C. Tata, and J. Wilson. 1994. "Sentencing and Information Technology: Incidental Reform." *International Journal of Law and Information Technology* 2(3):255–286.

Lovegrove, A. 1999. "Statistical Information Systems as a Means to Consistency and Rationality in Sentencing." *International Journal of Law and Information Technology* 7:31–72.

Marcus, M. Forthcoming. "Archaic Sentencing Liturgy Sacrifices Public Safety: What's Wrong, and How We Can Fix It." *Federal Sentencing Reporter*.

Miller, M. 1989. "Guidelines Are Not Enough: The Need for Written Sentencing Opinions." *Behavioral Sciences and the Law* 7:3–24.

———. 1992a. "Purposes at Sentencing." *Southern California Law Review* 66: 413–481.

———. 1992b. "True Grid: Revealing Sentencing Policy." *U.C. Davis Law Review* 25:587–615.

———. 1995. "Rehabilitating the Federal Sentencing Guidelines." *Judicature* 78: 180–188.

Miller, M., and N. Morris. 1985. "Predictions of Dangerousness." In *Crime and Justice: A Review of Research*, vol. 6, ed. Michael Tonry and Norval Morris. Chicago: University of Chicago Press.

Miller, M., and R. Wright. 1999. "Your Cheatin' Heart(land): The Long Search for Administrative Sentencing Justice." *Buffalo Criminal Law Review* 2:723–813.

Morris, N. 1953. "Sentencing Convicted Criminals." *Australian Law Journal* 27: 186–208.

———. "Towards Principled Sentencing." *Maryland Law Review* 37:267–285.

Parent, D. 1988. *Structuring Criminal Sentences: The Evolution of Minnesota's Sentencing Guidelines*. Stoneham: Butterworth Legal Publishers.

Potas, I., D. Ash, M. Sagi, S. Cumines, and N. Marsic. 1998. "Informing the Discretion: The Sentencing Information System of the Judicial Commission of

New South Wales." *International Journal of Law and Information Technology* 6(2):99–124.

Raggi, R. 1993. "Local Concerns, Local Insights: Further Reasons for More Flexibility in Guideline Sentencing." *Federal Sentencing Reporter* 5:306–308.

Rappaport, A. 2003a. "Unprincipled Punishment: The U.S. Sentencing Commission's Troubling Silence about the Purposes of Punishment." *Buffalo Criminal Law Review* 6, 00–00.

———. 2003b. "Rationalizing the Commission: The Philosophical Premises of the U.S. Sentencing Guidelines." *Emory Law Journal* 52:557–643.

Reitz, K. 1993. "Sentencing Facts: Travesties of Real-Offense Sentencing." *Stanford Law Review* 45:523–573.

———. 1997. "Sentencing Guideline Systems and Sentence Appeals: A Comparison of Federal and State Experiences." *Northwestern University Law Review* 91:1441–1506.

———. 2001. "The Disassembly and Reassembly of U.S. Sentencing Practices." In *Sentencing and Sanctions in Western Countries,* ed. Michael Tonry and Richard S. Frase. New York: Oxford University Press.

—. 2002. *Model Penal Code: Sentencing: Plan for Revision*. Philadelphia: American Law Institute. Available: http://www.ali.org/ali/MPC02Revision.htm.

Schild, U. 2000. "Statistical Information Systems for Sentencing: The Israeli Approach." *International Review of Law, Computers and Technology* 14:317–324.

Sifton, C. 1993. "Theme and Variations: The Relationship between National Sentencing Standards and Local Conditions." *Federal Sentencing Reporter* 5:31–33.

Simon, E., G. Gaes, and W. Rhodes. 1991. "ASSYST—The Design and Implementation of Computer-Assisted Sentencing." *Federal Probation* 55:46–55.

Stith, K., and J. Cabranes. 1998. *Fear of Judging: Sentencing Guidelines in the Federal Courts*. Chicago: University of Chicago Press.

Sweet, R. W., D. E. Van Hook, and E. V. Di Lello. 1996. "Towards a Common Law of Sentencing: Developing Judicial Precedent in Cyberspace." *Fordham Law Review* 65:927–950.

Tait, D. 1998. "Judges and Jukeboxes: Sentencing Information Systems in the Court Room." *International Journal of Law and Information Technology* 6(2): 167–189.

Tata, C. 1998. "'Neutrality', 'Choice', and 'Ownership' in the Construction, Use, and Adaptation of Judicial Decision Support Systems." *International Journal of Law and Information Technology* 6(2 :143–166.

Tonry, M. 1992. "GAO Report Confirms Failures of U.S. Guidelines." *Federal Sentencing Reporter* 5:144–155.

———. 1996. *Sentencing Matters*. New York: Oxford University Press.

———. 1997. "Salvaging the Sentencing Guidelines in Seven Easy Steps." *Federal Sentencing Reporter* 10:51–55.

Tonry, M., and N. Morris. 1990. *Between Prison and Probation: Intermediate Punishments in a Rational Sentencing System*. New York: Oxford University Press.

Tonry, M., and R. Frase, eds. 2001. *Sentencing and Sanctions in Western Countries*. New York: Oxford University Press.

TRAC Reports, Inc. 2002a. *Transactional Records Access Clearinghouse*. Available: http://trac.syr.edu.

———. 2002b. *TRACfed*. Available: http://tracfed.syr.edu.

U.S. Bureau of Justice Statistics. 2002. *Federal Justice Statistics Resource Center*. Available: http://fjsrc.urban.org.

U.S. Sentencing Commission. 2002. *Guidelines Manual*. Washington, D.C.: United States Sentencing Commission.

Van der Vinne, J., W. van Zwol, and M. Karnekamp. 1998. "A Sentencing Information System Named 'NOSTRA.'" *International Journal of Law and Information Technology* 6(2):230–234.

Waldfogel, J. 1991. "Aggregate Inter-Judge Disparity in Federal Sentencing: Evidence from Three Districts (D.Ct., S.D.N.Y., N.D.Cal)." *Federal Sentencing Reporter* 4:151–154.

———. 1998. "Does Inter-Judge Disparity Justify Empirically Based Sentencing Guidelines?" *International Review of Law and Economics* 18:293–304.

Wright, R. 1992. "Complexity and Distrust in Guideline Sentencing." *U.C. Davis Law Review* 25:617–637.

———. 1998. "Three Strikes Legislation and Sentencing Commission Objectives." *Law and Policy* 18:429–463.

———. 2002. "Counting the Cost of Sentencing in North Carolina, 1980–2000." In *Crime and Justice: A Review of Research*, vol. 29, ed. Michael Tonry. Chicago: University of Chicago Press.

Yellen, D. 1993. "Illusion, Illogic, and Injustice: Real Offense Sentencing and the Federal Sentencing Guidelines." *Minnesota Law Review*, 78:403–465.

PART III

Being There

6

Democracy and the Limits of Punishment: A Preface to Prisoners' Rights

Franklin E. Zimring and Gordon Hawkins

Graduate students and would-be lawyers can become interested in the subject of criminal justice for a variety of reasons. Crime is fascinating human drama, and social deviance is an important window into the larger context of conformity with social norms. Law enforcement and punishment are interesting and complicated phenomena. But many who write in this tribute to Norval Morris are part of a generation that was trained in the 1960s and 1970s, and who became interested in the subject of criminal justice because they wished to accomplish reforms that would carry social importance. Criminal justice then served as a magnet for would-be social reformers. Is it still? Should it be? Why might those who wish to promote important reform in a developed democracy imagine that a career in criminal justice would be a means to that end?

We think that trying to answer such questions is an important window into the strategic importance of limits on punishment in modern government and society. There were 30 years ago and are now two reasons why criminal justice might be considered an attractive subject for the aspiring law reformer. First, those processed through institutions of crime control and punishment are usually among the most disadvantaged of citizens— poor, members of minority groups, failures in education and employment. But in this respect, criminal justice is depressingly similar to public welfare and public health systems. This feature of criminal justice in developed nations does not make the criminal process into a specially attractive area for needed reforms. If one wants to help the poor, AIDS is far more important than prison reform. Education and job training are the vital engines of economic mobility. The criminal justice system is not a vehicle of social progress.

But the second respect in which the treatment of criminals is of special importance to the reformer is central to our thesis: criminals are the most feared and resented of a society's citizens. Public hatred of crime and criminals invites the use of extreme forms of governmental power to suppress and punish criminals.

The serious criminal offender—the rapist and the robber—is the least attractive case for claims to limit government power, but he is, for that reason, the most important frontier for defending the limits on that power. If the claim of human rights against government power is only as strong as its weakest link, that will almost always make the rules and limits of criminal punishment of central importance to respect for individual dignity as a limiting principle throughout government. Because punishment of criminals is the "weakest link" in the argument for limiting state power, those who try to keep the criminal system free from abuse of government power are guarding an important frontier.

It is only in the past three decades that penal reforms have been self-consciously included in any larger human rights agenda. The death penalty has been the cutting-edge issue of criminal punishment to be accorded human rights status, and this happened only in the 1980s and 1990s (Zimring 2003, ch. 2). A detailed analysis of criminal justice as a human rights issue has not yet emerged. We hope in these pages to make a small contribution toward studying criminal justice as a human rights question.

This essay will attempt four related tasks. The first section will explore some foundational issues on the question of limiting the powers of democratic governments to punish. In this first section, we will be dealing with a wide range of punishments. A second section will discuss two ways in which the modern politics of imprisonment in the United States generate the risks of excessively punitive conditions of confinement. The topic in this section is the political pressure on imprisonment, a much narrower concern than criminal punishment generally, but an important arena for testing the limits of government in American criminal justice. A third section will discuss both the principles of restraint and the strategies of governmental organization that might be used to limit punitive excesses in American prisons. A brief concluding note will argue for transplanting standards of decency from other areas of governmental function into prison policy.

We see the headings in the note as building toward a preface to the detailed discussion of "prisoners' rights" litigation in the United States, the topic addressed by James Jacobs in this volume. We hope to show why democracies need to develop restraints outside the popular political process to safeguard against excessive governmental power. The problems in recent policy that we identify provide a specific context for exploring the possibilities and the limits of strategies to protect human dignity in American prisons. Much of our analysis here is preliminary and unsystematic. Yet the enterprise we serve is an important missing link in the study of punishment and democracy.

Punishment and Governmental Power

To the extent that power held by government comes at the expense of restrictions on the liberties of individual citizens, there is a natural tendency for citizens to resent increases in governmental power and to desire limits on government. Where citizens have continuing power over governmental policy, new powers must be approved on the basis of the need for government to produce common benefits that citizens value more highly than the liberties they surrender. The need to justify governmental power in terms of collective gains that are more important than lost liberty is spread over the full range of governmental powers from taxation and spending to military force. Crime and punishment have a special strategic importance in this dynamic to establish the limits of governmental power because criminals are the most frightening and most unpopular citizens in a democratic state. Fear of crime means that citizens will cede authority to government for crime control that they might not be willing to surrender for other reasons. The public hostility toward criminals will support harsh punishments administered by government because criminals are to receive them. Citizens will approve conduct in the punishment and control of crime that they would hesitate to support or tolerate in other domains.

Because criminal punishments are the most extreme deprivations that government will inflict on any citizen, most enforceable limits in governmental power will be limits on criminal punishments. Further, because of hostility to criminal offenders, public opinion and democratic institutions will support punishments of high magnitude. Expanding power to punish in democracy will be easier than in other arenas of government operations, and limiting power through democratic institutions will be more difficult.

That the punishment enterprise is the boundary territory for the maximum exercise of negative government power explains the historic importance of criminal justice in the basic architecture of limited government. The Bill of Rights to the U.S. Constitution has eight amendments dealing with the relationship of government and individual citizens. Five of these eight amendments are chiefly concerned with criminal justice (4, 5, 6, 7, and 8).

Concern about excessive governmental power is external to the usual topics of effectiveness and individual desert in the determination of appropriate punishment. To worry about whether it is proper for modern governments to extinguish life as a criminal sanction is not to address either topics like deterrence or incapacitation that concern the effects of punishment on crime rates or to consider what particular punishment might be morally justified by the commission of a particular act. Restraints on government power of this sort are prior conditions to setting a scale of punishments based on individual desert or deterrence. The citizen is a potential victim in this setting both of criminals and of government; and he need not imagine himself a criminal offender to feel threatened by a government that is without restraints in pursuing its policies.

The external concerns that motivate restraints on punishment can produce debates in which the contestants are talking past each other, and in which differences of opinion exist even about the topic being debated. In many modern disputes about capital punishment, retentionists typically assume that the topic is crime control and therefore the issues are the individual desert of murderers and deterrence, while abolitionists see the topic as the appropriate limits of power in the modern state, a concern that has little use for criminological data or expertise. Often the debate is decided by which side succeeds in establishing its view of the topic under discussion.

What we are calling a "human rights" perspective tends to be most obvious in circumstances where citizens have special concerns about the organization and limits of government. Change of regime is one obvious circumstance where citizens have pressing concerns about limiting governmental power. The widespread abolition of capital punishment in Central and Eastern Europe after the end of Soviet domination is one recent example of this (Zimring 2003, ch. 2). A second is that the abolition of the death penalty in Western Europe after World War II was first evident in the nations that were defeated and changed regimes, that is, in Germany, Italy, and Austria (Zimring and Hawkins 1986). Only later did abolition spread to the major powers that were victorious, England and France.

All the major democracies in the world have substantial constitutional limits on their government's power to punish criminals, including prohibitions of torture, and all the major democracies except the United States and Japan prohibit the death penalty. All the developed democracies impose substantial minimal procedural conditions that must be met before punishing. The current pattern is that those nations with substantial democratic influence on government power also have more limits on punishment than nations with less citizen control on government, but this is no paradox. Authoritarian regimes do not choose to limit themselves and their citizens lack the power to force limits.

More interesting are the motives and mechanisms that limit punishment power in democracies. If a government responds to popular will, why not give it total discretion in the choice of punishment for criminal offenders? One problem with that position is that changing political circumstances is a risk that cannot be discounted. Governments may cease to be accountable, so that whatever safety came from popular control might disappear. But there is also a possibility of majority will supporting the excessive use of force. In almost all nations, discrete minority populations support restrictions on government power in part because of a fear of popular control. And while self-interested enthusiasm for limits on government power is easiest to imagine for those with conspicuous minority identities, there are few of us immune from being outvoted in a matter of important personal preference. All citizens are potential minorities on contested issues.

So the reason democratic regimes have more restrictions on government power than autocratic regimes is that democracies allow such limits to exist. We know this because the strongest support for limits on government will come from those who have recently experienced autocratic governmental excesses. Limits on government power are quickly imposed once iron curtains fall.

When we underscore the importance of limiting punishments in democratic governments, it is not because we regard punishment abuses as more of a problem in democracy (see, e.g., Greenberg 2001), but rather because abuse of punishment is a special threat to the positive values of liberal democracy.

How might a government constrained by limits on power tempt its citizens to remove such limits? Fear of crime and of criminals is one obvious technique, and this creates a strong motive for governments that desire additional power to exaggerate the danger of crime and criminals. The political task is to convince citizens that criminality is a greater threat to them than government excess. The motive is larger power to those in government. The major appeal is to fear.

Not all areas of criminal justice are of equal concern from a human rights perspective. The maximum dangers cluster at the extreme edges of the system—the most serious offenders, the most fear-inspiring crime problems, and the most extreme punishments.

The most serious and hated criminal offenders are the justification for new incursions of state power. The serial killer, the murderer of children, the terrorist bomber, the predatory sex offender, and the drug lord are the principal arguments put forward for extensions of the severity of punishments available and the length of incapacitation. Terrible crimes are always urged as the justification for terrible punishments. But more than the heinousness of individual offenders, the justification for new intensities of surveillance and punishment depends on the public's sense of insecurity in combating the particular problem that is urged as this year's necessity for the extension of state power. It is the citizen's sense of vulnerability more than his distaste for particular criminal offenders that justifies the extension of state power. A sense of public emergency thus becomes the leading enemy of moderation and of the limitation of government power. A powerful illustration of this general point is the aftermath of the September 11, 2001 events in the United States, where the extraordinary extensions of power were assembled in a piece of legislation labeled by its sponsors as the "Patriot Act."

The importance of public feelings of vulnerability about crime to support the expansion of punitive power explains not only the incentive of ambitious governments to scare their citizens but also the cyclicality of the public sense of emergency about particular crime problems. In late twentieth-century American experience, each campaign to make citizens feel acutely threatened had a relatively short effective life after the threatened Armageddon did not happen, from the war on drugs, to gang violence, to the juvenile super-predator. So that governments intent on consistent expansion of punishment powers felt the need to rotate the particular problems that were pushed to justify penal inflation. When drug wars are followed by panics about juvenile violence, the shift in topic may be the only way supporters of expansion in governmental power can generate consistent levels of public anxiety. Whether the concern with terrorists and terrorism in the aftermath of the World Trade Center's destruction in 2001 will have a more sustained career as the central justification for expanding governmental power is one of the important contingencies of the first decade of the twenty-first century. Is mass destruction sufficiently compelling to avoid becoming "last year's panic" in short order?

While extreme forms of criminality are the focus of support for extensions of governmental power, extreme forms of punishment attract the attention of the enemies of unlimited governmental power, particularly when a punishment is distinct from more standard penal measures in kind as well as degrees. Torture, beatings, and execution have been the targets of choice for human rights reformers, practices that inspire citizen empathy with the subject of the punishment, and types of deprivation that are easy to distinguish from more common penal measures such as imprisonment and fines.

Penal practices that differ from those in common use in extremity but not in kind are more difficult targets for the human rights reformer to identify and to attack. An illustration of this phenomenon, which we will discuss at some length in the next section, concerns what has come to be called "the supermax prison" that has proliferated throughout the United States since the 1980s. Designed to impose unprecedented levels of individual isolation and psychological deprivation, the supermax prison is nonetheless a more difficult target for the human rights reformer than canings or torture because the institution can be defended by government as merely another form of prison.

The general acceptability of imprisonment as a penal sanction then becomes that major premise in a syllogism; the minor premise is that these supermax institutions are prisons; and the conclusion is that therefore they must be acceptable penal measures. To date, these extraordinary institutions have not received the attention they deserve from either reformers or the wider community. This essay will show why a human rights approach to limits on prison is both more difficult than categorical prohibitions on types of punishment but necessary nonetheless.

•

Prisons and the Modern Politics of Punishment

Imprisonment is the most serious penal sanction that is frequently imposed in the modern state and a stunning example of the conflict and complexity involved in the protection of individual dignity during punishment. The imprisoning state administers an institution where the totality of the offender's life is under its control and restraint. For this reason, sociologists describe such facilities as "total institutions" (Goffman 1961). For the modern prisoner, the same government that condemns and wishes to punish him controls every aspect of the offender's daily life: eating and drinking, social contact, excreting, communication with the world outside the prison, exercise, light and darkness are all state-administered conditions in the modern prison.

In this section, we outline two recent developments in conditions of imprisonment in the United States. The first is political initiatives to make prisons even more unpleasant as a method of intensifying the punishment of criminals. The second is the construction of particularly terrible prisons in the service of special security. In this section we show why the political process might tolerate punitive abuses in these two contexts. In the next section, we explore whether it is practical to search for limits in legal controls.

The Politics of Gratuitous Deprivation

The totality of state power over individual life in prison means that the punitive impulse that inspires imprisonment could in theory influence every aspect of the conditions of confinement. Why should those who have murdered and raped get decent meals or the opportunity to communicate with family and friends? What is the argument for allowing those who are being imprisoned to be punished to enjoy movies on cable television or build their muscles in exercise rooms that have been equipped at public expense? One older version of objections to positive conditions in prison acquired the label "less eligibility," an argument that conditions in confinement should not be better than those available to the poorest members of the law-abiding community. But the broader argument we hear more recently is why not make the conditions of confinement in penal institutions punitive in all their details?

The contract between the rhetoric that supported concerns about less eligibility a century ago and the appeals associated with current efforts to reduce the privileges available in prisons is a useful introduction to the new politics of punishment in the United States. The hazard associated with "less eligibility" was as much a utilitarian as a moral concern. If prisoners were better off than the poor in the community, what was to make the poor fear prisons?

The modern political arguments do not compare prisoners with the poor, but instead favor making prison life less inviting for prisoners as a way of identifying with the concerns of crime victims. One branch of the modern politics of punishment begins with a premise that most if not all issues of criminal justice policy should be viewed as a status competition between criminal offenders and their victims. The politician asks whether the citizen cares more about the welfare of criminals or of crime victims. The implication is that the answer to that question should decide any question of justice system policy. To imagine every issue as a competition between victims and offenders can easily lead to assuming that everything done to disadvantage offenders in some way also helps victims. This image, which we have elsewhere called "the zero sum fallacy," leads also to the assumption that providing any comforts to prisoners, who are after all criminal offenders, is also a way of ignoring the interests of crime victims (Zimring, Hawkins, and Kamin 2001, ch. 11).

In this rendering, every decision about conditions of prison confinement can be seen as a competition between crime victims and criminal offenders, and the citizen is invited to show solidarity with the victims of crime by withdrawing family visits, cable television, weight rooms, and other gym equipment. Even prison policies that humiliate prisoners can be restated as a way of reinforcing the positive social status of crime victims by humiliating those who offended against them (e.g., the Maracopa County, Arizona Sheriff who makes jail inmates who have been caught masturbating wear pink pants on the outside of their jail uniforms). Once the assumption of a zero-sum relationship is accepted, the crime victim support rationale for making the environment of prisoners less tolerable has no apparent limit.

The 1990s produced a bumper crop of legislative and administrative attempts to make prisons more unpleasant, and not all of these were concerned with unimportant or merely symbolic details. State legislation and Corrections Department regulations were frequently passed concerning weight rooms and television privileges (Finn 1996).

Peter Finn of Abt Associates published a survey of the changes in prison and jail conditions imposed under the heading of "the no frills prison and jail" movement, with a range of examples:

In 1994 the Arizona legislature eliminated weightlifting equipment in state prisons and established a $3.00 co-payment for health care services.

In 1995, the Mississippi legislature mandated the phasing-in of striped uniforms with the word "convict" written on the back, banned private television and other equipment in cells.

The Arizona Department of Corrections reduced the number of items for sale in the prison store, reduced the amount of property and clothing inmates may keep in their cells, and the number and types of movies and television programs they may watch. (1996, pp. 35–36)

Many jails eliminate weightlifting equipment, free coffee, hot lunches, girly magazines, and reduce recreation time, television programming, visitations, and items for sale in the commissary (Finn 1996, p. 36).

Not to be outdone, the Alabama Department of Corrections introduced what were called "no frills chain gangs" in each of the state's three prisons in 1994. The punitive roots and deprivational intention of these wide-ranging policies are the only common thread we can imagine.

The federal Congress passed its own version of a "No Frills Prison Act" in 1996 that among other things provides that "[I]nmates serving a sentence for a crime that resulted in serious bodily injury to a victim are denied any television viewing and are limited to one hour a day of sports or exercise" (ibid., p. 36).

Legislation was also proposed to withdraw "good time" or "good behavior" credits to prisoners who file lawsuits that a court later classifies as frivolous, thus lengthening times of penal confinement as a sanction against the filing of lawsuits. This was also the era that produced "Megan's Laws" requiring released sex offenders location in a community to become public knowledge.

There are no obvious limits to the potential of this kind of politics to operate. However, since the actual incentives for victims and other groups to produce these negative impacts are not great, those restrictions that do receive legislative sanction will frequently have other constituencies who benefit from the restriction of privilege. The State Attorney Generals who must defend against inmate litigation are the real winners with good time restriction legislation.

Gratuitous restrictions on prisoners might not produce any real benefits to crime victims, but they have no powerful opponents either. Prison administrators might object to proposals that threaten the governability of prisoners and some administrators would also oppose the needless restriction of liberty and the denial of small comforts in prison. Thus, Finn reports that only 16 percent of prison administrators support television restrictions (Johnson, Bennett, and Flanagan 1996). The opposition of wardens to gratuitously downgrading prisons might not be a major bulwark against gratuitous restrictions, however, because prison administrators are not by themselves politically powerful in the legislative branch of state government. Once a political dynamic like the "zero sum" assumptions of victim's rights gets going, the political process can easily make for larger deprivations in the experience of imprisonment than are necessary or justifiable in a prosperous modern nation.

The Supermax Prison

A status competition of a rather different kind has contributed to the growth of the hyper-maximum security prison over the period since 1985. A persistent problem in any large prison system is the control of persistently disruptive, violent, and resistive prisoners. The traditional prison system was divided into institutions of minimum, medium, and high or maximum security, and some high security institutions had within their walls special units for isolation as either punishment or protection for inmates who posed special problems in general prison populations. In highly differentiated prison systems, entire prisons might acquire a reputation for housing special problem prisoners, as did Alcatraz and later Marion in the federal system and institutions like Sing Sing and Attica in New York. But the emergence of what Leena Kurki and Norval Morris call the "supermax prison" was something quite different from a section of a conventional facility being used for isolation or solitary confinement. The supermax enterprise was the building of an entire facility that was designed to house and control the very worst prisoners imaginable. The style of the supermax prison is a high tech-paranoia, which isolates the individual offender from contact with other prisoners and staff. Kurki and Morris use the common characteristics of five such institutions to sketch a composite portrait:

> The physical environment is similar in Tamms, Pelican Bay, Red Onion, and Indiana's and Texas's supermaxes. Cells are a combination of steel and concrete—toilet, sink, and door are steel, the rest is concrete. Exercise yards have concrete floors and walls, lack an outside view, and differ little from cells. They are often empty, although some may have an exercise bar, a basketball hoop and basketball, or a rubber handball. Cells do not have showers or their own exercise yards. When prisoners go to the shower or to the exercise yard, they are handcuffed and shackled and accompanied by several guards. Time and again, the environment is described as "old, hard, and austere" (Human Rights Watch 1997, p. 23) or "dull sameness in design and color" that reinforces detachment from the outside world (Madrid v. Gomez at 889 F Supp 1146 (1994)). Also, there are few differences in privileges between these facilities, for which detailed descriptions are available. Prisoners stay about twenty-three hours each day in their cells. They are allowed three to five showers per week, five to seven hours of exercise per week, and one to four visits per month. Some facilities allow phone calls, television, and radios to some of their inmates. In all, visitors stay behind a reinforced glass wall and conversations take place through a telephone. No work, programs, or leisure activities are offered. If social workers, nurses, or priests stop by, they stay behind the steel door. Organization and practice of medical and mental health care vary, but it is often a nurse or a medical technical assistant who screens incoming prisoners and decides whether a prisoner can see a doctor, psychologist, or psychiatrist. Reports on Indiana's supermaxes and Virginia's Red Onion indicate that inmates have real difficulties receiving adequate medical and mental health care (Human Rights Watch 1997, 1999). Madrid v. Gomez held that Pelican Bay's health care system was incapable of satisfying minimum constitutional standards and deliberately neglected medical needs of inmates. Ruiz v. Johnson (Ruiz v. Johnson, 154 F.Supp.2d 975 (2001)) found that the medical and psychiatric care systems of Texas prisons were "grossly wanting" (at 907), although not unconstitutional, but only since the present standards for proving constitutionality are "inordinately high" (at 892) and "permit inhumane treatment of inmates" (at 907). (p. 407)

This type of custom-designed freestanding institution of hyper-maximum security differs from the isolation units that were created in traditional prisons in significant respects. The cells and other areas where prisoners might be taken from time to time can be designed for isolation, to minimize the occasions when prison staff might be vulnerable in any interaction with inmates and to facilitate the prisoner's vulnerability wherever he might go to observation by staff and to forced physical removal. The second important feature of a designed supermax prison is its scale. Once an entire institution has been designed and constructed, an institution specially designed for the American prison's worst cases will exist with a capacity that will vary from several hundred to more than two thousand, and those spaces will be filled. So construction of these expensive special feature institutions commits the prison system to filling the facilities once they come into existence.

There are several reasons why the head of a prison system might wish to have a supermax prison in his institutional portfolio. There are some inmates in large prison systems—mentally ill, or violent or persistently and explosively resistant to institutional discipline—who are very difficult to maintain in standard conditions of imprisonment. So a special facility would make the continued custody of such prisoners less difficult. A second powerful incentive for building a supermax prison (and making it an unpleasant living prospect) is as a system-wide threat to secure the good behavior of all those who occupy space in conventional maximum security prisons. The system that builds a Pelican Bay (California's leading modern horror) can advertise that prison's unattractive features to all the other inmates in the system—the more problematic the conditions in such a prison, the better the deterrent. Adding on to the deep end of a prison system can thus provide a pervasive deterrent.

There is a third reason why administrators in prison systems would want to have supermax prisons of their own—as a status symbol. Once some major prison systems had built and opened supermax prisons, that type of facility became a normative part of any major state prison system. A system without a supermax prison was in effect acknowledging it was not in the correctional major leagues. The incentive that this kind of status symbolism presents is the real motive rather than the publicly provided rationale for a supermax project. Those who have been moved by the status symbolism of supermax prisons will find more practical sounding arguments for building such institutions, but we think the appeal of the supermax prison as status symbol is an important part of the explanation for the contagious enthusiasm for creating these prisons in the 1990s. While only one institution fit the supermax pattern in the early 1980s, by 2000 Kurki and Morris report 34 states operated supermaximum security units or prisons with nearly 20,000 beds (Kurki and Morris 2001). When an institution at that extreme in social control expands 20fold in 15 years, the probability that changes in penal fashion are responsible is difficult to dismiss.

There is a long list of separate threats that such institutions present to the welfare and autonomy of inmates. The isolation and sensory deprivation of the supermax prison are problematic even for the most difficult and deserving prisoner, and even when great care is taken to assure that unnecessary deprivations have not been imposed. But the structural tendencies for such prisons to abuse human rights beyond necessary boundaries are also extraordinary. When isolations and deprivations are based on the fears that a prison staff might have, how is the reality of the need to be tested? When the poor conditions of a supermax prison are advertised system-wide as a deterrent to disciplinary infractions, how can we be sure that all its advertised deprivations are truly necessary to security? When prisoners are kept far away from contact with the outside world, who will assure their safety and protect them from unwarranted deprivation of liberty?

Furthermore, the pressure to overuse facilities of hyper-maximum security is tremendous. Once a large-scale worst-case facility exists, it will be filled with the misfitting odds and ends of a major prison system. The number of "worst cases" will almost always expand to the limits of the space provided for them. The mentally ill are obvious candidates for the rigors of supermax prisons whether or not they require its security and despite the capacity of such places to exacerbate their emotional disorders. The hyper-security prison in the United States is by its nature pregnant with risk of serious human rights abuse.

Principles and Institutions of Limitation

The question we now confront is whether there are viable principles of limitation available to safeguard the prisons of the United States from unnecessary deprivations based on either citizen hostility expressed through the legislative process or the security concerns that metastasize into the supermax prison. The two problems noted—gratuitously punitive conditions of imprisonment and excessive deprivations of liberty in hyper-security prisons require separate analysis. Each presents difficult problems that show the stresses associated with legal reviews of practices of criminal punishment.

The gratuitous removal of prison amenities is a problem of modest size, and there is little cost associated with overturning the obvious examples of the genre. The supermax prison is a higher stakes problem. The potential for destructive abuses is great but the problems of separation of power and unnecessary interference with the management of prisons are quite real. Both the costs and needs of scrutiny are large.

Restricting Gratuitous Deprivation

The purest forms of gratuitous restrictions are those imposed by the political process—the legislation taking television away from prisoners or abolishing family visits. The simplest institutional arrangement to guard against punitive deprivation by legislation is to keep decisions about the details of prison administrations from the legislative branch of government. The general strategy of separating practical decisions on punishment from the most politically sensitive and symbolically oriented institutions of government was called "insulation" in our earlier discussion of punishment and democracy (Zimring, Hawkins, and Kamin 2001, ch. 10). The idea is to keep decisions about conditions of confinement from legislators. The argument is put forward that conditions of confinement are best decided by the experts who hold administrative power over prisons.

An institutional theory of separating power over correctional details from legislative bodies does provide limited protection from some forms of gratuitous punitive deprivation, but the prisoner protection that comes from a theory of administrative expertise is by no means complete. In the first place, legislative restrictions can always be framed as budgetary matters, to bring them within the traditional ambit of legislative control (i.e., "none of the funds allocated for the department of corrections shall be spent on television for prisoners"). Unless a reviewing body is willing to look behind the veil of budgetary authority, a formal prohibition on legislative setting of conditions of confinement will not provide much protection.

In the second place, the resort to administrative power might not protect the prisoner when the prison administration seeks to gain political favor by endorsing politically popular restrictions. To the extent that prison administrators need to curry favor with legislative bodies, they may endorse deprivations that have no functional role in prison administration. This certainly happened in the 1990s (Finn 1996).

The third problem with relying on the prison administrator to represent the interests of the prisoner is the very large number of situations where their interests conflict. Any power or autonomy one gives to the inmate in a prison is that much power that the staff and administration does not possess. Even when prison administrators oppose broad bans on inmate recreation and television, what they tend to favor is systems where small comforts are available to prisoners but only at the discretion of those who run the prisons (Finn 1996).

So there is no sense in which those who administer prisons have the neutrality that would make them ideal institutional agents to protect prison inmates from unnecessarily punitive deprivation. If neutral agencies of government would be the best hope for review of conditions of confinement, the choices are between executive branch personnel without any other responsibility for prison governance and judicial officers, either judges of general jurisdiction or judicial branch officers with special responsibility for prisons.

While constitutional courts are one necessary element of scrutiny for enforcing limits on governmental use of imprisonment, a variety of other executive branch controls are also helpful in maintaining human rights in prisons. Of particular value are executive officials with some administrative independence from the line and staff of a conventional department of corrections. An ombudsman or inspector general of the prisons has particular value when resources are devoted to the serious pursuit of oversight. When executive agencies operate effectively, they make the judicial system a last resort in the protection against abuse. And the capacity of executive offices to make scrutiny into an administrative routine assures that the combination of administrative and judicial oversight is much more effective than the judicial oversight alone.

The irony is that those prison systems most likely to have extensive administrative scrutiny for human rights abuses are also the places where the danger of abuses is the smallest. When a state like Alabama invents a "no frills chain gang," it is a safe bet that it will not also fund an aggressive inspector general to police against human rights abuses. The same insensitivity that invites abuses also inhibits the development of administrative controls.

Principles of Limit

But what should be the review standard for legislative acts that attempt to alter conditions of confinement for expressly punitive purposes. If the state legislature passes an act forbidding cable television services in maximum security prisons, what kind of claim should inmates be allowed to make against such regulations? Certainly there is little to suggest finding a positive legal or constitutional right of those in state custody to television service or free weights (Bryan 1995). Just as certainly, the absence of cable television should not be regarded as cruel and unusual punishment. Should judges or neutral ombudspersons have the power to order all reasonable services and amenities to those in prison?

But wouldn't that make the judge into the warden in fact of the prison? Any effort to impose such an open-ended set of conditions would become more of a usurpation of the normal authority of prison administrators than the legislative interference that removes the television service as an administrative option. Should the ban on television be considered a "Bill of Attainder" prohibited by the U.S. Constitution? But wouldn't that only preserve the television service of those who committed their crimes before the ban was passed?

There is a less artificial standard for review that may be available to courts that goes to the core of the problem posed by legislative ceremonies of punitive deprivation. A prohibition on gratuitously punitive legislative conditions could provide a method to curtail the all-but-transparently punitive provisions singled out in the last section without creating an open- ended invitation for second guessing administrative and legal authority on conditions of confinement. When a measure withholding a privilege, either by legislation or administrative action, appears punitive in intent, it could be subject to review on a due process standard that might put a nontrivial burden of justifying the condition on those who frame the rule. The prohibition of TV and weight rooms would be easy victims to any real judicial scrutiny, despite the creative imaginations of those who draft legislative findings of fact in modern government. The removal of good time credits for early release as a consequence of filing a frivolous lawsuit would also seem a likely candidate for invalidation.

But most traditional collateral conditions of imprisonment or felony conviction would survive challenge, unless they are plainly irrational in modern settings. The test case here is the permanent ban on a convicted felon's voting in many states that survives as a vestige of the "civil death" of a convicted felon in Anglo-American antiquity. It is punitive and irrational but also traditional, a close case for a standard that disapproves of the gratuitously punitive. Is history alone sufficient warrant for the perverse exclusion of the felon from political reintegration?

As a matter of principle, we see nothing wrong with a common law or constitutional rule that is suspicious of legislative disabilities that produce injury and indignity but serve no rational penal purpose. There is the danger that the standard might invite too much judicial interference, but judicial caution in application of such standards can help minimize that danger.

Scrutiny of the Supermax Prison

We believe that the supermax prison is one of the most important and one of the most complicated candidates for serious judicial scrutiny in the administration of criminal justice in the United States. The claim of prison systems that some prisoners are very dangerous is true, and security concerns for staff and other prisoners are a legitimate basis for preventive action. At the same time, there are a large number of important abuses in the supermax prisons that should be matters of high priority concern to the legal system.

There are five separate problem areas that require scrutiny in the modern supermax prisons. First, the worst of our hyper-security prisons impose some conditions on those they confine that no government should impose on any offender. Second, many such prisons confine persons who do not require conditions of security anywhere near the level of those that they currently suffer. Misclassification in security level imposes a terrible burden on the inmate that should be the basis for his reassignment to more appropriate conditions of confinement. Third, many of those who might have correctly spent some time in supermax prisons will stay too long. Fourth, many other troubled prisoners—the mentally ill, for example—are wrongly pushed into supermax prisons and are at risk for great harm from such misclassification. Fifth, many prisoners do not pose extreme security risks but have been transferred from other prisons as punishment for disciplinary infractions. The use of such a facility solely as punishment is a serious abuse of governmental power.

The five different problem areas listed in the previous paragraph are characteristics of the operation of most supermax prisons. In the aggregate, we would not be surprised if two-thirds of all those presently in hyper-security institutions do not currently belong in them. Further, we think there are common conditions in such institutions that should never be permitted in any prison.

But the different problems associated with supermax prisons need to be separately analyzed and addressed. The disciplinary transfer problem is quite different in its origins and its best solution than the dumping of mentally ill prisoners in supermax cells. With so many different problems, administrative monitoring and control of supermax prisons is absolutely essential to any effective responses to the problems of the hyper-security prison. But the strong interests that correctional administrators have in the operation of such institutions mean that internal administrative controls are always a necessary but never a sufficient condition for protecting against the abuse of governmental power in this deepest end of American imprisonment.

Principles and Implementation

What makes the supermax prison such a high stakes arena for enforcing limits on government punishment power is the great need to control such institutions coupled with the large difficulty and cost of intervening in the administration of the supermax prison to correct abuses.

The practical difficulty is not in creating standards for judging the appropriate conduct in a hyper-security prison. Each of the five different potential problems can produce a verbal formula that seems appropriate for separating abusive from necessary prison practices.

The verbal formula to describe those methods of isolation and control that should be totally prohibited should require a finding that a practice was cruel and degrading with a conclusion that it was not strictly necessary to the safe operation of the facility. But to measure the actual practices in a supermax prison against that kind of standard requires a detailed knowledge of how such prisons are and can be administered, as well as access to reliable data on the likely costs and effectiveness of alternative methods of achieving the same objectives that an abusive practice now serves. The well-prepared judge who decides whether a particular condition should be prohibited is an expert on prison operations and a sophisticated policy analyst. There are ample opportunities for error in making the complicated lesser-of-evil decisions that are implicated in the verbal formulas for judging conditions of hyper-security prisons.

The same contrast is found between the relatively easy task of formulating a standard and the complicated job of implementing the same standard when considering the use of supermax prison as a punishment for non-dangerous prisoners who violate institutional rules at other institutions. The use of unnecessary physical restraint and isolation for solely disciplinary reasons is a problematic correctional approach that we would think should be classified as abusive. But how can one scrutinize institutional records to separate out dangerous from disliked prisoners when the sending prison will try to make all their outcasts look dangerous?

Of course, the non-dangerous mentally ill should be kept out of supermax prisons, but how can we judge who among the mentally disturbed prisoners are dangerous? And what should a judge do if there are no suitable institutional settings for those mentally disturbed prisoners who have been improperly pushed into hyper-security confinement?

Policing a hyper-security prison for abuses of power can quickly involve many of the nightmare scenarios that have produced criticisms of structural injunctions and judicial management of other governmental institutions. Much more than approving or prohibiting particular practices is undertaken when neutral institutional actors scrutinize the operations of a hyper-security institution.

But there are two quite different ways of accounting for the exceptional costs of this kind of review procedure. On the one hand, it can be assumed that the redundancy and exceptional scrutiny are the high cost of maintaining any independent scrutiny of imprisonment. This characterization regards the inspection for abuses as an enterprise that is separate from the business of keeping people in prisons, it is a human rights add-on that is not an integral part of the machinery of criminal justice.

On the other hand, the reason that the hyper-security prison calls for so much scrutiny is its extraordinary potential for government abuse. The institution itself is located so close to the outside margin of permissible punishment that the need for its special scrutiny is obvious and inherent. From that perspective, the complexities and costs of special precautions to guard against abuse are a necessary part of deciding as a society that this problematic institution should be created. The only way that a decent society can build a Pelican Bay is with ample apparatus to make certain that its potential for harmful abuses of human dignity is being closely monitored. The scrutiny is an essential part of the cost of the hyper-security prison in a decent state. If that cost is too great, we should not build the problematic institution.

Prison Reform as Transplant Surgery

One question of methodology confronts any effort to correct conditions of punishment because they do not conform to a particular critical standard of decency—where does the critic who finds the penal practice deficient obtain an independent standard of decency to make such a judgment? A variety of methods for assessing standards of decency have been debated in courts that render decisions about the standards for cruel and unusual punishment under the U.S. Constitution. The only standard to judge the behavior of state government that has been used without great controversy is the penal practices of other U.S. states. On questions of decency and the morality of penal practices, some justices oppose any arguments based on the practices and standards in other countries (see *Stanford v. Commonwealth of Kentucky*, 492 U.S. 361 (1989)). Those who are critical of judicial efforts to limit government powers to punish frequently suggest that the standards of decency invoked by critics are either arbitrary individual values or elitist prejudices not suited to be substituted for the will of the majority. So where might the critic of penal excesses find standards of decency to use in the criticism of penal practices with moral weight and social credibility?

We wish to return to our description of the strategic importance of criminal justice in the first part of this essay to suggest one method of obtaining standards of decency for American penal practices that has substantive credibility. Our earlier argument is that public fear and resentment make the criminal justice process one where a society's usual standards of decency and restraint might not be observed. This vulnerability is what makes appropriate restraint by government in the criminal justice field so broadly important. But the special pressures that often distort practices in criminal justice also are a signal that one natural place to find good standards of decency in practice that can be projected into criminal justice is from related areas of government operation without the distortive fear and hostility found in criminal justice. Practice in noncriminal justice fields provides some measure of what constitutes minimum standards when fear and loathing are not powerful pressures.

Our earlier analysis made the conclusion that:

> In one key respect, the punishment of criminals is not a frontier issue for consideration of the obligation of the state to its citizens. Criminal justice is not the area where governments can be expected to innovate in the extension of opportunities and entitlements to citizens. Such innovations will usually first be extended to dependant populations with much higher social reputations than criminals—the elderly, children and to those handicapped through no fault of their own. The strategic role of the criminal offender is in defining the absolute minimum obligation of state to citizen, so that adequate provisions for prisoners are a defensive necessity. (Zimring and Hawkins 2002, p. 252)

Our suggestion now is that the standards of decent treatment that exist with noncriminal dependant populations, "the elderly, children and those handicapped through no fault of their own" are a useful measure of standards of decency that can be applied to conditions of penal confinement as well.

Take the question of the treatment of mentally ill prisoners in the supermax facility. One measure of the decency of their treatment is whether the same conditions imposed on the mentally ill in supermax prisons would be approved or allowed in public and private hospitals for persons with the same mental health problems. If not, an additional question is whether the conviction status of the mentally ill inmate should make a critical difference. The reference to public standards in noncriminal justice fields is both a disciplined and appropriate way to construct measures of decent conditions that are specific to American culture and values.

A second example of such logic concerns the access of jail and prison inmates to smoking opportunities. Whenever persons are wholly confined in state institutions, a rule against smoking in public buildings becomes a total prohibition against smoking. The argument is made in jails and prisons that such a prohibition protects nonsmoking inmates and staff from the harms of "passive smoking." Perhaps, in the age of the "no frills" prison, there is more than a possibility of punishment as a motive for prohibiting smoking. We suggest that the policies and principles about opportunities to smoke found in military barracks and state mental hospitals should also apply in prisons as well, unless there are good reasons why different levels of smoking control are needed. And the way that the smoking problem is handled in other institutions of adult confinement provides insight into the actual motives for policy in prisons and jails.

This sort of transplantation of standards of decency from areas of governance that do not suffer the distortions of criminal justice suggests another perspective on the function of the criminal justice reformer. One technique of assuring that the distortive pressures that operate in criminal justice do not corrupt the government is to perform a sort of transplant surgery of healthy values and appropriate practices found in other domains of governmental activity. This form of transplant protects the most vulnerable areas of government operation from corruption and thus protects the health of the entire governmental organism. Norval Morris has confessed that he once thought of combining medicine and law as a career. In this important sense, perhaps he did.

The Consolations of an Uphill Struggle

What can this general review tell us about prisoners' rights in the immediate future? The strategic role of the criminal offender is in defining the absolute minimum obligation of state to citizen, so that adequate provisions for prisoners is a defensive necessity. Assuring the human dignity of the murderer and the rapist is not a strategy for expanding the entitlements of school children and senior citizens; instead it is a strategy to prevent the erosion of citizen claims against government, to prevent regressions applied to the least popular of dependant populations, which might thereafter be applied more broadly.

The defensive significance of offenders' interests in the human rights dynamic has two implications when thinking about the future efforts to protect human dignity in prisons. The first is that the entirety of a human rights agenda can never be exclusively based on offenders' interests. The defense of prisoners' rights is always a necessary but never a sufficient condition for a human rights agenda.

A second corollary of the defensive strategic position of offenders' interests is that efforts to protect this particular flank will be much more important in bad times than in good times. In periods characterized by good will and the growth of government concern for citizens, the advocacy for offenders' rights will be somewhat easier in its own right and less necessary for the protection of other vulnerable populations.

When a social climate turns threatening, the defence of offenders' interests becomes at once tactically more difficult and strategically more important. It is during eras of bad feeling that the interests of vulnerable populations are most at risk. The path of least resistance to the erosion of individual rights will always be to target those domestic enemies assembled in the criminal justice process.

So there is some consolation in the current low esteem of prison reform in the United States early in the twenty-first century. The same features of politics and society that make the advocates of prison reforms unpopular also make those who question the government's hegemony in penal institutions an indispensable element in defence of human liberty.

References

Bryan, D. 1995. "U.S. Courts Hand the Debate over Inmate Privileges to Corrections Officials." *Corrections Compendium* 20(6):2–3.

Finn, Peter. 1996. "No-Frills Prisons and Jails: A Movement in Flux." *60-September Federal Probation*, 35.

Goffman, Erving. 1961. *Asylums: Essays on the Social Situation of Mental Patients and Other Inmates*. Garden City, N.Y.: Anchor Books.

Greenberg, D. F. 2001. "Striking Out in Democracy." *Punishment & Society: The International Journal of Penology* 4(2):237–252.

Human Rights Watch. 1997. *Cold Storage: Super-Maximum Security Confinement in Indiana*. New York: Human Rights Watch.

————. 1999. *Red Onion State Prison: Super-Maximum Security Confinement in Virginia*. New York: Human Rights Watch.

Johnson, W. W., K. Bennett, and T. J. Flanagan. 1996. "Getting Tough on Prisoners: A National Survey of Prison Administrators." Paper prepared for the annual meeting of the Academy of Criminal Justice Sciences, Las Vegas.

Kurki, Leena, and Norval Morris. 2001. "The Purposes, Practices, and Problems of Supermax Prisons." In *Crime and Justice: A Review of Research*, vol. 28, ed. Michael Tonry. Chicago: University of Chicago Press.

Zimring, Franklin. 2003. *The Contradictions of American Capital Punishment*. New York: Oxford University Press.

Zimring, Franklin, and Gordon Hawkins. 1986. *Capital Punishment and the American Agenda*. Cambridge: Cambridge University Press.

————. 2002. "Criminal Justice, Ethics of: Aspects of Human Dignity." *International Encyclopedia of the Social and Behavioral Sciences*, vol. 5, pp. 2949–2954.

Zimring, Franklin, Gordon Hawkins, and Sam Kamin. 2001. *Punishment and Democracy: Three Strikes and You're Out in California*. New York: Oxford University Press.

7

Prison Reform amid the Ruins of Prisoners' Rights

James B. Jacobs

Prisons and jails need continuous "reform" because there are constant financial, political, administrative, psychological, and even biological pressures threatening to undermine conditions, practices, and programs. Penal institutions often seem to be in decline if not in crisis (Christianson 1998). At the beginning of the twenty-first century, it remains a tremendous challenge to keep prisons and jails safe, clean, hygienic, operational, and humane (Stern 1998).

In our 1,400 federal and state prisons and many thousands of county jails and local lockups, conditions and operations are only to a limited extent determined by correctional ideologies and philosophies. Humane values and correctional "philosophies" are important, but they are insufficient to ensure humane conditions. Resources and administrative competence are far more important (see Lin 2000; Bottoms 1999).

Money does not guarantee decent prison conditions and operations, but lack of money assures the opposite. At present, our states and localities are experiencing very serious budget crises that may persist for years. State and local officials are combing through their programs to identify places to make budget cuts. Jails and prisons will certainly be a prime candidate. While imprisonment has been wildly successful in the late twentieth century in garnering support for more beds in more facilities, that is entirely different than garnering support for maintaining and improving intra-prison conditions, operations, and programs.

Unlike practically all other programs, penal institutions have no political constituency, except perhaps for the prison officers' unions in some states (e.g., California). Prisoners are not seen as among the "deserving poor." Allocating scarce resources to improve or maintain humane prison conditions (in contrast with spending money to provide more beds) will not win votes or acclaim. Thus, when it comes to choosing whether to cut funding for prisons and jails, schools, higher education, roads, and health care, prisons and jails will always be the first choice unless public officials are forced (by courts, riots, or something else) to spend the money (see Berk and Rossi 1977).

How budget reductions impact on jail and prison conditions, practices, and programs is an important topic for empirical research. We can expect, at a minimum, that expenditures for maintenance and renovations will suffer. Prisons do not age gracefully. Many penal institutions are more than 50 years old, some of the largest institutions date from the nineteenth century. Maintenance, much of it performed by prisoners themselves, is often shoddy. There is always a crying need for repairs to plumbing, electricity, heating, windows, painting, kitchens, grouting, and so on.

When money is scarce, prison officials will not be successful in their attempts to upgrade out-of-date industrial equipment and workshops. As the machinery wears out or becomes obsolete, intra-prison worksites and vocational training programs are cut back and shut down; certainly, no new ones are opened. "Unemployment" and idleness increase. Even small budget items fall victim to the budget cutters. Athletic equipment and televisions are not replaced. The prison library stops making acquisitions. There are fewer special events and not enough staff on duty to supervise them. In contrast to the decline in living conditions, inmate expectations have risen steadily over the last century as the general societal living standard has steadily improved. Thus, prison conditions that inmates of past generations might have considered endurable, today's prisoners will experience as unendurable. As prison conditions and operations deteriorate, inmate morale decreases and staff morale follows suit.

Maintaining the physical infrastructure is not the only, or even the most important, challenge of prison reform. The crisis in state and local budgets also impacts on salaries and the number and type of positions that can be funded. Sufficient attention, especially academics', has never been paid to the importance of the human infrastructure of prisons and jails and its management. (There are approximately 440,000 persons working in adult corrections; 260,000 are uniformed correctional officers.) It takes many capable and dedicated people to run a penal institution efficiently and safely—for example, wardens, assistant wardens, and other central office administrators, shift commanders, cell block sergeants, vocational teachers, industrial foremen, and treatment personnel. Indeed, it takes intelligence, maturity, and confidence to function effectively as a line correctional officer in a cell house, recreational area, or kitchen/dining room. And even all of the efforts of competent people at the institutional level can go for naught if the correctional department's central office is marked by incompetence.

Jails and prisons are hard on staff as well as inmates (Lombardo 1981). Locked in like the prisoners, employees are exposed on a daily basis to unpleasant, dangerous, and unhealthy conditions (noise, odor, hostility, violence, disease, and high levels of stress). They spend their working lives in close interaction with inmates loaded with anger, self-loathing, violent impulses, manipulative personalities, mental illness, and infectious diseases, including tuberculosis, hepatitis, and HIV. There are complicated and fractious divisions among the inmates based upon race, gang affiliation, personal fealties, feuds, and animosities (see Morris 1995). Given such working conditions, it is hardly surprising that prison staff, especially without competent training, support, and supervision, burn out or worse. Very high staff turnover and daily absenteeism are the reality in many penal facilities, greatly complicating, if not overwhelming, effective management. The risk and reality of staff corruption, capitulation to inmates, and brutality constantly threaten the goal of a humane and smooth functioning organization.

Recruiting, training, nurturing, promoting, and improving prison personnel should be seen as a prerequisite and top priority for prison reform. Unfortunately, little attention is given to identifying the qualities needed for prison staff, recruiting and training such people, identifying potential leaders and developing their expertise, retaining the most capable people, and structuring rewarding careers in corrections. Recruitment is typically haphazard, training cursory and shallow (often half of the recruits are gone within the first six months), work unpleasant, stressful, dangerous, and unhealthy. Promotions are not keyed to competence. Status is low. It is not surprising that most employees do not find prison work satisfying.

Many good people quit; there is a constant flow of the most competent staff to the private sector and to other public sector jobs. Staff turnover undermines administrative systems. Those left behind feel "stuck." Absenteeism proliferates. Management positions go unfilled. Decisions are left hanging. Morale plummets. It becomes harder to recruit new employees into an organization that is "troubled," chaotic, and dangerous.

Even in the best of times, it is a major challenge to maintain decent prison conditions. But the beginning of the twenty-first century is not the best of times for prisons and jails, fiscally or politically. Pay is extremely low, given the magnitude of the responsibility and the difficulty of the work. In January 2001, going into the current fiscal crisis, the average annual starting salary for correctional officers was approximately $24,000; the average maximum salary was $38,000.[1] The average minimum salary for wardens was $54,250, while the average maximum salary was $86, 275. If salaries fail to keep pace with inflation, or actually lose ground, the forces of demoralization become even stronger so that recruiting and retaining competent replacement will become even tougher.

Crowding is the relentless opponent of humane prison conditions, over-whelming improvements to physical plant, programming, and staff. At the turn of the twenty-first century, despite massive prison construction in the previous two decades, most American prisons operate at more than 100 percent rated capacity, some at much more than 100 percent.[2] Mass incarceration reigns as the entrenched criminal justice policy of the United States (Garland 2001). While, in the last few years, prison population growth has slowed down, there has certainly been no reversal; there remains plenty of pent-up demand for prison beds—desire for more severe sentences, desire to punish new crimes, desire for more "productive" (in terms of arrests/convictions) police work (see Hallinan 2001).

The prevailing law and order politics, embraced by both political parties, has produced a chronic crowding problem that affects every aspect of institutional life. The greater the crowding, the more and greater the negative impacts; a smaller percentage of inmates has any kind of job or educational placements. Less recreational space/time per prisoner means a much less satisfactory recreational program (e.g., more people competing for a ball or a game opportunity). The waiting list to see doctors and counselors lengthens. More prisoners are crammed into cells where they spend more hours per day (in many cases practically all 24 hours). Less space and less privacy generate more friction and conflict. The same number (or fewer) prison officers for more inmates means less supervision and declining safety. Rising prison population without commensurate increases in staff and improvement to the built environment inevitably and inexorably undermines prison conditions. Moreover, the prevailing ethos is not sympathetic to prisoners (Zimring, Hawkins, and Kamin 2001). To the contrary, there is political pressure to cut back on or cut out "amenities" like weight lifting and college programs and to establish "no frills prisons." Such cuts are all the more likely in the context of serious public sector budget crises. And such cuts, of course, contribute to the spiral of decline.

Sources of Prison Reform

What are the forces that operate to counteract the pressures that constantly undermine prison conditions, programs, and operations? In the last half century, the most important, by far, has been the willingness of judges, especially federal judges, to enforce prisoners' rights, especially the right to be free from cruel and unusual punishment. Other forces that, in the past, have generated pressure for humane prison conditions, and that may play a role in the future, are prisoners' riots and protests, correctional leaders' lobbying and innovations, advocacy and watchdog groups' campaigns, and privatization.

Rise and Fall of the Prisoners' Rights Movement

The heyday of the prisoners' rights movement roughly spanned the period from 1960 to 1980. Prisoners challenged every aspect of the prison regime, from censorship to disciplinary confinement, from prohibitions on wearing jewelry to no-contact rules in the visiting room, from denial of access to the Bible and Koran to racial discrimination in cell and work assignments, from lack of access to the courts to arbitrary disciplinary procedures (Jacobs 1980). The lawsuits with the largest impact on the institution of imprisonment were class actions challenging the constitutionality, under the Eighth Amendment's cruel and unusual punishment clause, of the totality of prison conditions, including cell size, quality of lighting, ventilation, sanitation, nutrition, and medical care (Feeley and Rubin 1998; Schlanger 1999).

Unlike other areas of court-initiated social change, the U.S. Supreme Court did not play a powerful role in the prisoners' rights movement. True, there were a few decisions in the early years that guaranteed religious freedom and access to the courts. *Wolff v. McDonald* (418 U.S. 539 [1974]), a case about prison discipline, supplied the most stirring language by announcing that no iron curtain separated prisons from the rest of American society. But there is no single watershed Supreme Court decision to match *Brown v. Board of Education* (for school desegregation) or *Roe v. Wade* (for abortion rights). In the area of prisoners' rights, the most important decisions were rendered at the district court level and were strongly rooted in the facts, the conditions and operations at particular prisons and jails (Jacobs 1995).

The prisoners did not win most of their cases but, in the early years, they won many. The prison officials, used to ruling as autocrats, were arrogant and ineffective witnesses. They could rarely point to written rules and regulations; existing rules were vague and authoritarian (e.g., "insolent eyeballing" and "unruly conduct"). And even when the inmates did not prevail, their litigation reinforced the point that prisons are sociopolitical institutions that must function under the rule of law and that prisoners are citizens behind bars entitled to constitutional protections (see Jacobs 1977, 1980).

The active involvement of courts in prisoners' rights cases meant that prison reform that was not achievable in the political arena was achievable in the judicial forum. Federal judges examined every aspect of prison conditions and operations in a way that had never been done before, and they (even "conservative" judges) found many of these conditions deplorable and unconstitutional. Wide-ranging and thorough reform was imposed upon prisons, which were ordered to provide prisoners decent light, heat, cell space, showers, food, safety, sanitation, nutrition, recreation, medical care, and, to some extent, fair and rational procedures (see Feeley and Rubin 1998).

The potential of judicially driven prison reform is much weaker at the turn of the twenty-first century. Forward momentum has been halted and, arguably, the willingness and ability of courts to set and enforce minimum standards of decency in jails and prisons is waning. How and why this reversal happened is a subject that will take years to understand fully, but understand it we must if we are to understand the potential and limits of prison reform in the twenty-first century.

Perhaps all social movements carry the seeds of their own reversal. In the case of the prisoners' rights movement, a clash between the political branches of government and the judiciary was inevitable. The political branches always preferred to allocate resources to causes and constituencies that produce votes, certainly not to inmates of prisons and jails. On occasions, governors and powerful legislators publicly defied or vilified the courts. More frequently, they ignored or dragged their feet with respect to compliance with court orders, and explicitly or implicitly encouraged prison officials to do the same. This led to some very protracted, sometimes decades-long struggles between, on the one side, plaintiffs' counsel and special masters working for the courts and, on the other side, local and state officials (see, e.g., Martin and Ekland-Olson 1987). (Over the years, however, many front-line prison officials came to see that their working conditions and jobs generally would be easier and more satisfying if the court-mandated changes were implemented. In some cases, they welcomed and even colluded in the prisoners' lawsuits.)

Conservative scholars excoriated federal judges for being duped by plaintiff prisoners and for handing down decisions that undermined the authority of savvy prison officials (DiIulio 1987). The Supreme Court and lower federal courts' support for prisoners' rights lawsuits steadily diminished in the 1980s and 1990s (see Branham 1976). It is not so much that the courts reversed themselves (although the Supreme Court did rein in lower courts on a number of occasions with decisions like *Turner v. Safley*, 482 U.S. 78 [1987]), as that the courts drew a line in the sand: "this far and no further." Most existential rights have been recognized in whole or in part, and the principle that the Eighth Amendment protects prisoners from inhumane conditions (admittedly difficult to define) has become part of our constitutional jurisprudence. Nevertheless, the Supreme Court has made it abundantly clear that federal courts must show substantial deference to prison officials (e.g., *Rhodes v. Chapman*, 452 U.S. 337 [1981]) and that the exigencies of prison organization necessarily mean that constitutional rights in prison cannot be exercised as freely and fully as on the outside (e.g., *Baxter v. Palmigiano*, 425 U.S. 308 [1976]; *Hudson v. Palmer*, 468 U.S. 517 [1984]).[3]

The most profound blow to the prisoners' rights movement was passage of the Prison Litigation Reform Act of 1995 (PLRA) (Pub.L. No. 104–134; 110 Stat. 1321, Sections 801–810), an ideologically motivated federal law that represents the political branches' efforts to prevent the judiciary from recognizing and enforcing prisoners' rights (Kuzinski 1998). The PLRA, a plank in the Republicans' "contract with America," but signed without protest by President Bill Clinton, sought to deter prisoners from filing federal lawsuits, lawyers from representing them, courts from granting them wide-ranging equitable relief, and special masters from enforcing court decrees.[4] What is more, the PLRA allows prison officials to open up and cast off reforms, long ago agreed to in negotiated settlements with plaintiff prisoners.[5]

The PLRA's first strategy is to increase litigation costs to prisoners in order to deter or prevent them from suing their captors. The law requires prisoners to exhaust all administrative (grievance-type) remedies before filing a lawsuit. It also puts financial barriers in their way. Whereas for decades inmates could avoid filing costs by bringing their suits *in forma pauperis*, the PLRA requires even the most impecunious prisoners, as long as they have money in their prison accounts, to pay a filing fee. Moreover, a prisoner who has had three previous lawsuits dismissed must pay the full filing fee in advance. Furthermore, the PLRA instructs the court not to waive certain litigation costs (e.g., transcripts of depositions) that could be levied against a losing prisoner plaintiff.

The PLRA's second strategy is to make it more difficult for prisoners to obtain legal representation in institutional litigation. Until passage of the PLRA, prisoners' rights attorneys, like all other civil rights lawyers, were entitled to "reasonable compensation" from the defendant government in the event they were successful; that provided an incentive for private attorneys to take on prisoners' cases that they thought had a reasonable chance of succeeding. The PLRA caps an attorney's fee at 150 percent of the total monetary judgment awarded the inmate or 150 percent of the hourly rate paid to criminal defense lawyers for representing indigent federal criminal defendants, whichever is the lesser. This makes it financially difficult or impossible to take on cases that, while important in principle, are not likely to produce large monetary judgments for the plaintiff inmates. The law redefines "reasonable compensation" for lawyers representing prisoners to 150 percent of the hourly rate authorized for court-appointed criminal defense lawyers rather than the market-based rate that previously applied.

Third, the PLRA limits the remedies that federal judges can impose in prisoners' rights cases. Courts may neither grant nor approve any relief other than money damages, "unless the court finds that such relief is narrowly drawn, extends no further than necessary to correct the violation of the federal right, and is the least restrictive means necessary to correct the violation of the federal right." In other words, the PLRA seeks to restrict courts to redressing individual grievances (restricted to compensating inmates for physical injury) and not the problems of classes of plaintiffs. Even if plaintiffs can vault the class action hurdle, relief must be limited to correcting the specific constitutional violations giving rise to the suit. In addition, judges cannot impose population caps except in circumstances in which other, less intrusive relief, have failed to remedy the constitutional violation. Only a specially convened three-judge panel can impose a cap.

Federal judges have enforced their remedial decrees in condition of confinement cases by appointing special masters to operate as the judge's eyes and ears on the scene. The special master, often with the assistance of a staff, has devoted full-time or substantial part-time attention to a particular case, has carried out investigations on compliance, hired special consultants to draw up standards and strategies for reform, and reported to the court on the defendant prison officials' progress. On occasion, the special masters have sought to have defendant prison officials held in contempt for dragging their heels. The importance of the role of special master in late twentieth-century prison reform cannot be exaggerated; the expertise, persistence, and negotiating skills of many of these masters is the single most important factor in the success of major institutional reform litigation.[6] The PLRA attempts to neutralize special masters by limiting their remuneration to 150 percent of the hourly rate for counsel appointed to represent indigent defendants in federal criminal cases, a fraction of what masters have been awarded in the past. The hope of the PLRA's sponsors is that the most experienced and competent special masters will be driven from the field.

Finally, defendants are entitled to termination of any prospective relief two years after it is granted, unless the court finds a "current and ongoing violation" of the federal law. The PLRA even opens up old consent decrees, agreements negotiated between prisoners' lawyers and the state. While they are under attack by prison officials, the courts are instructed to treat them as null and void.

The PLRA is an extraordinary politico-legal event, representing a broadside attack on the whole jurisprudence of prisoners' rights and, what is more, an attempt by the legislature to supplant the courts as the ultimate arbiter of what prison conditions and operations are acceptable. Nevertheless, it would be an exaggeration to say that the PLRA and conservative court decisions have eliminated the prisoners' rights movement as a source of prison reform in the twenty-first century. Some prisoners' cases will be successfully brought in state courts, although those courts historically have been far less receptive to prisoners' complaints than the federal courts. Crafty litigators have found ways around some of the PLRA's restrictions and some federal judges who resent the congressional effort to curtail their jurisdiction seek ways to reach results they think are just. Some prison and jail conditions and operations will be so deplorable and violative of humane standards that prisoners' rights lawyers will have no difficulty overcoming the hurdles that the PLRA places in their path. Parties can contract around the provision allowing for consent decrees to sunset in two years.

A final caveat: the prison reform litigation of the late twentieth century may have contributed to the emergence of a new form of super-maximum-security incarceration that scrupulously respects the letter of the law, while constituting a prison regime remarkable for a new form of inhumanity, marked by massive control and minimal interpersonal human contact. These institutions utilize high-tech security with remote controlled gates, voice recognition equipment, and omni-present surveillance. To find these "state of the art" institutions unconstitutional would take a wholly new understanding of human suffering and "cruel and unusual punishment" as well as breathtaking judicial ingenuity and audacity (see *Madrid v. Gomez*, 889 F. Supp. 1146 [N.D. Cal. 1995]). How could such institutions be reformed when, according to a new model, they are the quintessence of reformed?

Prison Riots and Protests

Prisoners have little influence over the prison conditions, operations, and programs. Indeed, they are disenfranchised in most states. Ironically, perhaps, inmates' main contribution to prison reform has been due to riots. Major jail/prison riots (e.g., Attica, N.Y. 1971; New Mexico 1980; Strangeway Prison [U.K.] 1989) have focused media attention and thus public attention on these institutions, led to the formation of prestigious committees (New York State Special Commission 1972; Woolf 1991) and to sensible recommendations for reforms aimed at ameliorating the conditions and practices that caused the riots. Although the record on following through on such recommendations is spotty, there is no doubt that riots and fear of riots generates some pressure to address prisoners' and staffs' grievances.

We cannot dismiss the possibility that in the twenty-first century riots will turn out to be an important force for addressing inhumane prison conditions, but there is no reason to predict that this will happen. In the last decade or two, U.S. penal institutions have become much more riot-resistant. Prison officials have more and better anti-riot hardware (including rubber bullets, gas bombs) and SWAT units, better anti-riot training and more sophisticated strategies for dealing with disturbances. The "hardening" of penal facilities over the last generation has made rioting less likely and, if it occurs, more controllable.

Prisoners have also been known on rare occasions to engage in self-mutilation, hunger strikes, and other types of protests to make known their grievances and to bring about improvements in the conditions of their confinement (see Cummins 1994). While a possible source for future prison reform, these kinds of protests are not very likely. American prisoners historically have not been good at or experienced in organizing and protesting. Moreover, it would be extremely difficult, within the context of its conflict-ridden inmate culture, for prisoners to effectively organize and demonstrate for prison reform. Finally, such protests would have to be extremely dramatic to draw public and political attention and achieve results.

Professionalism as a Force for Reform

There have always been particular prison officials (e.g., Thomas Mott Osborne in New York and Alexander MacConochie in Norfolk Island), themselves reformers, who have pressed for more humane penal conditions (see Morris 2002). While historically the point was not always obvious to them, prison officials have a substantial community of interest with prisoners in safe, humane, and constructive prison conditions, operations, and programs. This point is now widely recognized. What was new in the latter decades of the twentieth century was the emergence of the American Correctional Association, a professional prison officials' organization that linked professionalism to safe, clean, efficient, and richly programmed penal institutions (see American Correctional Association 2002).

Whereas at previous points in U.S. history, prison staffs have seen themselves locked in a zero-sum struggle with prisoners over authority, many of today's prison officials are much more professional and sophisticated than their predecessors. They are graduates of colleges and universities, much more closely tied to mainstream society, more integrated with public administration generally, less politicized, and more likely to define themselves as professional public sector managers whose aim is to secure the most resources they can toward the goal of safe, secure, and humane institutions. When living conditions are safe and relatively pleasant for inmates, working conditions for employees will be safe and relatively pleasant. When inmates feel that rules and procedures are fair and uniformly enforced, there will be fewer challenges to staff authority. When inmates are busy, there will be less violence and conflict; staff will find their work more relaxed and more rewarding.

Professionalism is very important to the self-identity of today's prison wardens and managers. For almost two decades the American Correctional Association (ACA) has promulgated best practices standards for jails and prisons and has encouraged its members voluntarily to seek "accreditation" of their institutions. (The process involves an ACA team carrying out a thorough evaluation of compliance with ACA standards.) Managers of more than 1,200 jails and prisons have invested millions of dollars in training and renovation in order to comply with ACA standards.

Nevertheless, while prison officials may become more important as a force pushing for decent and rational prison reform, there are limits to what they can accomplish. For one thing, it remains unclear how much professionalization can take place around a sense of mission as limited and lackluster as safe and secure warehousing of convicted offenders. For another thing, for today's correctional professional to survive and advance in state politics, it is necessary to be a team player, loyal to the governor. Lobbying is mostly confined to the executive branch where prison officials compete with representatives of other government agencies for position on the governor's list of priorities. In this competition, their great disadvantage is that they do not provide services for a politically significant constituency. They have to compete with government agencies that represent powerful and politically salient groups. Furthermore, the top corrections officials can only lobby so much and so openly. As members of the governor's team, they cannot denounce, embarrass, or threaten the governor and his or her administration. Only the guards' union could play the role of a no-holds-barred pressure group and perhaps they will do so more aggressively in the years to come (see generally, Parenti 1999).

Even without more resources, prison officials could contribute to better prison conditions and operations by being capable and imaginative managers, who are good problem solvers, get the most out of their staffs, promote fairness, and keep morale high. The National Institute of Corrections has made important but limited contributions to professionalizing and training the managerial ranks of prison officials. In the twenty-first century, there is enormous opportunity for improvements in professional educational programs in prison administration. An expanded federal National College of Corrections that offered year-round short and long courses for middle and upper corrections managers could make an enormous contribution to the operation of our prisons.

Privatization as a Force for Reform

It certainly could be argued that one reason prison conditions have historically been so bad is that penal institutions have, for most of U.S. history, been handed over to a public monopoly that has no or little incentive to innovate, to do things better or more efficiently. Americans, at least at this point in our history, are likely to think of competition as being the great engine of innovation and efficiency. If the operation of prisons is farmed out to a variety of private sector contractors, would we not reap a benefit in terms of better managed prisons? Unlike public prison departments, private prison providers would have a powerful incentive to perform well so that they would be hired to run more institutions in more states. Indeed, a highly publicized failure would be very bad for business (see Harding 1997).

The private prison companies are run by some of the best known and most highly respected former public sector prison managers. If successful, privatization would allow them to earn more money and to leverage their expertise over more institutions. In theory, they could, by use of financial incentives, hire the best people, promote them more flexibly, and adopt all sorts of innovations that would not be possible in the public sector. Moreover, the private prisons could be seen as laboratories for reform where, unfettered by muscle-bound bureaucracies, managers could experiment with new administrative strategies and ideas. Any successes that they achieve could be replicated in other institutions, public and private.

So far the jury is still out on whether private prisons have been a positive force for American corrections. Many studies have failed to confirm that private prisons have produced better prison regimes (Greene 2003a, 2003b; Greene et al. 1999). Indeed, there have been disturbing cases of chaotic and unsuccessful private prisons. Nevertheless, I think there is reason to believe that private prisons, in some form, can and will be a positive force in American corrections in the twenty-first century.

Perhaps the public sector officials who contract for and supervise the contracts of private prisons will have to develop greater expertise in performing their role. The same fiscal pressures that drive down conditions and operations in public prisons lead public officials to focus primarily or solely on cost in contracting for and evaluating private prison providers. If cost is going to be the only criteria on which public contractors are going to evaluate private prisons, it will hardly be surprising that the resulting institutional regimes do not do well on all sorts of measures of good conditions, operations, and programs. You get what you pay for.

Citizens Prison Reform Groups

There have always been idealistic private citizens, some of them ex-prisoners, who have dedicated themselves to improving the lot of jail and prison inmates. Groups like the John Howard Association, the Fortune Society, the Osborne Association, and Prison Fellowship Ministries in the United States, the Howard League in the United Kingdom (Schone 2001), and Amnesty International, which investigates prisons all over the world, have played a positive role throughout the twentieth century in bringing deplorable conditions to public attention and in campaigning for better conditions and more resources. Sometimes these groups have achieved formal or quasi-formal status in corrections by being given authority to freely visit prisons and make reports (see, e.g., Morgan 2001).

While these publicly spirited NGOs will undoubtedly continue to be a force for prison reform in the twenty-first century, their role is limited by several realities. First, there are today far more prisons and prisoners than there were a generation ago, but the size of the NGO prison reform groups has not grown commensurately. Thus, there are fewer prison reformers to monitor far more institutions and inmates. Second, in a period of fiscal crisis, these organizations, which depend upon private donations, will have to struggle just to keep running. It will become harder and harder to prevent layoffs and reduction of activities. It will also be harder to wring concessions and initiatives out of public officials when these officials are under pressure from groups and constituencies of all types.

New Sources for Prison Reform

The best hope for a brand new source of prison reform would come from adoption of some sort of national service program or ethos that would require or encourage young Americans to give one or two years of service to their country (see Moskos 1988). Just as tens of thousands of young people today serve a stint in the armed forces and just as other young people, under the auspices of Americorps, tutor and mentor youth, build affordable housing, teach computer skills, clean parks and streams, run after-school programs, and help communities respond to disasters, thousands could be directed to our correctional facilities where they could work (for a national service stipend) in office jobs, in the visiting room, as counselors, teachers, or staff aids to the administrators, or as line officers.

Consider the benefits that would flow from filling 10 percent of prison staff positions with young people meeting their national service responsibility. At a minimum, they would inject an "outsiders" presence into the closed world of the prison. Because these young people would be available to bear witness to deplorable conditions and staff brutalities and illegalities, they would deter them from occurring and help remedy them when they do occur. In effect, they would undermine the prison's equivalent of the "blue wall of silence." They would bring to the parochial prison society new ideas and perspectives that might make operations more efficient and fair. They would create a much stronger link between the prison and the larger society.

A corps of young National Service volunteers would help the prisons run more smoothly. Extra hands could improve the records office, the commissary, the visiting room, the school, and the infirmary. In addition, the program would provide a pool of potential recruits that would otherwise not be available to corrections.

Perhaps most importantly if, over time, tens or hundreds of thousands of young people had a first-hand experience working in prisons, they might form the basis for an informed and active political constituency for prison reform. At a minimum their participation in the society's core institution of punishment would democratize the institution of punishment and bolster the prison's legitimacy.

Admittedly, there is no reason to predict that Congress will establish a national service system any time soon. Nevertheless, volunteerism remains a powerful theme in U.S. society and recent years have seen the formation of Peace-Corps-type organizations in education and the environment. Some states (e.g., Texas) have experimented with internships in corrections. A program of short-term service in corrections might appeal to an idealistic element among today's youth. We will not know until we have tried.

Conclusion

The twenty-first century has begun with American prisons and jails under more than usual pressure. The national inmate population is at an all-time high, indeed six times higher than it was in the early 1970s. Hundreds of prisons have been opened in the last two decades. Thousands of correctional personnel have been hired. Experienced officials have been spread thinner and thinner over more and more institutions. Still, a crowding crisis endangers the smooth and humane operation of this American gulag. And a serious fiscal crisis now calls into question the capacity of state and local governments to manage their much-expanded penal facilities and inmate populations consistent with humane and constitutional standards.

Funding and administering decent penal facilities is one of the toughest challenges our society faces and one of the most important. Yet political realities do not assign the task a high priority. For the last several decades the courts took over the role of monitoring the prisons and guaranteeing that conditions be kept to certain standards. Now the courts are in retreat, and there is no other actor available to pick up the slack. In my view, only a national service program aimed at prisons and jails would supply the manpower and energy to really make a significant impact. But I have floated the idea before and regrettably have never seen it seriously discussed.

Of course, we should always be modest in trying to make future forecasts. Forces now unforeseen may come to the rescue of our prisons and jails. Perhaps today's fiscal crisis will prove to be short-lived? Perhaps our two-decade-long experiment with mass incarceration will suddenly and dramatically reverse itself? Perhaps the courts will get a second wind and come roaring back into prison cases? Perhaps one or more horrific riots will persuade the populace and the politicians that prison conditions cannot be ignored? Perhaps a wave of humanitarianism, stimulated by the voices of humanists like Norval Morris, will capture the imagination and spirit of a new generation that will take more seriously its responsibility to ensure that all citizens under state confinement are treated with respect and decency (Morris and Jacobs 1974).

Notes

1. These figures are taken from the *2001 Corrections Yearbook* (Camp and Camp 2002). Line officers can increase their take home salary by working overtime. But working a lot of overtime may also take its toll on individuals and the organization.

2. According to the *2001 Corrections Yearbook* (Camp and Camp 2002), as of January 1, 2001, states reported that their penal institutions were operating at 107.2 percent of capacity. Rhode Island reported operating at 88.9 percent capacity, while Washington State reported operating at 135.7 percent of capacity.

3. *Baxter* held that Miranda warnings need not be given inmates facing disciplinary hearings. *Hudson* held that, under the Fourth Amendment, prisoners have no reasonable expectation of privacy in their cells and that destruction of their property does not constitute an unconstitutional "seizure" because the exigencies of prison security require that prison officials have authority to seize inmates' property.

4. There is a growing research literature on the extent to which prisoners' lawsuits, before the PLRA, were a burden on the federal judiciary. Professor Margo Schlanger (2003) has carried out the most comprehensive research. She finds that in 1995, inmates filed over 40,000 new federal civil lawsuits, 15 percent of the federal civil docket. Of course, many of these complaints were given very short shrift. In 1997, just two years after passage of the PLRA, the number of inmate filings had declined 30 percent.

5. Before passage of the PLRA, the Supreme Court had opened the door to opening up and modifying old consent decrees in *Rufo v. Inmates of Suffolk County Jail*, 502 U.S. 367 (1992).

6. Professor Norval Morris served as special master in *Williams v. Lane*, 1988–1992, which dealt with the conditions and operations of protective custody at Illinois's Stateville Penitentiary and in *K.L. v. Edgar*, 1993–1996, which dealt with conditions in Illinois's mental hospitals. The jurisdiction of both cases was the Northern District of Illinois.

References

American Correctional Association. 2002. *Standards for Adult Correctional Institutions*. 4th ed. Washington, D.C.: American Correctional Association.

Berk, Richard A., and Peter H. Rossi. 1977. *Corrections Reform and State Elites*. Boston: Ballinger Press.

Bottoms, Anthony E. 1999. "Interpersonal Violence and Social Order in Prisons." In *Prisons, Crime and Justice: A Review of Research*, vol. 26, ed. Michael Tonry and Joan Petersilia. Chicago: University of Chicago Press.

Branham, Lynn S. 1976. *The Law of Sentencing, Corrections, and Prisoners' Rights*. 5th ed. 2002. West Group.

Camp, Camille G., and George M. Camp. 2002. *2001 Corrections Yearbook*. Middletown, Conn.: Criminal Justice Institute.

Christianson, Scott. 1998. *With Liberty for Some: 500 Years of Imprisonment in America*. Boston: Northeastern University Press.

Cummins, Eric. 1994. *The Rise and Fall of California's Radical Prison Movement*. Stanford, Calif.: Stanford University Press.

DiIulio, John, Jr. 1987. *Governing Prisons: A Comparative Study of Prison Management*. New York: Free Press.

Feeley, Malcolm M., and Edward L. Rubin. 1998. *Judicial Policy Making and the Modern State: How the Courts Reformed America's Prisons*. Cambridge: Cambridge University Press.

Fitzgerald, Mike. 1977. *Prisoners in Revolt*. Harmondsworth: Penguin.

Garland, David. 2001. *The Culture of Control: Crime and Social Order in Contemporary Society*. Oxford: Oxford University Press.

Greene, Judy. 2003a. "Bailing Out Private Jails." In *Prison Nation: The Warehousing of America's Poor*, ed. Tara Herival and Paul Wright. London and New York: Routledge Press.

———. 2003b. "Lack of Correctional Services: The Adverse Effects on Human Rights." In *Capitalist Punishment: Prison Privatization and Human Rights,* ed. Andrew Coyle, Rodney Neufield, and Allison Campbell. Atlanta: Clarity Press.

Greene, Judy, et al. 1999. "Comparing Private and Public Prison Services and Programs in Minnesota: Findings from Prison Interviews." Minneapolis: University of Minnesota Law School Institute on Criminal Justice. Available: http://www.law.umn.edu/centers/crimjust/sentence.php.

Hallinan, Joseph. 2001. *Going up River: Travels in a Prison Nation.* New York: Random House.

Harding, Richard. 1997. *Private Prisons and Public Accountability.* New Brunswick, N.J.: Transaction Pub.

Howard League. 1975. Boards of Visitors of Penal Institutions: Report of a Committee Set up by Justice, the Howard League for Penal Reform, the National Association for the Care and Resettlement of Offenders.

Jacobs, James B. 1977. *Stateville: The Penitentiary in Mass Society.* Chicago: University of Chicago Press.

———. 1980. "The Prisoners Rights Movement & Its Impacts." In *Crime and Justice: An Annual Review of Research,* vol. 2, ed. Norval Morris and Michael Tonry. Chicago: University of Chicago Press.

———. 1995. "Judicial Impact on Prison Reform." In *Punishment and Social Control,* ed. Thomas G. Blomberg and Stanley Cohen. New York: Aldyne de Gruyter.

Johnson, Robert. 1996. *Hard Time: Understanding & Reforming the Prison.* Boston: Wadsworth Publishing Co.

Kuzinski, Eugene J. 1998. "The End of the Prison Law Firm? Frivolous Inmate Litigation, Judicial Oversight, and the Prison Litigation Reform Act of 1995." *Rutgers Law Review* 29:361–399.

Lin, Ann Chih. 2000. *Reform in the Making: Implementation of Social Policy in Prisons.* Princeton: Princeton University Press.

Lombardo, Lucien X., 1981. *Guards Imprisoned: Correctional Officers at Work.* New York: Elsevier.

Martin, Steve J., and Sheldon Ekland-Olson. 1987. *Texas Prisons: The Walls Came Tumbling Down.* Austin: Texas Monthly Press.

Mathiesen, Thomas. 1990. *Prison on Trial: A Critical Assessment.* London: Sage.

Morgan, Rod. 2001. "International Controls on Sentencing and Punishment." In *Sentencing and Sanctions in Western Countries,* ed. Michael Tonry and Richard S. Frase. New York: Oxford University Press.

Morris, Norval. 1995. "The Contemporary Prison: 1965–Present." In *Oxford History of the Prison: The Practice of Punishment in Western Society,* ed. Norval Morris and David J. Rothman. New York: Oxford University Press.

———. 2002. *Maconochie's Gentlemen: The Story of Norfolk Island and the Roots of Modern Prison Reform.* New York: Oxford University Press.

Morris, Norval, and James B. Jacobs. 1974. "Proposals for Prison Reform." *Public Affairs Pamphlets,* no. 510.

Moskos, Charles. 1988. *A Call to Civic Service: National Service for Country and Community*. New York: Free Press.

New York State Special Commission on Attica. 1972. *The Official Report*. New York: Bantam Books.

Parenti, Christian. 1999. *Lockdown America: Police & Prisons in the Age of Crisis*. London: Verso.

Schlanger, Margo. 1999. "Beyond the Hero Judge: Institutional Reform Litigation as Litigation." *Michigan Law Review* 97: 1994–2036.

———. 2003. "Inmate Litigation." *Harvard Law Review* 116(6): 1555–1706.

Schone, J. M. 2001. "The Short Life and Painful Death of Prisoners' Rights." *Howard Journal* 40:70–82.

Stern, Vivien. 1998. *A Sin against the Future: Imprisonment in the World*. Boston: Northeastern University Press.

Woolf, Lord Justice H. 1991. *Prison Disturbances, April 1990: Report of an Inquiry*. London: H.M. Stationery Office.

Zimring, Franklin, Gordon Hawkins, and Sam Kamin. 2001. *Punishment and Democracy: Three Strikes and You're Out in California*. New York: Oxford University Press.

PART IV

Coming Out

8

Questioning the Conventional Wisdom of Parole Release Authority

Kevin R. Reitz

This essay examines the advisability of including parole release discretion within the design of American sentencing systems as an important means for fixing the length of prison terms actually served by offenders. U.S. jurisdictions divide sharply on this question today. Sixteen states and the federal system have abolished the release authority of parole boards, including a majority of sentencing guideline jurisdictions. There is a slow but long-term trend in the direction of abrogation. Four states cancelled their parole boards' release authorities in the 1970s, six jurisdictions did so in the 1980s (including one that later changed its mind), and eight more took the step in the 1990s (Petersilia 2003, figure 2.1). In 1994 the American Bar Association endorsed the movement, recommending that time served in prison should be determined by sentencing judges subject only to formulaic good-time reductions, all within a framework of sentencing guidelines (American Bar Association 1994, Standards 18–2.5, 18–3.21(g), and 18–4.4(c)). The American Law Institute, now in the early stages of a revision of the Model Penal Code, must likewise confront this policy issue (see American Law Institute 2002a). It is possible that a new Model Code will seek to add momentum to the abrogationist tendency, or the ALI may seek to slow or reverse the trend. Strong views on both sides have already been aired in the Institute's debates.

Norval Morris's work stands at the center of this controversy. In *The Future of Imprisonment* in 1974, he mounted an influential attack on the theory and practice of back-end release decisions as entrusted to parole boards. He argued that such discretion should be eliminated or, where this was politically unfeasible, reconfigured (Morris 1974, pp. 31–45). In contrast with many other critics of the day, however, Morris did not claim that a perceived collapse of rehabilitation theory should be the underlying motivation for removal of the boards' authority (compare Wilson 1975; Frankel 1973; von Hirsch and Hanrahan 1979). Instead, Morris wanted to preserve as much room as possible for rehabilitation, or "facilitated change," inside prison walls (Morris 1974, p. 27, ch. 2). He posited that the mission of prison programming was crippled when the term-fixing decision was left hanging for months or years. By making the date of freedom turn in part upon an inmate's apparent engagement in programs, Morris argued that the system encouraged inauthentic participation (making prisons "schools of dramatic arts"), and also failed to limit enrollment to true volunteers—those who recognized their need for help and wanted to do something about it (see also Morris and Tonry 1990, p. 193; Morris 1993, pp. 831, 833–834). Morris suggested that the elimination of back-end release discretion, by addressing these corrosive defects, would do a great deal to *enhance* rehabilitative possibilities during confinement.

This chapter revisits the question of parole release discretion raised in the 1974 edition of *The Future of Imprisonment*—before any American state had yet experimented with abolition—in light of accumulating experience in the two-thirds of U.S sentencing systems that have retained a paroling authority and the one-third that have not. The first section of the chapter asks whether parole release discretion can be shown to advance the goals of the sentencing system, using Morris's theory of limiting retributivism as a frame for discussion. The second section then examines the performance of parole-release abolition jurisdictions against other jurisdictions for their differing experiences of prison population growth over the past three decades.

Two assumptions stand alongside the chapter's analysis. First, the question of supervision of released prisoners, often denoted as "parole supervision," is in no way implicated by the discussion. The issue here is who should decide when prisoners are released. The chapter assumes, and the author hopes, that adequate supervision and support will be afforded to ex-prisoners during their difficult transitions back into free society regardless of how the timing of release is determined. Second, I take as given that a well-ordered process for granting good-time or earned-time credits is a desirable feature of a prison system. The question posed in these pages is whether a parole release mechanism is needed *in addition to* the provision of good-time allowances in the neighborhood of 20 or 25 percent. A modest amount of play in confinement terms can assist prison administrators in maintaining discipline and can be used as an incentive to encourage inmates to participate in prison programming, but the device should be routinized and should carry basic protections on prisoners' behalf. The presumption should be that good-time credits will be granted in the absence of established reasons for their retraction, and good-time allowances should vest during the progress of a prison term so that vindictive staff or fellow inmates cannot engineer their withdrawal at an eleventh hour short of release (see Morris 2002). With these starting premises in place, we may proceed to the main subject at hand.

Does Parole Release Discretion Advance the Goals of the Sentencing System?

The stated advantages of parole release discretion often include claims that an agency with such authority can: predict with reasonable accuracy an individual prisoner's likelihood of reoffending (this can be restated in terms of the board's ability to discern when a prisoner has been rehabilitated); provide incentives to many prisoners to behave well in confinement and to participate seriously in prison-based programs, thus making their rehabilitation more probable; mitigate harsh pronounced sentences in individual cases and act overall as a force in favor of lenity in sentencing; facilitate prison population control in times of institutional overcrowding; and reduce disparities in sentences imposed by trial judges (see Bottomley 1990, p. 322, table 1; compare Burke 1995, p. 33).

Focused consideration of the policy desirability of discretionary release requires more than reciting a laundry list of objectives, however. The assembled goals must be related to the fundamental considerations that bear on the question of *durations* of confinement as a matter of punishment theory. We must also ask how well parole boards have done (or can be expected to do) in furthering those purposes when compared with other actors in the sentencing system.

Morris's Limiting Retributivism

This section examines parole release discretion under Norval Morris's theory of limiting retributivism (LR), adapted to the question of how long prison sentences should be in particular cases (see Morris 1974, 1982; Morris and Tonry 1990). Because LR is a hybrid theory that incorporates and gives structure to all of the mainstream retributive and utilitarian goals of punishment, readers who do not subscribe to LR may nonetheless find that their preferred objectives are addressed in the following analysis.

Richard Frase (chapter 4 in this volume) has given thoughtful treatment to the elements of LR theory and its growing acceptance in the United States and the Western world (see also Frase 1997). Thankfully, therefore, this essay can dispense with exegesis and proceed to LR's application to the question at hand. Two preliminary notes may be useful, however.

First, one of the great strengths of LR, as conceived by Morris, is that it attempts to capture and give shape to the impulses felt by conscientious decision makers in the rough and unhappy world of real criminal punishments. It is a flexible theory built upon human experience, not a theory that wages war on familiar thought processes (Frase, chapter 4 in this volume). When applying LR to questions of parole release, this essay works in the same spirit.

Second, LR theory has already won a place as a cornerstone of early drafting efforts for a new Model Penal Code (American Law Institute 2002b, Revised Section 1.02(2) and comment). One can foresee that debates of sentencing reform across American jurisdictions, to the extent they are influenced by ALI discussions and recommendations, will be somewhat more concentrated on explicit LR criteria than in the past. Quite apart from his contributions to the law of prison release, Morris's LR framework promises to have long and expanding influence on sentencing law and policy.

The Retributive Range

Morris's LR theory builds upon the idea that, while a retributive assessment of how much punishment is deserved is a necessary step in every sentencing decision, such an assessment can seldom be made with precision. There are few judges, philosophers, or other experts who can say that a particular offender who has committed a serious imprisonable crime—let us assume a forcible date rape with a maximum penalty of 10 years—deserves exactly *x years* in prison. Imagine a judge who has decided that a term of about five years in time actually served would be an appropriate retributive response in such a case (after the judge has weighed everything she knows about the offender, the harm to the victim, and the circumstances of the crime). We cannot ask our hypothetical judge, but it would not be shocking to learn that, deep in her heart, she remains in some doubt about the absolute correctness of her ruling. She might also think a term of four years, or six years, or possibly seven, to be within reason on desert grounds alone. Perhaps she even grappled with such a range of possibilities before the necessity of handing down a decision drove her to an exact number. Her thought process, which never alighted on a single penalty that was unmistakably appropriate, might have been spread along a continuum like the one pictured here:

Clearly Excessive:	10 years
Probably Excessive:	8–9 years
Possibly Excessive:	6–7 years
Possibly Too Lenient:	5 years

Probably Too Lenient: 3–4 years
Clearly Too Lenient: 1–2 years, or probation

Human experience tells us that retributive perceptions are often blurred. This is not to say that they never come into sharp focus. They gather clarity when removed further and further from the fuzzy middle ground. For example, we might expect our hypothetical judge—and most other people equally familiar with the case—to balk without hesitation at a low sentence of one or two years for the date rapist and to rule out altogether any term of probation (cf. *State v. Chaney*, 477 P.2d 441 [1970]). At the other extreme, and again assuming full knowledge of aggravating and mitigating facts, the judge might be equally resolute that a prison term of nine or 10 years would be unjustly harsh, as would all longer terms and the death penalty (which are not available in any case under the statute of conviction). LR theory requires decision makers to select sentences inside the boundaries of penalties that are clearly excessive and those that are clearly too lenient, always staying within the plausible retributive range. (Within the permissible range of severity, utilitarian purposes of punishment may also be weighed, and these considerations will be discussed later.) When in doubt about arriving at a hard decision in this world of approximations, Professor Morris has enjoined sentencers to err in the direction of "parsimony" (Morris 1974, pp. 60–61).

Such judgments of desert have bearing on decisions about prison durations and dates of release, and we could choose to design a sentencing system that asks parole boards to apply LR reasoning to their cases. For present purposes, however, the important questions are whether we *want* such judgment calls to be made by parole boards, and whether there are adequate reasons to delay their determination for months or years during which prisoners serve uncertain sentences.

A desert theorist might claim that sentencing judges, often aided by the scaling of offenses by a sentencing commission, are the most appropriate officials to make final retributive evaluations relevant to sentencing (see Monahan 1982, pp. 111–112; Frase, chapter 4 in this volume). In this conception, desert-based judgments are made at the front end of the punishment chronology, in highly visible administrative and adjudicative forums, all before the offender has begun to serve his sentence. Many commentators have argued that judges should have the last word in such matters, and that no additional information accumulates during prison terms that can or should reinform the retributive judgments made by sentencing courts (von Hirsch and Hanrahan 1979; Kress 1980).

This is an especially powerful argument within any theory that measures desert solely against the offense committed or the offense supplemented by the offender's criminal record (see, e.g., von Hirsch 1993). These referents do not change or become more knowable between the sentencing hearing and later parole board hearings. It is thus problematic to explain why a parole board is needed to revisit the considered moral pronouncement of the sentencing judge. Indeed, it can seem pernicious to have the parole board doing this, given that the procedural safeguards attendant to back-end decision making fall far short of those in a criminal courtroom. When retribution is the subject on the table, or so the argument goes, we should greatly prefer judicial decision makers over parole officials.

If this conclusion holds appeal (it does for me), that is all the more reason to test it carefully. Some people, for instance, might quarrel with the premise that desert-based sentencing should respond narrowly to present offenses and criminal history. Their moral intuition, which is the foundation of all desert theory, tells them that punishments should be measured by more expansive criteria. This alone would not threaten the preference for judges as decision makers, however. For purposes of argument, we may broaden our conception of the factual bases relevant to desert to include many things having to do with the offender's past, the circumstances of the crime, and the harm to the victim—all without creating any new justification for back-end release discretion. The factors just mentioned are ripe for consideration on the day of the sentencing hearing and will if anything be harder to reconstruct when the parole board finally meets, perhaps years down the line. A proponent of parole release must find narrower ground to stand on. If someone is willing to take the view that an offender's just punishment should turn in part on his *post-sentencing behavior*, or other post-sentencing developments, then we have the kernel of an argument that paroling authorities should share in the retributive evaluation of sentence length.

It would be dogmatic to rule out such considerations. Almost certainly, officials who now exercise delayed release discretion bring their moral sensibilities to their jobs, along with their other intellectual equipment. Consider, for example, a prisoner who has been denied parole repeatedly because of a series of in-prison infractions including fights with other inmates, drug use, theft, and belligerence toward prison staff. The parole board members were likely thinking a great deal about risk and rehabilitation each time they denied release, but it is difficult to believe that they were able to cleanse their minds entirely of moral reactions to the inmate's "bad" conduct. If we then imagine another prisoner, who has been rule-compliant and has devoted huge effort to work and education programs (or, to make the example more sympathetic, he has rescued a guard during a prison uprising), it is likewise hard to imagine that parole boards will stand aloof from all feelings that the "good" prisoner has earned or deserves an early release date—even conceding that they will probably weigh other, more utilitarian, factors as well.

Here it is useful to recall that Morris's LR theory is respectful of the ways in which real-world decision makers approach their tasks. If it is true that parole and corrections officials instinctively believe that the moral desert of prisoners during confinement should have some bearing on their length of stay, we should think carefully before attempting to legislate in the opposite direction. My own view is that these concerns can be captured adequately in a well-designed system of good-time or earned-time, and that too much scope is given to retributive evaluations of in-prison conduct if we have the parole board doing so, as well. But this is a matter of preference rather than fierce belief. Much depends on whether one believes in redemption as a moral phenomenon, and the degree to which one is willing to trust criminal justice officials to recognize its occurrence.

A wholly different desert-based argument is sometimes offered in favor of back-end release discretion: that final retributive judgments are best made only when considerable time has passed after the commission of offenses. On this view, judges are too close to their cases and sometimes cannot free themselves from the raw emotions and public visibility that may surround a sentencing proceeding. Parole boards, in contrast, are portrayed as having greater detachment and the freedom of generally operating outside the glare of publicity. Months or years after an extremely unpleasant event such as a serious crime, in other words, we can expect cooler heads to prevail. In its most unapologetic form, this argument goes further to suggest that the back-end release system allows the sentencing judge to announce a penalty in open court that (by design) sounds much more formidable than the system will actually produce. The afterglow of the sentencing hearing, and the next day's headlines, will satisfy the common person's appetite for a cathartic punishment, but neither the corrections system nor the defendant will really pay the advertised price. As Franklin Zimring has put it, "In a system that seems addicted to barking louder than it really wants to bite, parole (and 'good time' as well) can help protect us from harsh sentences while allowing the legislature and judiciary the posture of law and order" (Zimring 1976, p. 15).

If we accept these claims, then very little weight should ever be given to the retributive reasoning of sentencing judges. The true sentencer ought to be an entirely separate agency, with power to effect vast alterations in judicial penalties not only on desert grounds, but on all other grounds. (If judges are too caught up in the moment or are too conflicted to adjudge desert, they of course cannot be trusted with utilitarian purposes either.) To rest easy with this state of affairs, we must endorse a formal courtroom process for sentencing that is symbolic but intentionally misleading. We must also be prepared to believe that crime victims and the general public will not realize what is happening. None of this sounds terribly palatable or realistic.

There is also grave reason to doubt that parole boards are in fact politically insulated decision makers, and that the tugs of publicity and victim sentiment do not tell upon their actions. Through the 1980s and 1990s, parole boards across the country became visibly more risk averse in their release decisions, often jolted by a single but terrifying episode of criminality by a releasee. As Norval Morris has written, *all* systems of release will experience horrific failures in a small number of cases. Yet paroling authorities are poorly constituted to withstand the pressures of an impossibly difficult job (Morris 2002, p. 183). At any rate, most histories of parole boards in action do not engender confidence in their dispassionate powers of analysis (see, e.g., Rothman 1980, pp. 159–201; Rideau and Wikberg 1992, pp. 124–147).

Nothing can ever be proven beyond dispute, especially where deontological theories of punishment are concerned, but the upshot of this short analysis of LR principles, retributive reasoning, and prison release is this: I hope most readers will agree that the permissible range of punishment established by considerations of desert should be fixed at the front end of the sentencing process rather than the back end. Judges, perhaps in collaboration with sentencing commissions, should have responsibility for such judgments, but the parole board should not play a major role. If there is any place for desert-based adjustments of dates of release, they should be narrowly tailored to post-sentencing behaviors and events.

General Deterrence

Morris's LR theory allows criminal sentences to vary within the range of retributively permissible severity if there is a good utilitarian reason to move up or down within the range. I consider each of the utilitarian goals of punishment in turn, beginning with general deterrence (see Morris 1974, pp. 60, 79). Deterrence, as an act of communication to the society at large, would seem a function best discharged at the sentencing hearing itself through the judge's pronouncement of a penalty in open court. The formality and solemnity of most courtrooms, the public aspect of their proceedings, the stature of most judges, and the opportunities for participation extended to offenders, victims, and other concerned parties—all augur in favor of a maximized deterrent effect, at least within the realm of what is realistically possible. There is evidence that general deterrence is better effected through increases in the certainty of punishment following criminal conduct that through increases in the severity of threatened punishments (von Hirsch et al. 1999, pp. 45, 47–48). If the designers of a sentencing system were to take these empirical findings to heart, then the goal of general deterrence would have small importance to the question of prison durations, or to the question of who should make durational decisions.

Is there any substantial argument that an agency with back-end release authority should share discretion over the length of prison terms to enhance the pursuit of general deterrence? It does not seem likely. Such later-in-time discretion will tend to weaken the inhibitory force of judicial sentences once it is widely known that only a fraction of sternly voiced prison terms will really be served. Courtroom sentences that lack street credibility may have insidious effects more widespread than those upon potential criminals who are weighing their odds. General deterrence is sometimes allied with the idea that the criminal law can have an educative effect on citizens at large, inculcating habits of mind that the legal order means business and must be respected (Andenaes 1952, pp. 179–180). Within this more diffuse understanding of general deterrence, parole release can produce negative ripple effects among those who see it as a failure of the legal system to keep its promises—or worse, among those who see it as a corrupt mechanism for hoodwinking the public.

In some times and places, parole release has been an unpopular institution, and one that threatens people's beliefs in the rectitude of the justice system. Campaigns to abolish parole release discretion have flown under the banner of "truth in sentencing," suggesting that the alternative is a system that tells lies. I would not like to say that what is popular or unpopular should be the sole touchstone of criminal law reform, but we are here focused upon general deterrence and public perceptions as one part of a larger picture. In order to find a comfortable resting place for back-end release discretion as an aid to general deterrence, we would have to return to the "bark and bite" approach discussed earlier, in the hope that the public can be bamboozled while being deterred from crime, all the while remaining respectful of a judicial system that engages in false advertising.

Incapacitation (and Rehabilitation)

Theories of incapacitation and rehabilitation, two sides of the same coin, resound as traditional justifications for parole release discretion. The flip side of releasing prisoners when we think they are rehabilitated is continuing to confine them when we think they remain crime-prone (see Packer 1968, p. 55). In some cases, where the prospects for an offender's rehabilitation are believed to be slim or none, the policy of incapacitation predominates and pushes toward the longest period of confinement morally allowable (Zimring and Hawkins 1995, ch. 4). Norval Morris has said that such cases may be countenanced in LR theory and others agree (Morris and Miller 1985; Ruth and Reitz 2003, ch. 4).

Is a parole board with back-end release authority necessary or useful to the goal of extended confinement of dangerous criminals within retributive limits? The answer depends on whether the parole board, through observation of an offender's in-prison behavior, is in a better position to predict post-release recidivism than the sentencing court had been months or years earlier. For three decades, Professor Morris has reported firmly that this is not the case. In 1974 Morris wrote:

> Protracted empirical analysis has demonstrated . . . that *predictions of avoidance of conviction after release are no more likely to be accurate on the date of release than early in the prison term.* . . . Neither the prisoner's avoidance of prison disciplinary offenses nor his involvement in prison training programs is correlated with later successful completion of parole or with later avoidance of a criminal conviction. (Morris 1974, p. 35, citing Goldfarb and Singer 1973, pp. 278–282; Hood and Sparks 1970, pp. 183–192)

In 2002 Morris reiterated this statement: "The blunt truth is that at the time of sentencing as good a prediction as to when the prisoner can be safely released can be made as at any later time during confinement" (Morris 2002, p. 186). It may seem counterintuitive that long observation of an inmate can yield no reliable information about his future conduct. Yet it is not wholly paradoxical that a prisoner's ability to navigate in the structured and artificial prison environment should tell us little about his functionality outside. Norval Morris quoted his colleague Hans Mattick as saying, "It is hard to train an aviator in a submarine" (Morris 1974, p. 16). Once released, the former inmate is reimmersed in the same world of temptations, personal deprivations (which are probably more acute than before his confinement), and criminogenic forces that landed him in the penitentiary in the first place.

No existing body of research has mounted a serious challenge to Morris's general claim that paroling authorities gain no predictive abilities superior to those of sentencing courts. A group of Canadian researchers have come closest to calling Morris's dictum into question, but the evidence they have assembled is preliminary and only suggestive. Their thesis is that predictions of future criminality in all settings depend on both "static" factors (things an offender cannot change, such as age, gender, and childhood experience) and "dynamic" factors (that can be altered, such as antisocial attitudes, educational attainment, and use of or abstinence from drugs) (see Andrews and Bonta 1994, p. 165; Gendreau, Little, and Goggin 1996, p. 597). In a recent meta-analysis, Paul Gendreau and his coauthors cumulated 131 predictive studies of great variety and reported that dynamic predictors (as defined by the authors) had proven overall to be just as important, or slightly more important, than static predictors in reaching the best possible forecasts of future criminal acts (ibid., p. 588).

Based on this finding, Gendreau et al. offered the policy recommendation that "reclassification" of offenders should be performed at different times when mapping out criminal justice or other crime-preventive interventions. This speaks only obliquely to the question of parole release, but others have taken the matter further. Joan Petersilia, in a recent and important book on parole and reentry, has made the Gendreau study one basis for her recommendation that American sentencing systems should retain or restore the release discretion of parole boards (Petersilia 2003, ch. 5, recommendation 5). Petersilia is a respected voice in the criminal justice research community, and it is important to ask whether in this instance the knowledge base supports her prescription.

In fact, the evidence is far from compelling. First, it is important to stress that the Gendreau study gave limited attention to parole decision making. The meta-analysis did not specifically address prediction as part of the parole release process, nor were results separately reported for predictions by parole boards, and only a small minority of the 131 studies in the survey had been performed in the parole release setting. Moreover, the dynamic factors that Gendreau et al. found to hold predictive value across multiple studies included a preponderance of factors that parole boards or corrections officials cannot usefully observe. For example, parole boards would be nonplussed if told they should monitor whether or not the offender in question has socialized with other offenders, has experienced family discord, especially with a significant other, has gotten married, has found and held a good job, has increased his income, or has changed his address (see Gendreau, Little, and Goggin 1996, p. 597). These things are all geared toward observation of behavior in the free society and are present—if at all—in distorted ways in the prison setting. The most powerful of the dynamic predictors, which the Canadians have given the enigmatic name "criminogenic needs," is defined as "antisocial attitudes supportive of an antisocial lifestyle and behavior regarding education, employment" (ibid.). This is a dangerously vague criterion that could be applied in large part according to the likes and dislikes of corrections officials (see Jones 1996, p. 61; Underwood 1979, p. 1443). Most importantly, the meta-analysis included no findings whatever on the questions of whether and when predictions of future offending are seen to improve because changes in dynamic variables have been noted. The authors disclosed (and speculated) that "While very few studies have assessed how well changes over time within dynamic factors predict recidivism, the data suggest that changes in criminogenic needs may produce strong correlations in that regard" (Gendreau, Little, and Goggins 1996, p. 588). This, however, is exactly the information we need, comparing predictive power at *time 1* and *time 2*. Specifically, in the parole release context, we need to know whether predictions at *time 1* (judicial sentencing) are better or worse than predictions at *time 2* (parole release hearing). Gendreau and his coauthors—and the existing literature of prediction more generally—do not help us answer this question (see Rice, Harris, and Quinsey 2002, p. 591).

The Gendreau study provides slight support for an across-the-board recommendation that parole release discretion should be retained (where it exists) or restored (where it has been extinguished). The Gendreau results are provocative and should be enough to encourage future research into "dynamic" factors that are within the purview of paroling authorities (but see Rice, Harris, and Quinsey 2002, pp. 591–592). A number of in-prison interventions have been associated with lowered recidivism rates following release, and it may be that means can be developed to identify which inmates, at what stage in the game, have absorbed such crime-suppressive benefits (see, e.g., Bushway and Reuter 2002; Anglin and Hser 1990). Until useful evidence is found, however, it is unsound to give an enormous share of sentencing discretion to an agency that is flying in the dark. Years ago, Marvin Frankel wrote that he had nothing against indeterminate sentences for some offenders—but they should be made available only in cases where it can be shown that the criminal justice system possesses a rehabilitative intervention with some reasonable prospect for success and where the system can claim the ability to identify successes and failures "with a decent approach to precision" (Frankel 1973, pp. 98–100). It seems to me that Frankel had it right. We should be open to future research and should take steps to encourage it. In the meantime, we should not design entire sentencing systems on unsupported hopes.

Rehabilitation (and Incapacitation)

Before weighing the parole board's competency to further the goal of rehabilitation, we confront an important philosophical obstacle. Many distinguished scholars, including Norval Morris, H. L. A. Hart, and Marvin Frankel, have argued that considerations of rehabilitation should never be permitted to influence the decision of whether or not a convicted offender will be imprisoned. Taking this idea one step further, as Morris has done, it might likewise be said that hopes for an offender's rehabilitation should not be allowed to prolong the *duration* of the prison term he would otherwise serve (see Morris 1974, p. 18; Hart 1968, p. 26; *United States v. Bergman*, 416 F. Supp. 496 [1976] at 499; American Bar Association 1994, Standard 18–3.12[a][iii]; National Conference of Commissioners on Uniform State Laws 1980, § 3–102[5]; Packer 1968, p. 67). If we accept this second proposition—which is much stronger than the first in practice, but difficult to separate from it on principled grounds—then the leading rationale for parole release discretion has been removed completely from the table. One intended effect of the parole board's operation is unabashedly to keep selected prisoners confined for additional months and years—sometimes many years—while everyone waits for the rehabilitative process to take hold. The reader who is committed to proposition number two should read no further into this section, for it has already been established to his or her satisfaction that the goal of offender rehabilitation can provide no basis for the institution of parole release discretion.

Without doing sustained battle against the combined forces of Morris, Hart, Frankel, and others, I nonetheless proceed on the contrary assumption that sentence severity should in some instances, and within appropriate limits, be allowed to vary in the pursuit of rehabilitation. This prospect requires a friendly amendment to Morris's approach, borrowing from his LR framework, to posit that the exact term of confinement may be adjusted up or down *within the permissible retributive range* if there is good reason to suppose that the offender's rehabilitation will be facilitated by a longer or shorter stay.

Consider, for example, the case of a repeat offender convicted of a violent crime in the middle range of seriousness, who has a history of severe drug and alcohol dependency. Research shows that a sentence of two or three years of confinement with intensive substance abuse treatment (even if the offender does not participate voluntarily) stands a realistic chance of bringing the offender's addiction under control and reducing or eliminating his propensity for crime. The research also tells us that success rates in such programs are correlated with longer time periods of intervention. Three years would be better than two (see Anglin and Hser 1990). Finally, assume that the sentencing judge (or someone else entrusted to speak for the values of the community) would conclude on retributive grounds that the penalty deserved by the offender falls somewhere in the range of one-to-three years of institutionalization.

In such a case, should LR theory allow the sentencing court to select a three-year term at the high end of the retributive range? To put the question most vividly, we must assume that the judge would have chosen a shorter sentence in the absence of information about the efficacy of longer treatment doses. For anyone who thinks that the judge should have the power, or should even be encouraged, to pursue the most effective treatment option within the LR range, even if it means a penalty more severe than the judge would have imposed on retributive grounds alone, the "friendly amendment" to Morris's analysis has gained an important foothold. Further illustrations could press matters further, but we must return to the central question at hand: Assuming *arguendo* that durations of prison terms may sometimes vary based on rehabilitative motivations, but always within retributive limits, does a back-end paroling authority have a role to play in juggling and applying these concerns?

The bulk of this question has already been addressed in the preceding section, which explored the empirical evidence for the supposition that parole boards can detect, based on their observation of in-prison behavior, when an inmate may safely be released into free society. If we believed that parole boards were good at this, and were substantially better than sentencing courts at forecasting the future behavior of prisoners, there would be some reason to delay the term-fixing decision. That case has not yet been made, but might usefully be explored in future research and in pilot programs for specific kinds of offenders.

There is a somewhat different argument based on rehabilitation theory, however, that might still support the existence of back-end release discretion. Joan Petersilia and others have reasoned that it is always important to give inmates incentives concerning their own futures, and that the effectiveness of prison programs will be increased if prisoners believe that their early release depends on authentic participation (Petersilia 2003, ch. 2; Stivers Ireland 2001, p. 17). This argument supposes that holding the date of release in suspense can help prisoners muster the commitment necessary to work toward positive change, provided also that prisoners have reasonable confidence that the paroling authority will recognize and reward their honest efforts.

To the extent that these are common-sense assertions about human nature (that positive incentives are good, that people should believe they have a stake in their own futures), it is interesting to note that they are exactly contrary to the observations of Norval Morris and other experienced observers of the psychology of confinement. Morris has long argued that the coercive edge of the parole board's release discretion actually destroys the best chances for obtaining inmates' genuine involvement in prison programming. In Morris's telling, back-end release discretion is most likely to encourage play-acting, or other behavior designed to ingratiate the inmate with prison staff—not real commitment to change. Further, there is little in the annals of parole history to support the idea that prisoners have placed their trust in parole boards to make objective decisions based on legitimate criteria. Quite the contrary—and prisoners' suspicions about the unlovely nature of the boards' deliberations has often been well founded (Rothman 1980, pp. 159–201; Rideau and Wikberg 1992, pp. 124–147). Even apologists for parole release discretion concede the point that decision making in the past has been unsystematic and that a structured approach would be a novelty (Burke 1988, pp. xiv–xv).

If the question were simply one of intuition, it would be hard to choose between the opposing views that discretionary release helps, or hurts, the potential for in-prison rehabilitation. Professor Petersilia, however, relying on unpublished research performed by Connie Stivers Ireland, argues that there is now empirical foundation for the belief that discretionary release is a better way to help prisoners achieve a law-abiding lifestyle than a system of determinate release. Using data from the U.S. Justice Department's National Corrections Reporting Program (NCRP), collected from 30 states and the federal system, and multi-regression analysis, Stivers Ireland reports that "those released from prison via a mandatory mechanism were less than half as likely to successfully complete parole than those released from prison under discretionary (parole board) systems." Without regression, mandatory releasees were 75 percent less likely to succeed on parole (Stivers Ireland 2001, p. 13). These findings give some credence to the claim that back-end release discretion, as presently exercised in American jurisdictions, is having a net positive effect on ex-prisoners' behavior.

In fact, the results are highly suspect. The most evident problem with the Stivers Ireland study is the disproportionate importance of data from a single determinate state, California. Among the 30 jurisdictions in the NCRP sample used by Stivers Ireland, California supplied more than one-quarter of all prison releasees and more than one-half of all releasees from legal systems that had eliminated parole release discretion (Stivers Ireland 2001, p. 27, table 1). Stivers Ireland's findings do not really tell us how determinate release is working in all 17 jurisdictions across the country that have such an arrangement. We are primarily seeing how it plays out in California.

This is an enormous problem because California, for idiosyncratic reasons, has the highest rate of revocation of post-release supervision of any state in the union. In 1995, at the time of the Stivers Ireland study, California's failure rate on parole was a staggering 77 percent. Among all other states, the average failure rate was 47 percent. California's outlier status is confirmed in more recent data. In 1999 parolees were more than twice as likely on average to succeed in other states than in California. Fully two-thirds of prison admissions in California in 1999 were due to parole revocations—roughly twice the percentage across other states (Bureau of Justice Statistics 2001, pp. 12–13). More tellingly still, the flow of prison admissions due to revocations in California was far greater than in any other state that had abolished parole release discretion, and more than three times the average rate among other determinate states (see table 8.1).

Compared with other states that have abolished parole release discretion, California is the only jurisdiction that has produced revocation numbers well above national averages. As a whole, the "non-California" determinate states experience a flow of revocations (measured as a share of prison admissions) somewhat below the national benchmark. I would not like to make the claim that determinate sentencing structures have some tendency to produce a kinder and gentler machinery of sentence revocation, however. Large observable variations in revocations are almost certainly the result of institutional and policy differences in parole supervision arrangements across jurisdictions, rather than any difference in

Table 8.1. Percent of Prison Admissions that were Parole Violations in Determinate States in 1999

Jurisdiction	Percent of prision admissions that were parole violations
California	67.2
Maine	40.9
Illinois	27.3
Indiana	9.6
Minnesota	32.1
Florida	6.9
Washington	10.5
Oregon	25.1
Delaware	25.3
Kansas	38.2
Arizona	23.0
North Carolina	12.8
Mississippi	9.7
Virginia	11.1
Ohio	17.6
Average among Indeterminate States Other than California	20.7

Source: Bureau of Justice Statistics 2001b, p. 13, table 19.

release practice. The important point is that any study based on a dataset dominated by California, that uses sentence revocations as an outcome measure, is playing cards with a fixed deck.

What happens to Stivers Ireland's main finding if we redact the anomalous California numbers? In 1995, using raw data, prisoners released by discretionary authorities nationwide succeeded on parole at a rate of 54.2 percent, while those released in "non-California" determinate systems succeeded at a rate of 64 percent. The removal of California does not simply soften Stivers Ireland's conclusions; it reverses them. In every year through the remainder of the 1990s the same pattern holds: Without California fouling the data, it could be argued that prisoners who have served time in determinate systems are in general *more* rehabilitated upon release than those who have languished in indeterminate systems.[1] In a qualified way (see the next paragraph), we might say that Norval Morris has been vindicated.

It is dangerous to draw firm policy conclusions from these statistics. Aside from allowing one outlier state to overwhelm the sample, Stivers Ireland's methodology labors under an important conceptual difficulty that plagues much of recidivism research. Simply put, it is a serious error to equate failure rates on post-release supervision with the actual behavior of prison releasees. The states are far too different in their revocation practices to allow us to consider the data compatible from state to state. In any jurisdiction, the number and rate of revocations depends to some degree on the good or bad conduct of parolees, to be sure, but it also depends at least as much on what might be called the "sensitivity" of the supervision system to violations. Sensitivity varies with formal definitions of what constitutes a violation, the intensity of surveillance employed by parole field officers, the institutional culture of field services from place to place, and the severity of sanctions typically used upon findings of violations. Judging by the great differences in revocation patterns shown in table 8.1, which are found throughout the literature of post-release supervision, it is hard to avoid the conclusion that high or low revocation rates are more the result of the system's sensitivity to violations than any large difference in the post-release conduct of offenders from place to place. One must be supremely cautious about drawing conclusions from a methodology that equates low revocations in a given state with successful in-prison rehabilitation.

In summary, we possess no evidence whatever that discretionary prison release, as opposed to determinate release, facilitates rehabilitation. As I said earlier when the topic was prediction, this does not mean that a hypothesized connection between release mechanism and future behavior does not merit future study. It does, and we may someday discover that for some categories of offenders, in some circumstances, there is indeed a link. But we should be wary of building important components of a sentencing system, especially rules and processes that apply indiscriminately to all prisoners, upon an empirical knowledge base that remains nonexistent.

Does the Abolition of Parole Release Discretion Contribute to Ungoverned Prison Expansion?

Unless the preceding discussion has taken a serious wrong turn, neither Morris's limiting retributivism, nor any of the traditional deontological or consequentialist philosophies of punishment, offers compelling justification for a sentencing system that places a large reservoir of discretion in a parole release agency. The argument cannot end here, however, for it is possible to favor the existence of discretionary release on other grounds. One such justification is the belief that back-end release authority works in general to shorten prison sentences and as a check upon prison population growth. There are many people who hold a committed humanitarian view that the United States overincarcerates offenders by a large margin, has done so for a long time, and that the problem has greatly worsened in the last quarter century (see, e.g., Dyer 2000; Mauer 1999; Parenti 1999). From such a perspective, it is tempting to be attracted to *any* feature of a sentencing system that appears to incline in the direction of fewer inmates or shorter sentences—quite apart from whether the preferred feature can be justified through fine-grained analysis of retributive or utilitarian premises (see Zimring and Hawkins 1991, p. 206).

My own opinion is that deincarceration should not be favored as a blanket prescription (for more analysis, see Ruth and Reitz 2003, ch. 4; see also Piehl, Useem, and DiIulio 1999). Still, let us assume that there are sizable constituencies who are so disposed, and who feel that back-end release discretion should be preserved (or reinstated) in American sentencing systems because it is believed to further a deincarceration agenda. In such a frame of mind, it is still worth asking whether parole release discretion really is associated with restraint in the use of confinement.

A similar concern is the belief that the abolition of back-end release authority allows pressures toward prison growth to become ungovernable because there is no longer a flexible release valve at the back door of institutions. Thus, we have become accustomed to hear charges that determinate sentencing, where it has been adopted, has been a powerful contributor to late twentieth-century prison growth. This indictment is sometimes made specific to parole release and is sometimes broadened to include sentencing guidelines and other determinate reforms as alleged engines of punitive expansionism. On this view, the quintupling of incarceration rates that occurred nationwide from 1972 to 2002 would have been ameliorated if all U.S. jurisdictions had retained their former indeterminate sentencing laws.

These speculations are invariably voiced without empirical support. They have entered the conventional wisdom because they *seem* correct and because they line up with one notorious example of determinate sentencing reform gone awry. Most lawyers, judges, and academics are aware that the federal sentencing system, which abolished parole release in 1987 while instituting felony sentencing guidelines, has worked over the past 14 years to balloon the federal imprisonment rate. Per capita confinement in federal prisons grew 206 percent from 1987 to 2002—a rate impressively greater than the swift nationwide growth among the states of 102 percent over the same period (Bureau of Justice Statistics 2003, p. 4, table 4; 2002c, p. 495, table 6.24). In the decade prior to parole abolition and guidelines, the federal prisons had been expanding more slowly than the national average. Empiricists know the dangers of extrapolating from a sample size of one. Too often, however, the federal experience is taken as conclusive evidence that all determinate sentencing reforms will produce the same results.[2]

If we broaden the inquiry from the 11 percent of U.S. prison inmates housed for federal crimes to include the 89 percent under state jurisdiction (Bureau of Justice Statistics 2002b, p. 1), our observations about the effects of parole release abolition shift dramatically. Indeed, it quickly becomes apparent that the federal system bears little resemblance to any state system that has abolished parole or has instituted guidelines for sentencing and is the poorest of starting points for generalization (see Knapp and Hauptly 1992; American Bar Association 1994, pp. xxv – xxvii; Tonry 1996, chs. 2 and 3; Reitz 1996). When policy makers consider the future design of a state's sentencing system, the pertinent knowledge base should be drawn from other states. This is the approach of the remainder of this essay.

Indeterminacy, Determinacy, and the Expansionist Era

Although it is frequently asserted today that determinate sentencing reform has been an instrument of prison growth, there was a widespread belief mere decades ago that *indeterminate* sentencing systems were peculiarly associated with prison expansionism (see Allen 1964, pp. 34–35; Tappan 1958, pp. 531–532; American Bar Association 1980, pp.18–66; Walker 1998, p. 120). It is ironic that perceptions have flipped, but the kernel of wisdom here is that such broad-brush statements are almost always oversimplifications. Historically speaking, it is clear that the structural design of a sentencing system does not dictate by itself whether and how quickly the prisons will grow. In the late nineteenth century and for the first 70 years or so of the twentieth century, American sentencing systems were increasingly taken over by indeterminate sentencing reform (they were *all* indeterminate by the 1930s) (Walker 1998, p. 122). Across this period the nation's prisons grew slowly but relatively steadily. From 1880 to 1980 the state prisons enlarged by 832 percent compared to national population growth of 351 percent (Cahalan 1986, p. 29, table 3–2; Bureau of Justice Statistics 1988, p. 13, table 1; U.S. Bureau of the Census 1975, part 1, p. 8, Series A 6–8; U.S. Bureau of the Census 2001). There were some years of declining incarceration rates, however, most notably around World War II and through the 1960s. Indeed, the performance of America's sentencing systems of the 1960s was quite striking and may have been etched indelibly in the minds of deincarceration advocates: prison rates went down in that decade despite skyrocketing crime rates and a boom economy. The nation could have paid easily for more prisoners, but indeterminate sentencing systems were (temporarily) not delivering that result (see Ruth and Reitz 2003, pp. 18–22, 77–80).

In studying the track records of indeterminate versus determinate punishment structures, this section focuses on the current era of prison expansionism from 1972 to 2002. During these years the state and federal prisons swelled seven times over from a combined inmate population of 196,092 to 1,440,655 and the national imprisonment rate (for state and federal prisons, excluding local jails) rose from 94 per 100,000 in 1972 to 427 in 2002 (Bureau of Justice Statistics 1988, p. 11, table 1; 2003, p. 1; U.S. Bureau of the Census 1982). The main goal of the analysis is to refute the oversimplification that determinate sentencing reforms such as parole abolition and sentencing guidelines have fueled the incarceration explosion to any greater degree than "unreformed" indeterminate systems. In the following pages, state-by-state analysis supports the following conclusions:

- Although all state prison systems have grown very appreciably in the last three decades, rates of imprisonment vary widely across jurisdictions and some state prison systems have grown much faster than others.
- Prison growth over the last three decades has been the most explosive in states that have retained indeterminate sentencing struc-

tures, and the highest incarceration rates nationwide are also found in indeterminate jurisdictions.

- On average, prison growth has been slower in states that have abolished parole release discretion than in states that have retained such discretion.
- Prison growth has been most restrained in those states that have abolished parole release discretion in conjunction with the introduction of sentencing guidelines.

Franklin Zimring and Gordon Hawkins, in their classic book *The Scale of Imprisonment*, pointed out that the punishment systems in the 50 states and U.S. federal system were so markedly different from one another that they should be seen as "fifty-one different countries." Working with figures from 1980, the state with the highest imprisonment rate (then North Carolina) had more than 10 times the prison rate of the state with the lowest rate (New Hampshire) (Zimring and Hawkins 1991, pp. 137, 149). In 2001 decades of prison explosion had compressed the ratios a little, but the state at the top of the scale (Louisiana with a prison rate of 800 per 100,000) out-incarcerated the state at the bottom (Maine, 127 per 100,000) by more than a factor of six (Bureau of Justice Statistics 2002b, p. 4, table 4). If we count both prisoners and jail inmates, the state with the highest "total incarceration" rate in 2001 was still Louisiana (1,013 inmates per 100,000 population), with Maine at the low extreme (222 per 100,000) (Bureau of Justice Statistics 2002a, p. 13, table 16).

Looked at another way, there are a few U.S. jurisdictions today whose incarceration practices are almost comparable with those of the most punitive Western European nations. The highest incarceration rate among Western European nations in 2000 was Portugal, with a rate of 127 per 100,000 population, followed by England and Wales with a rate of 124 (see Elkins and Olagundoye 2001, p. 3, figure 2). These high-end confinement nations line up with low-end imprisonment states in the United States (e.g., Maine with a 2001 prison rate of 127 per 100,000), although a truer comparison between European and American practices should refer to total confinement rates (jail as well as prison), where the low-end states in the United States in 2001 were Maine (222 per 100,000) and Vermont (226) (Bureau of Justice Statistics 2002a, p. 13 table 16). There are many other American states, however, that outstrip any known standard of confinement on Earth, even in the Third World (The Sentencing Project 2001). When the deincarceration literature points out that the United States is the world leader in confinement, it is properly talking about states like Louisiana and Texas, but the characterization does not fit jurisdictions like Vermont and Minnesota. These brief observations should demonstrate that it is nonsensical to talk about *"the* American sentencing system" as though it were a monolithic whole, just as it is dangerous to make general statements about nationwide practices using aggregated data. Each state should be examined on its own or categorized according to its sentencing structure and actual practices.

The years of exploding prisons in America have been for the most part years in which indeterminate sentencing remained the structure of choice across the country. A simple mathematical exercise illuminates the point. When inmate counts were assembled in 2001, the United States had experienced 24 years of uninterrupted prison growth. The large governmental units that participated in that growth were the 50 states, the federal system, and the District of Columbia—52 jurisdictions in all. Multiplying years by jurisdictions, there were a grand total of 1,248 "jurisdiction-years" in this expansionist period. How many of these jurisdiction-years took place with an indeterminate sentencing system in place, and how many jurisdiction-years unfolded with determinate sentencing systems? From 1972 to 1973, all U.S. sentencing systems were indeterminate, yielding a total of 52 "indeterminate jurisdiction-years"—and this number continued to add up until California and Maine became the first determinate states effective in 1976. Counting all jurisdiction-years in the 17 jurisdictions where parole release discretion has been abolished, there were a total of only 237 from 1972 to 2001 compared to 1,033 jurisdiction-years of systems retaining parole release (counts based on data in Petersilia 2003, ch. 2, table 2.1). If we define "determinate sentencing reform" more broadly to include parole release abolition *and/or* the implementation of sentencing guidelines, there have been a total of 330 jurisdiction-years of determinate reform during this expansionist period—or 26 percent of all jurisdiction-years.[3] No matter how one counts, the prison expansion era remained overwhelmingly a period of parole release retention and indeterminacy. On the face of things, the determinate sentencing reforms have been of too recent origin, and are insufficiently widespread, to have massed into a dominant force behind national trends of prison growth.

Let us now focus on states that have, or have not, abolished parole release authority. In 2001 eight of the ten states with the highest prison rates nationwide were jurisdictions that retained parole release discretion. Nine of the 10 states with the highest rate of prison population growth from 1995 to 2001 were likewise parole release jurisdictions. Nearly all of the national leaders in confinement rates are Southern states, so it may be that there are regional forces at work that have driven up prison populations that are independent of the sentencing structures in operation. One can test for this by examining confinement practices within separate regions. If one assembles a list of the five states in 2001 with the highest prison rates in each of the four regions of the Northeast, Midwest, South, and West, 15 out of the total of 20 regional leaders in imprisonment are parole release states (Bureau of Justice Statistics 2002b, p. 4, table 4, p. 5, table 5, p. 6, table 6). Even when looking region-by-region, the pattern holds of indeterminacy at the top of the carceral heap.

It is also revealing to look at rates of change in incarceration practices of individual states, rather than standing populations. Standing counts reflect historical and cultural forces at work long before the advent of sentencing reform. For instance, some of the parole-release abolition states with low inmate counts today were already low incarceration jurisdictions when they eliminated parole release. We must find some means to take account of such pre-reform realities and also the fact that different states have always had drastically different confinement levels no matter what kinds of sentencing structures they have employed. In an attempt to make such corrections, figure 8.1 charts the experience of all states that have abolished parole release for a period of five years or longer, using the states' pre-abolition prison rate as a common baseline. For each state, the

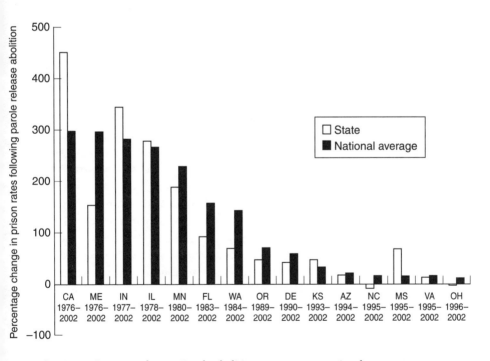

Fig. 8.1. Prison rate change: Parole abolition states versus national averages.

Sources: Bureau of Justice Statistics 2003, p. 4 table 4; 2002c, p. 495 table 6.24; 1998, p. 3 table 3; 1997, p. 3 table 3; 1996, p. 3 table 2; 1995, p. 3 table 2; 1988, p. 12 table 1; U.S. Bureau of the Census 1982; 2002.

chart displays the total *percentage* growth in the state's imprisonment rate from the effective date of parole abolition through the present and compares that rate of growth with the national average across all states for the same time period.

Figure 8.1 delivers a surprising message. Of the 15 parole abolition states in the figure, only five have experienced growth in prison rates that has outstripped the national average among all states in the years since abolition took effect. With the exceptions of California and Mississippi, the five states that have experienced above average growth have not been far above average. In contrast, the 10 abolition states with below average growth have for the most part been significantly below the nationwide benchmark. Figure 8.1 does not establish that parole release abolition invariably pushes inmate counts up or down. It appears that either outcome is possible, and many other factors are surely at work. Figure 8.1 is, however, wholly unsupportive of the claim that parole release abolition always, or usually, speeds up incarceration growth as compared with parole release retention. The general drift of things over three decades has been in the other direction.

Parole Abolition and Sentencing Guidelines

For those who work in the field of sentencing reform, the desirability of a single design feature of a sentencing system, such as the mechanism for prison release, is seldom considered in isolation. The final punishment outcome in the typical prison case is determined by a kaleidoscope of decisions and decision makers, including the police, prosecutor, defense lawyer, trial judge, probation officer, sentencing commission (if there is one), appellate courts (in some jurisdictions), prison officials, parole release authorities (where they still exist), and parole revocation authorities (see Zimring 1976; Knapp 1993; Reitz 1998). It makes limited sense to extract a lone actor or decision point to try to explain the operation of the system as a whole. For example, we saw earlier that prison admissions in California have been driven primarily by revocations of post-release supervision. Revocation practice seems a much more important determinant of incarceration trends in California than the state's arrangement for prison release decisions. Future studies of parole release authority in California and elsewhere should surely give greater attention to the *reincarceration* discretion of parole boards, little discussed in the existing literature, as an important systemic mechanism for undoing release decisions, however they are made.

To broaden the analysis of the essay, this section examines the performance of parole release abolition in states that have also created sentencing commissions and enacted sentencing guidelines. Beginning with Minnesota in 1980, a total of nine states have deliberately reallocated sentencing authority over prison durations by removing it entirely from parole boards at the back end of the decisional chronology and repositioning it at the front end of the system, where it is now concentrated in the sentencing commission and the courts (for a jurisdiction-by-jurisdiction count, see Reitz 2001). If the guidelines are not too restrictive, the judiciary acquires a substantial amount of new authority in such a system, since judicial sentences will now bear close resemblance to the punishments actually experienced by offenders. If sentencing courts comply with guidelines most of the time, either voluntarily or because the guidelines have a degree of legally binding force, the sentencing commission also inherits some of the discretion formerly possessed by a parole release agency (Knapp 1993, p. 684; American Law Institute 2002a, pp. 28–32).

The systemic interactions of (1) the addition of guidelines to a sentencing structure and (2) the subtraction of parole release authority are complex, and most are far afield from the present discussion. We are here concerned with the impact of sentencing reforms on the course of prison population growth. Figure 8.2 speaks directly to that issue, using the same manner

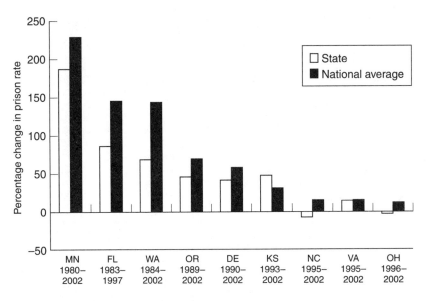

Fig. 8.2. Prison rate change: Guideline states that have abolished parole release versus national averages.

Sources: Bureau of Justice Statistics 2003, p. 4 table 4; 2002c, p. 495 table 6.24; 1997, p. 3 table 3; 1996, p. 3 table 2; 1995, p. 3 table 2; 1988, p. 12 table 1; U.S. Bureau of the Census 1982; 2002.

of display as figure 8.1. It charts the histories of prison expansion in the nine sentencing-guideline/parole-release abolition states (let us call them SGPRA states), from the date of reform through 2002, and compares those states against national trends over the same time.

The major finding in figure 8.2 is that eight of the nine SGPRA states have experienced post-reform rates of prison expansion below the national benchmarks for equivalent periods. The one state with an above average growth rate was not dramatically higher than the mean. The overall pattern is striking, especially when the SGPRA systems are compared with the available alternatives. Through the 1980s and 1990s there was no other structural design among up-and-running American sentencing systems that produced inhibitory effects on prison growth as reliably as those experienced in SGPRA states. Of those states that abolished parole release *without* the introduction of sentencing guidelines, more than half were high growth states, defined against nationwide trends. Among sentencing guideline states where parole release discretion was *not* abolished, more than half have also been high growth jurisdictions. And finally, as we have seen throughout this essay, indeterminate sentencing systems have long been the nation's leaders in imprisonment rates and imprisonment growth. A formal count of these observations, based on data from 1980 to 2002, is presented in table 8.2.

These observations are consistent with, but add nuance to, previous empirical analyses of sentencing guideline reforms. In a 1995 study, Thomas

Table 8.2. States above and below the National Mean for Prison Rate Expansion by Type of Sentencing Structure, 1980–2002

	Number of low-growth states	Number of high-growth states
SGPRA states	8	1
Guideline states retaining parole release	2	4
Parole abolition states, no guidelines	2	4
Traditional indeterminate systems	9	20

Note: States are classified based on the sentencing structure in place in 2002, provided that structure had been in operation for at least five years. Otherwise, a state is classified according to the sentencing system in use for 17 or more years of the 22-year period. For states that have undergone sentencing reform, the classification as "high-growth" or "low-growth" was calculated for the years after the reform was instituted. One state falls outside this pattern: Florida was an SGPRA state from 1983 through 1997, or 14 years of the 22-year period. During this time it was a low-growth state by a substantial margin (60 percentage points). From 1997 through 2002, Florida has operated as a parole-abolition jurisdiction without sentencing guidelines. During this latter period, Florida has been a low-growth state by a small increment (less than one percentage point). Rather than double-count the state, I include Florida as one of the SGPRA jurisdictions in the table.

Sources: Bureau of Justice Statistics 2003, p. 4, table 4; 2002c, p. 495, table 6.24; 1999, p. 3 table 3; 1998, p. 3 table 3; 1997, p. 3 table 3; 1996, p. 3 table 2; 1995, p. 3 table 2; 1988, p. 12 table 1; U.S. Bureau of the Census 2002; 1982.

Marvell found that sentencing guidelines were strongly associated with slower prison growth than in comparable non-guideline jurisdictions wherever sentencing commissions had made conscious efforts to restrain prison expansion (Marvell 1995). Researchers Jon Sorenson and Don Stemen at the Vera Institute of Justice recently concluded that sentencing guidelines of all varieties were correlated with lower imprisonment rates than those in non-guideline states at the end of the twentieth century, including states that had been incarceration leaders before the advent of guideline reform (Sorenson and Stemen 2002). The data presented in figure 8.2 suggest that the abolition of parole release discretion has been a particularly important component of the success of some sentencing commissions in deliberately managing the use of correctional resources.

Why should this be so? Part of the answer is the happenstance of policy preferences in SGPRA states. Most jurisdictions that have created SGPRA systems have done so in the hope of slowing or stopping preexisting cycles of incarceration expansion, prison construction, and spiraling correctional expenditures. For a time in the 1990s, this was the single most important reason why states undertook the ambitious project of sentencing guideline reform (Orland and Reitz 1993, pp. 839–840). With the severe state budget crunch of the early 2000s, this may continue to be a strong motivation toward SGPRA reform in additional states (see Wilhelm and Turner 2002). But there is no necessary connection between the SGPRA machinery and restraint in the use of confinement. If the same states had chosen to use an identical structural framework to *accelerate* their use of incarceration, they likely would have succeeded at that goal as well. There are only two sentencing guideline systems that were created deliberately to work sharp increases in aggregate punishments—the federal system and the guideline system in Pennsylvania. Both have succeeded smashingly (Reitz 2001).

Still, it is important to emphasize that SGPRA reform, in most of the places where it has occurred to date, including a majority of all parole-release abolition states, has not been intended to accelerate the growth of incarceration or push up the average length of prison stays. The small scholarly literature of parole release usually gets this fact wrong (Petersilia 2003, ch. 2 conclusion; Stivers Ireland 2001, pp. 7, 16–17). Indeed, I know of no SGPRA jurisdiction that had such a policy goal in mind except the federal system.

From a deincarceration perspective, all of this may not be very reassuring, since the policy makers who brought in SGPRA reforms with one set of expectations may easily change their minds in later years—or be replaced by other officials who decide to turn the system toward greater severity. In 1976, before any American sentencing guideline system had taken effect, Professor Zimring noted that the character of determinate sentencing systems could be changed in an instant by erasing one set of presumptive sentence provisions and substituting larger numbers. Zimring thought this was very likely to happen, given political pressures on criminal justice decision makers and the acute temptation to make sweeping "get-tough" changes in law following a single horrendous criminal episode (Zimring 1976, pp. 16–17) (with determinate sentencing legislation, "it takes only an eraser and pencil to make a one-year 'presumptive sentence' into a six-year sentence for the same offense"). The hypothesized vulnerability of determinate punishment systems to punitive policy shifts is now sometimes abbreviated with reference to "Zimring's eraser."

Let us put aside those who would think it a good thing that SGPRA systems are able to respond effectively to the will of publicly elected officials or to populist notions of appropriate sentences. They may be numerous, but they belong to a different discussion. The constituencies who are worried about Zimring's eraser are those who fear that a sentencing system's political responsiveness will generally, in the long haul, incline toward undue harshness in punishments. There is no way to refute absolutely these suspicions about the possible future, but we now have 25 years of subsequent experience since Zimring created the eraser metaphor, and this was a quarter century of unprecedented toughness in crime response. Even during the expansionist period, the vast majority of SGPRA systems were not visibly overwhelmed by draconian impulses.

History is always complicated, so it is important to qualify the previous statement. The typical state that has employed an SGPRA structure for any length of time has experienced some years in which state policy makers wanted to turn the system toward greater severity, and other years in which different priorities have prevailed. In Minnesota, for example, in the late 1980s, three high-profile crimes in Minneapolis parking lots caused the legislature to instruct the sentencing commission to ratchet up guideline penalties for serious violent offenses. The changes were dramatic, doubling presumptive sentence ranges in some categories (Frase 1993b, pp. 359–360). For a number of years following these amendments, the rate of growth in the Minnesota prisons outstripped national averages. On the other side of the coin, however, most years under the Minnesota guidelines have been years of relative restraint in the use of prison resources. The sentencing commission, in Minnesota as in other SGPRA states, provides the legislature with correctional population projections on a periodic basis, and these also accompany proposed changes in sentencing legislation or guidelines. Legislatures have been known to balk at the high cost forecasts that can attend new laws, or to soften the laws' terms before they are enacted. Or else they have found ways to offset punishment increases in one part of the criminal code with a lightening of penalties elsewhere (see Frase 1993a; Boerner and Lieb 2001; Wright 2002). During some years, therefore, the SGPRA systems provide effective tools to retard punitive expansionism that would otherwise occur—and this ends up being a significant thing even if it does not happen every year. Over the long term, the broken cadence of punitiveness in some years, and restraint in others, seems to yield a pattern of slower prison growth than in indeterminate jurisdictions that always, year-in and year-out, lack the systemic controls of the SGPRA system.

As a matter of abstract theory, a parole board could be just as effective at managing the use of prison resources as a sentencing guideline commission, but this has not often worked in practice in the past 20 or 30 years. Part of the reason, noted by Michael Tonry, is that sentencing commissions are able to address in-out decisions as well as sentence durations. Parole boards, in contrast, have no say over who comes into the prisons in the first instance, and thus are lacking one critical lever for the management of prison use (Tonry 1996, p. 27). An even more important concern may be the susceptibility of parole boards to political influence and a natural institutional drift toward severity in practice. I cannot think of a catchy term like "Zimring's eraser" to describe the phenomenon, but most parole boards in the 1980s and 1990s became stingier in their release decisions (Austin 2002, p. 3). Sometimes parole release practice changed in reaction to a single publicized incident, as in Pennsylvania following the police killing committed by parolee Robert "Mud Man" Simon in 1995 (PR Newswire 1995; Pennsylvania Law Weekly 1998, p. 2). In my own home state of Colorado, and in some other states, the word on the street is that the parole boards have become more risk averse than they used to be and are increasingly aware that they will not draw criticism for keeping someone in prison for too long, while an error in the opposite direction could be catastrophic—a syndrome observed many years ago by Professor Morris (see Morris 1974, p. 48).

In contrast, most parole-release abolition jurisdictions, including all SGPRA states, decided to build in the "early release" probabilities of a discretionary release system when they moved to determinate release. The expected behavior of a parole board was incorporated actuarially into the new determinate or guideline sentences when the systems were redesigned. This always requires considerable explanation to the public, who have to be made to understand that a two-year prison sentence under the new regime is actually tougher than, say, a five-year sentence under the former law. Provided this hurdle can be surmounted, however, the early release assumptions embedded in the typical guideline system are now harder to erode than are the behaviors of line officials who make discretionary release decisions. In the latter instance, a telephone call from the governor would probably suffice. In a sentencing commission state, meetings, public notice, projections, and debate must precede any change of similar consequence, and people from all sectors of the criminal justice system and across the political spectrum will have the opportunity to weigh in. Determinacy, with its concomitant advantages of systemic planning, may not be severity-prone by nature. And Zimring's eraser, at least in the setting of sentencing guidelines, is perhaps not so worrisome an office supply as may have appeared 25 years ago.

Conclusion: Important Issues Outstanding

The current scholarship concerning the question of parole release discretion is hardly robust, despite the urgent relevance of the question to the development of sentencing law nationwide. This essay is only a small contribution to an inadequate literature, but it is one that challenges many fundamental assumptions in common currency. The essay was not written to settle matters, but to lay the groundwork for future policy debate at a higher level of sophistication, with a more sound factual foundation, than often supplied by the conventional wisdom of the day. In focusing on both theory and data, the presentation here has been inspired by Norval Morris's work and teaching—and has yielded the happy surplusage of supporting much of what Morris has been saying about prison release decisions for many years.

There are many important questions concerning parole release, of course, that have not been addressed in this short discussion. One critical issue is the poor process constraints that have historically surrounded parole board decision making (see, e.g., Davis 1969, pp. 126–133). While courts are accustomed to working with enforceable decision rules, open proceedings, a right to appointed counsel for indigent offenders, explication of their decisions on the record, and appellate review of their rulings, parole board decision making never has—and probably never will—be attended by many or all of these safeguards. If we have faith in the regularity of parole board decisions, it must to some extent be a blind faith or one founded on our trust in the competence and professionalism of board members. Here again, however, the history of parole in America counsels caution. The system of patronage appointments has seldom given us parole boards with deep expertise in the behavioral sciences or with any professional credentials that would make them superior to (or competitive with) judges in the fixing of prison durations. It is always easy to say that more qualified persons should therefore be recruited to the task, but criminal justice reform is most likely to founder when it is built on the assumption that the human capital within the system can be dramatically improved. Such change takes generations if it can be brought about at all. If we are realists, we must design institutions for criminal punishment that will function well with the same people, or nearly the same, who are presently attracted to jobs in the field.

This essay has also given inadequate attention to the *reincarceration* discretion of parole boards, which is the mirror image of release discretion. For many offenders, especially in some states, the probabilities that their prison sentences will really end upon first release are small. Although numerous jurisdictions have experimented with the routinization of release discretion, efforts to comprehend or impose structure on parole revocations are still in their infancy. We have much evidence that reincarcerations in some jurisdictions occur in large numbers for technical violations of parole that would, on their own merits, never justify a term of confinement (Petersilia 2003, ch. 7). What is clearer still is that we simply do not know enough about parole revocations from state to state to build sound policy. This knowledge vacuum must sooner or later be addressed.

A number of readers of an early draft of this essay commented that a compelling argument against parole release agencies as they are presently constituted in American law should not be accepted too quickly as proof that better constructed arrangements for delayed release decisions would be equally infirm. The point is well taken. Perhaps new vehicles for judicial reconsideration of prison terms should be available for some classes of offenders, including those who have received the longest sentences. Special humility about the correctness of legal rulings—and the opportunity for later reflection by the sentencing judge—are perhaps warranted when those rulings affect not years but decades of human lives. It may also be the better part of wisdom to encourage ongoing experimentation with treatment and reentry programs fueled in part by early release incentives, provided reasonable evaluations are performed along the way. Such efforts might produce defensible algorithms for release decisions that seem beyond our reach today. I am receptive to these possibilities and hope that many readers will be as well.

Finally, this essay has not addressed the content of rehabilitative programs that should be made available within prisons, the level of investment governments should make in such programs, the aftercare services that should be offered to newly released offenders, and the evaluation efforts that should regularly attend such interventions to help us to know which ones are working and which are not. All of these matters probably have greater potential to influence offenders' future behavior than the inherited device of parole release discretion. Also, as one reader of an early draft commented, it may be unfair to dismiss the role of discretionary release conceived as part of a prison system dedicated to the rehabilitation of prisoners, when in fact "the parole board in most cases is not part of a structured system designed to rehabilitate anyone" (Bushway 2003). I am sure that many other people of good faith feel the same way.

On the narrow question at hand, however, this essay has shown that it is presently difficult to justify the allocation of large authority over prison durations to a parole board if we are to build the case on the fundamental goals of sentencing collected in Morris's theory of limiting retributivism. It is not altogether impossible to cobble together an argument, but one must go through convolutions in order to do so, or be willing to place one's bets on empirical findings that have not yet been recorded. In addition, this essay has shown that common preconceptions that parole release acts as a force toward lenity in prison sentences, and that parole release abolition is associated with greater severity, are seriously out of kilter with actual experience. On balance, prison populations have grown more slowly in parole-release abolition jurisdictions than elsewhere, and the slowest growth patterns among all American sentencing systems in recent decades have prevailed in parole abolition states that have also instituted sentencing guidelines. It would be well for future debate to take stock of these surprising facts.

Notes

I owe thanks to many generous colleagues who provided comments (some of them extensive) on an earlier draft of this essay, including Shawn Bushway, Paul Campos, Richard Frase, Patrick Furman, Sandra Guerra-Thompson, Lackshman Guruswamy, Kim Hunt, Connie Stivers Ireland, James Jacobs, Susan Jones, Kay Knapp, Benjamin Lerner, Mark Loewenstein, Gerard Lynch, Theodore McKee, Marc Miller, Daniel Meltzer, John Monahan, Norval Morris, Hiroshi Motomura, Robert Nagel, William Nagel, Scott Peppet, Joan Petersilia, William Pizzi, Curtis Reitz, Michael Smith, Michael Tonry, Patricia Wald, Philip Weiser, Marianne Wesson, Ahmed White, Ronald Wright, and Franklin Zimring.

1. In 1999, e.g., an ex-prisoner was 18 percent more likely to succeed on post-release supervision in a determinate regime. I am neither qualified nor equipped to redo the regression analysis performed by Stivers Ireland, but I have contacted her with the suggestion, which she has received graciously. The flip in the raw numbers is so compelling that there is little doubt Stivers Ireland's regression results would change dramatically once the California data are excised.

2. I can no longer count the number of people who have told me that, when first studying the prospect of state-level sentencing reform, they had to spend considerable time overcoming their strong negative views of the current federal

system. (This was my own experience, as well, when I entered the sentencing policy field in the late 1980s.) The published scholarship of sentencing law and policy exacerbates the problem of knowledge and perception focused too much on one system, by devoting nearly exclusive attention to federal law (see University of Colorado Law Review 1993).

3. The additional increment of sentencing guideline jurisdiction-years (exclusive of those guideline systems in parole-release abolition states) may be reproduced using the effective dates reported in Reitz 2001, adding 11 jurisdiction-years to take account of the discontinued sentencing guideline systems that were in force in Wisconsin from 1986 to 1995 and in Louisiana from 1993 to 1995.

References

Allen, Francis A. 1964. *The Borderland of Criminal Justice*. Chicago: University of Chicago Press.

American Bar Association. 1980. *Standards for Criminal Justice, Sentencing Alternatives and Procedures*. 2d ed. Boston: Little, Brown and Co.

———. 1994. *Standards for Criminal Justice: Sentencing*. 3d ed. Chicago: ABA Press.

American Law Institute. 2002a. *Model Penal Code: Sentencing, Plan for Revision*. Philadelphia: American Law Institute.

———. 2002b. *Model Penal Code: Sentencing, Preliminary Draft No. 1*. Philadelphia: American Law Institute.

Andenaes, Johannes. 1952. "General Prevention—Illusion or Reality?" *Journal of Criminal Law, Criminology & Police Science* 43:176–198.

Andrews, D. A., and James Bonta. 1994. *The Psychology of Criminal Conduct*. Cincinnati: Anderson.

Anglin, M. Douglas, and Yih-Ing Hser. 1990. "Treatment of Drug Abuse." In *Drugs and Crime, Crime and Justice: A Review of Research*, vol. 13, ed. Michael Tonry and James Q. Wilson. Chicago: University of Chicago Press.

Austin, James. 2002. *The Need to Reform Parole Board Decision-Making*. Lexington, Mass.: American Probation and Parole Association.

Boerner, David, and Roxanne Lieb. 2001. "Sentencing Reform in the Other Washington." In *Crime and Justice: A Review of Research*, vol. 28, ed. Michael Tonry. Chicago: University of Chicago Press.

Bottomley, A. Keith. 1990. "Parole in Transition: A Comparative Study of Origins, Developments, and Prospects for the 1990s." In *Crime and Justice: A Review of Research*, vol. 12, ed. Michael Tonry and Norval Morris. Chicago: University of Chicago Press.

Bureau of Justice Statistics. 1988. *Historical Statistics on Prisoners in State and Federal Institutions, Year-end 1925–86*. Washington, D.C.: Bureau of Justice Statistics.

———. 1995. *Prisoners in 1994*. Washington, D.C.: Bureau of Justice Statistics.

———. 1996. *Prisoners in 1995*. Washington, D.C.: Bureau of Justice Statistics.

———. 1997. *Prisoners in 1996*. Washington, D.C.: Bureau of Justice Statistics.

———. 1998. *Prisoners in 1997*. Washington, D.C.: Bureau of Justice Statistics.

———. 1999. *Prisoners in 1998*. Washington, D.C.: Bureau of Justice Statistics.

———. 2001. *Trends in State Parole, 1990–2000*. Washington, D.C.: Bureau of Justice Statistics.

———. 2002a, *Prison and Jail Inmates at Midyear 2001*. Washington, D.C.: Bureau of Justice Statistics.

———. 2002b. *Prisoners in 2001*. Washington, D.C.: Bureau of Justice Statistics.

———. 2002c. *Sourcebook of Criminal Justice Statistics—2001*. Washington, D.C.: Bureau of Justice Statistics.

———. 2003. *Prisoners in 2002*. Washington, D.C.: Bureau of Justice Statistics.

Burke, Peggy B. 1988. *Current Issues in Parole Decisionmaking: Understanding the Past; Shaping the Future*. Washington, D.C.: National Institute of Corrections.

———. 1995. *Abolishing Parole: Why the Emperor Has No Clothes*. Lexington, Mass.: American Probation and Parole Association.

Bushway, Shawn. 2003. Personal correspondence to Kevin R. Reitz, January 31, 2003 (on file with author).

Bushway, Shawn, and Peter Reuter. 2002. "Labor Markets and Crime." In *Crime*, ed. James Q. Wilson and Joan Petersilia. Oakland, Calif.: ICS Press.

Cahalan, Margaret Warner. 1986. *Historical Corrections Statistics in the United States, 1850–1984*. Washington, D.C.: Bureau of Justice Statistics.

Davis, Kenneth Culp. 1969. *Discretionary Justice: A Preliminary Inquiry*. Urbana: University of Illinois Press.

Dyer, Joel. 2000. *The Perpetual Prisoner Machine: How America Profits from Crime*. Boulder, Colo.: Westview Press.

Elkins, Mike, and Jide Olagundoye. 2001. *The Prison Population in 2000: A Statistical Overview*. London: Home Office.

Frankel, Marvin E. 1973. *Criminal Sentences: Law Without Order*. New York: Hill & Wang.

Frase, Richard S. 1993a. "Implementing Commission-Based Sentencing Guidelines: The Lessons of the First Ten Years in Minnesota." *Cornell Journal of Law and Public Policy* 2:279–337.

———. 1993b. "The Role of the Legislature, the Sentencing Commission, and Other Officials under the Minnesota Sentencing Guidelines." *Wake Forest Law Review*. 28:345–379.

———. 1997. "Sentencing Principles in Theory and Practice." In *Crime and Justice: A Review of Research*, vol. 22, ed. Michael Tonry. Chicago: University of Chicago Press.

Gendreau, Paul, Tracy Little, and Claire Goggin. 1996. "A Meta-Analysis of the Predictors of Adult Offender Recidivism: What Works!" *Criminology* 34:575–607.

Goldfarb, Ronald L., and Linda R. Singer. 1973. *After Conviction*. New York: Simon & Schuster.

Hart, H. L. A. 1968. *Punishment and Responsibility: Essays in the Philosophy of Law*. New York: Oxford University Press.

Hood, Roger, and Richard Sparks. 1970. *Key Issues in Criminology*. New York: McGraw-Hill.

Jones, Peter R. 1996. "Risk Prediction in Criminal Justice." In *Choosing Correctional Options That Work: Defining the Demand and Evaluating the Supply*, ed. Alan T. Harland. Thousand Oaks, Calif.: Sage Publications.

Knapp, Kay A. 1993. "Allocation of Discretion and Accountability within Sentencing Structures." *University of Colorado Law Review* 63: 679–705.

Knapp, Kay A., and Denis J. Hauptly. 1992. "State and Federal Sentencing Guidelines: Apples and Oranges." *University of California, Davis Law Review* 25: 679–694.

Kress, Jack M. 1980. *Prescription for Justice*. Cambridge, Mass.: Ballinger Press.

Marvell, Thomas B. 1995. "Sentencing Guidelines and Prison Population Growth." *Journal of Criminal Law and Criminology* 85:696–709.

Mauer, Marc. 1999. *Race to Incarcerate*. New York: New Press.

Monahan, John. 1982. "The Case for Prediction in the Modified Desert Model of Criminal Sentencing." *International Journal of Law and Psychiatry* 5:103–113.

Morris, Norval. 1974. *The Future of Imprisonment*. Chicago: University of Chicago Press.

———. 1982. *Madness and the Criminal Law*. Chicago: University of Chicago Press.

———. 1993. "Comments to Franklin E. Zimring, Drug Treatment as a Criminal Sanction." *University of Colorado Law Review* 64:831–835.

———. 2002. *Maconochie's Gentlemen: The Story of Norfolk Island and the Roots of Modern Prison Reform*. New York: Oxford University Press.

Morris, Norval, and Marc Miller. 1985. "Predictions of Dangerousness." In *Crime and Justice: An Annual Review of Research*, vol. 6, ed. Michael Tonry and Norval Morris. Chicago: Chicago University Press.

Morris, Norval, and Michael Tonry. 1990. *Between Prison and Probation: Intermediate Punishments in a Rational Sentencing System*. New York: Oxford University Press.

National Conference of Commissioners on Uniform State Laws. 1980. *Model Sentencing and Corrections Act*. Washington, D.C.: Law Enforcement Assistance Administration.

Orland, Leonard, and Kevin R. Reitz. 1993. "Epilogue: A Gathering of State Sentencing Commissions." *University of Colorado Law Review* 64:837–845.

Packer, Herbert L. 1968. *Limits of the Criminal Sanction*. Stanford, Calif.: Stanford University Press.

Parenti, Christian. 1999. *Lockdown America: Police and Prisons in the Age of Crisis*. New York: Verso.

Pennsylvania Law Weekly. 1998. "Judge: Inmates are Unfairly Denied Parole." *Pennsylvania Law Weekly*, October 26, 1998, p. 2.

Petersilia, Joan. 2003. *When Prisoners Come Home: Parole and Prisoner Reentry*. New York: Oxford University Press.

Piehl, Anne Morrison, Bert Useem, and John J. DiIulio, Jr. 1999. *Right-Sizing Justice: A Cost–Benefit Analysis of Imprisonment in Three States*. New York: Center for Civic Innovation at the Manhattan Institute.

PR Newswire. 1995. "Pennsylvania Gov. Ridge Announces Probation and Parole Reforms; New Mission Community Safety." *PR Newswire*, June 27, 1995.

Reitz, Kevin R. 1996. "The Federal Role in Sentencing Law and Policy." *Annals of the American Academy of Political and Social Sciences* 543:116–129.

———. 1998. "Modeling Discretion in American Sentencing Systems." *Law & Policy* 20:389–428.

——— 2001. "The Status of Sentencing Guideline Reforms in the United States." In *Penal Reform in Overcrowded Times*, ed. Michael Tonry. New York: Oxford University Press.

Rice, Marnie E., Grant T. Harris, and Vernon L. Quinsey. 2002. "The Appraisal of Violence Risk." *Current Opinion in Psychiatry* 15:589–593.

Rideau, Wilbert, and Ron Wikberg. 1992. *Life Sentences: Rage and Survival Behind Bars*. New York: Times Books.

Rothman, David J. 1980. *Conscience and Convenience: The Asylum and its Alternatives in Progressive America*. Boston: Little, Brown and Company.

Ruth, Henry, and Kevin R. Reitz. 2003. *The Challenge of Crime: Rethinking Our Response*. Cambridge, Mass.: Harvard University Press.

The Sentencing Project. 2001. *U.S. Surpasses Russia as World Leader in Rate of Incarceration*. Washington, D.C.: The Sentencing Project.

Sorenson, Jon, and Don Stemen. 2002. "The Effect of Sentencing Policies on Incarceration Rates." *Crime and Delinquency* 48:456–475.

Stivers Ireland, Connie. 2001. "Impacts of Discretionary Parole Release on Length of Sentence Served, Percent of Imposed Sentence Served, and Recidivism." Master's thesis. Irvine: University of California.

Tappan, Paul W. 1958. "Sentencing under the Model Penal Code." *Law and Contemporary Problems* 23: 528–543.

Tonry, Michael. 1996. *Sentencing Matters*. New York: Oxford University Press.

Underwood, Barbara D. 1979. "Law and the Crystal Ball: Predicting Behavior with Statistical Inference and Individualized Judgment." *Yale Law Journal* 88: 1408–1448.

University of Colorado Law Review. 1993. "A Symposium on Sentencing Reform in the States." *University of Colorado Law Review* 64:645–847.

U.S. Bureau of the Census. 1975. *Historical Statistics of the United States: Colonial Times to 1970, Bicentennial Edition*. Washington, D.C.: Bureau of the Census.

———. 1982. *Preliminary Estimates for the Intercensal Population of Counties, 1970–1979*. Washington, D.C.: Bureau of the Census.

———. 2002. *Time Series of Intercensal Population Estimates: April 1, 1990 to April 1, 2000*. Washington, D.C.: Bureau of the Census.

von Hirsch, Andrew. 1993. *Censure and Sanction*. Oxford: Clarendon Press.

von Hirsch, Andrew, and Kathleen J. Hanrahan. 1979. *The Question of Parole: Retention, Reform, or Abolition?* Cambridge, Mass.: Ballinger Publishing Co.

von Hirsch, Andrew, Anthony E. Bottoms, Elizabeth Burney, and P.-O. Wikstrom. 1999. *Criminal Deterrence and Sentence Severity: An Analysis of Recent Research*. Oxford: Hart Publishing.

Walker, Samuel. 1998. *Popular Justice: A History of American Criminal Justice*. New York: Oxford University Press.

Wilhelm, Dan F., and Nicholas R. Turner. 2002. "Is the Budget Crisis Changing the Way We Look at Sentencing and Incarceration?" *Federal Sentencing Reporter* 15:41–49.

Wilson, James Q. 1975. *Thinking about Crime*. New York: Basic Books.

Wright, Ronald F. 2002. "Counting the Cost of Sentencing in North Carolina, 1980–2000." In *Crime and Justice: A Review of Research*, vol. 29, ed. Michael Tonry. Chicago: University of Chicago Press.

Zimring, Franklin E. 1976. "A Consumer's Guide to Sentencing Reform: Making the Punishment Fit the Crime." *Hastings Center Report* 6:13–21.

Zimring, Franklin E., and Gordon Hawkins. 1991. *The Scale of Imprisonment*. Chicago: University of Chicago Press.

———. 1995. *Incapacitation: Penal Confinement and the Restraint of Crime*. New York: Oxford University Press.

9

The Future of Violence Risk Management

John Monahan

> Injustice and inefficiency invariably flow from any blending of the criminal-law and mental health powers of the state. Each is sufficient unto itself to achieve a just balance between freedom and authority; each has its own interested constituency; when they are mixed together, only the likelihood of injustice is added. (Morris 1982, p. 31)

Despite this prescient warning, a blending of the criminal justice and mental health systems is exactly what is happening in the United States, and what may be on the verge of happening in the United Kingdom as well. On the mental health side, the blending has taken the form of a resurgent emphasis on the state's police power as the principal justification for the civil commitment of people with serious mental disorder who have committed no crime but who are believed to be "dangerous to others." The result has been the first significant loosening of the 1960s-era libertarian-oriented standards for involuntary treatment as a hospital inpatient, and the first meaningful laws ever that allow for involuntary treatment in the community. On the criminal justice side, the blending has come as statutes have proliferated, and been upheld, authorizing the indefinite civil commitment in a mental hospital of convicted offenders who are believed to have a "mental abnormality"—which need not rise to the level of a "mental disorder"—and are found likely to recidivate. To date, these statutes have been limited to offenders convicted of sexually violent offenses, but proposals have been introduced in the United States and in the United Kingdom to expand them to the perpetrators of any form of violent act.

Both of these moves toward convergence have been facilitated by developments in the professional technology that enables their operation: violence risk assessment. After two decades of largely depressing research on the abilities of mental health professionals at predicting violence, the journals are suddenly replete with guardedly optimistic studies indicating that actuarial instruments may succeed where clinicians have failed. For the first time, relatively accurate assessments of the risk of violence that a patient or offender poses may be within the realm of science rather than science fiction.

This essay is organized in three sections. First, I consider how the mental health system is coming to resemble the criminal justice system, as standards for inpatient and outpatient commitment become focused on the crimelike concept of danger to others. Second, I address how the criminal justice system is coming to resemble the mental health system, as "mental disorder" is diluted to "mental abnormality" for the purpose of triggering the commitment of those offenders found likely to offend again. Finally, I review developments in the technology of violence risk assessment that allow both the mental health variant and the criminal justice variant of what might be called "violence risk management" to be in the ascendance.

Mental Health: Disorder and Danger

In this section, I consider separately developments in existing statutes authorizing the civil commitment of nonoffenders who are believed to have a "serious" or "major" mental disorder—generally taken as schizophrenia, major depression, and bipolar disorder—and the creation of new statutes authorizing the civil commitment of similar persons to treatment in the community, usually referred of as "outpatient commitment." In addition, I address forms of "mandated community treatment" other than outpatient commitment that are being used to induce the receipt of mental health services in the community. Each of these developments is motivated by the same thing: public fear of people with mental disorder. Indeed, playing the "violence card" has been frankly promoted by one of the most visible figures in the "treatment advocacy" movement:

> Laws change for a single reason, in reaction to highly publicized incidents of violence. People care about public safety. I am not saying it is right, I am saying this is the reality. . . . So if you're changing your [civil commitment] laws in your state, you have to understand that. . . . It means that you have to take the debate out of the mental health arena and put it in the criminal justice/public safety arena. (Jaffe 1999)

Inpatient Commitment

All states have statutes allowing certain people who have a mental disorder to be civilly committed as an inpatient in a psychiatric facility. As stated by Gostin (2002, p. 210):

Civil commitment is the detention (usually in a hospital or other specially designated institution) for the purposes of care and treatment. Civil commitment, like isolation and quarantine, is both a preventive measure designed to avert risk, and a rehabilitative measure designed to benefit persons who are confined. Consequently, persons subject to commitment usually are offered, and sometimes are required to submit to, medical treatment. Civil commitment is normally understood to mean confinement of persons with mental illness or mental retardation, but it is also used for containing persons with infectious diseases, notably tuberculosis, for treatment. (p. 210)

Prior to the late 1960s, involuntary commitment to psychiatric hospitals was justified primarily by a paternalistic concern for people who were seen to be "in need of treatment." Beginning in the late 1960s, however, public protection began to dominate as a rationale for commitment, and risk of behavior harmful to others—called "dangerousness" in statutes and court decisions—became a primary focus of legal attention (Appelbaum 1994). Typically, to qualify for involuntary civil commitment in a psychiatric facility, the individual has to be "seriously mentally disordered," and because of this disorder, to be either "dangerous to others" or "dangerous to self." While there was a flurry of interest in the constitutionality of commitment statutes during the 1970s, the U.S. Supreme Court left no doubt that such laws would be upheld, provided that adequate procedural safeguards were in place, such as proof of disorder and dangerousness by clear and convincing evidence (e.g., *Addington v. Texas*, 441 U.S. 418 (1979)).

Advocates for the family members of people with mental disorder have long argued that these 1960s-era state civil commitment statutes were written so narrowly and with so many procedural protections that many people who need mental health services but refuse to adhere to those services—refuse, according to this view, because their disorder rendered them incompetent to make treatment decisions (Grisso and Appelbaum 1998)—were effectively left untreated. These advocates urged looser due process protections and longer time limits on hospital treatment. For two decades, a combination of civil libertarian and fiscal concerns thwarted moves in this direction.

In the past several years, however, the tide has turned in many states. This development has less to do with an increase in legislative compassion for people with mental disorder than with a shift in the lobbying tactics of the treatment advocates. As mentioned earlier, advocates of reinvigorated commitment statutes, no longer appealing to humanitarian concerns, have explicitly sold their approach by playing on already exaggerated public fears of violence committed by people with a mental disorder (Pescosolido et al. 1999). These advocates frame their arguments in terms of evocative frequencies rather than bland probabilities. For example, Torrey and Zdanowicz (1998) write that "approximately 1,000 homicides a year are committed nationwide by seriously mentally ill individuals who are not taking their medication," and not that the annual likelihood of being killed by such an individual is approximately .0000036 (i.e., 1,000 out of 273,000,000 Americans will die in this manner each year). These advocates are quite open about their motivation: they *want* to frighten the general public about violence by people with mental disorder, in the hope that this fear will translate into less libertarian laws and more funding for mental health services (Satel and Jaffe 1998).

Examples of the new, more treatment-oriented commitment statutes include South Dakota, which extended the time frame over which a violent act could be predicted to occur by deleting the word "very" from the previous statutory language that had read "very near future" (S.D. Codified Laws, § 27A-1–1 (2001)). Likewise, Minnesota in 2002 removed the requirement that dangerousness be "imminent" (2002 Minn. Chapter Law 335). Wyoming in 1999 broadened the definition of "dangerous to himself or others" to include not only "death" and "serious physical injury," but also "destabilization from lack of or refusal to take prescribed psychotropic medications for a diagnosed condition" (Wyoming Stat., § 25–10–101(a)(ii) (2001)). Similarly, in 2002, the Wisconsin Supreme Court, in *State of Wisconsin v. Dennis H.* (2002 Wisc. Lexis 505 (July 12, 2002)), upheld a statute authorizing the commitment of people with mental disorder who, if left untreated, will lose their "ability to function independently in the community."

Outpatient Commitment

More dramatic than the loosening of existing civil commitment statutes for inpatient hospitalization has been the proliferation of new statutes allowing for civil commitment to *outpatient* treatment for people with mental disorder. Mandating adherence to mental health treatment in the community through outpatient commitment has now become the most contested issue in mental health law (Swartz and Monahan 2001). There are three types of outpatient commitment. The first is a variant of conditional release from a hospital: a patient is discharged on the condition that he or she continues treatment in the community. The second type is an alternative to hospitalization for people who meet the legal criteria for inpatient treatment: they are essentially given the choice between receiving treatment in the community and receiving treatment in the hospital. The third type of outpatient commitment is preventive: people who do not currently meet the legal criteria for inpatient hospitalization but who are believed to be at risk of decompensation to the point that they will qualify for hospitalization if left untreated are ordered to accept treatment in the community (Gerbasi, Bonnie, and Binder 2000).

Although 40 U.S. jurisdictions have statutes that nominally authorize outpatient commitment, until recently few states made substantial use of these laws. With the 1999 enactment in New York State of "Kendra's Law" (New York Mental Hygiene Law, § 9.60), named after a woman pushed under a subway by a man with an untreated mental disorder, nationwide interest in outpatient commitment (euphemistically termed "assisted outpatient treatment" in the New York statute) has greatly increased. Kendra's Law mandates adherence to mental health treatment in the community for persons who meet a number of statutory qualifications, including that the person is suffering from mental illness and "because of mental illness is unlikely to participate voluntarily in recommended treatment and . . . needs assisted outpatient treatment to prevent a relapse or deterioration which would likely result in serious harm to the person or others." Kendra's Law has withstood a number of constitutional challenges in New York State courts. For example, in the case of *In re Urcuyo*, 714 N.Y.S.2d 862 (2000), the court held:

> Clearly, the state has a compelling interest in taking measures to prevent these patients who pose such a high risk from becoming a danger to the community and themselves. Kendra's Law provides the means by which society does not have to sit idly by and watch the cycle of decompensation, dangerousness and hospitalization continually repeat itself.

Since the enactment of Kendra's Law in late 1999, over 7,000 people have been evaluated in New York State for outpatient commitment.[1] Kendra's Law is seen as a model for outpatient commitment bills being introduced in other states. In this regard, in September of 2002, the California legislature passed, and the governor signed, "Laura's Law" (AB 1421) (also named for a woman killed by an individual with untreated mental disorder), explicitly modeled on the New York outpatient commitment statute. Outpatient commitment bills are currently under consideration in Florida, Texas, Minnesota, Maryland, and Utah.

Does outpatient commitment "work" at reducing future treatment as a hospital inpatient and future violence in the community? Two randomized controlled trials of outpatient commitment have been published. The first—the Duke Mental Health Study—followed patients who had been involuntarily hospitalized and given a court order for mandatory community treatment after discharge. Patients randomly assigned to the control group were released from the court order. For patients randomly assigned to the experimental group, the outpatient commitment order remained in effect for varying periods of time, depending on whether a psychiatrist and the court believed the patient continued to meet legal criteria.

In bivariate analyses, the control and outpatient commitment groups did not differ significantly in hospital outcomes, although in repeated measures analyses outpatient commitment group assignment did reduce the odds of readmission (Swartz et al. 1999). However, when the data from the experimental group were disaggregated into those patients who were under outpatient commitment for at least six months and those patients who were under outpatient commitment for less than six months, strong differences emerged. Patients on outpatient commitment for a sustained period had significantly fewer hospital readmissions and hospital days than control subjects. Additional analyses revealed that sustained outpatient commitment was associated with reduced hospital readmissions only when it was combined with a higher intensity of outpatient services. The prevalence of violence to others during the year after discharge was also significantly lower among patients receiving at least six months of outpatient commitment compared to controls and to those who received less than six months of outpatient commitment (Swanson et al. 2000). Extended outpatient commitment also reduced criminal victimization and arrests (Hiday et al. 2002).

The second randomized controlled trial—the Bellevue Study—also followed patients who had been hospitalized and given a court order for mandatory community treatment after discharge (Steadman et al. 2001). A court-ordered outpatient commitment group was contrasted with a control group over a one-year follow-up period. Both experimental and control groups received a package of enhanced services including intensive community treatment.

No significant differences between the control and experimental groups were found in follow-up hospitalizations, arrests, or other outcomes. A significantly smaller portion of both the experimental and control groups were hospitalized during the year of the follow-up than had been hospitalized during the previous year. The researchers concluded that enhanced services made a positive difference in the post-discharge experiences of both experimental and control groups, but that "the court order itself had no discernible added value in producing better outcomes."

It would appear, therefore, that the only two randomized controlled trials of outpatient commitment are in agreement that improving the availability and quality of mental health services leads to positive outcomes, but yield conflicting results regarding the value added by legally mandating patients' participation in those services. Both of these studies have methodological limitations that make resolving this conflict difficult (Appelbaum 2001).

Other Forms of Mandated Community Treatment

Much of the strident policy debate on outpatient commitment treats it as if it were simply an extension of commitment as an inpatient and views outpatient commitment within the same conceptual and legal framework historically used to analyze commitment to a mental hospital. Increasingly, however, it is becoming apparent that concepts developed within a closed institutional context do not perform as intended in the much less structured context of the open community. To take only one example, in the 1979 case of *Addington v. Texas* (441 U.S. 418), the U.S. Supreme Court raised the standard of proof necessary for the state to invoke inpatient commitment from "preponderance of the evidence" to "clear and convincing evidence." In reaching this decision, the Court focused on "the individual's interest in not being involuntarily confined," and held that "civil commitment constitutes a significant deprivation of liberty that requires due process protection."

In the context of outpatient commitment, however, the individual is not being physically "confined" or "deprived of liberty"—the individual is free to move about in the open community as he or she chooses—as long as periodic office appointments for psychotherapy or medication are kept. Must the state now meet the same heightened standard of proof when it wants to invoke outpatient commitment as the Court 25 years ago said it must to invoke inpatient commitment? Currently available, institutionally based concepts are not helpful in answering this question.

Rather than viewing outpatient commitment as a simple extension of commitment to a mental hospital, outpatient commitment may be seen as only one of a growing array of legal tools now being used to insure treatment adherence in the community. It is only in relation to these other forms of "mandated community treatment" that outpatient commitment can be adequately understood (Monahan et al. 2001a).

What are these other forms of mandated community treatment? People with severe and persistent mental disorders are often dependent upon goods and services provided by the social welfare system, including disability benefits and housing. Their access to these goods and services may be tied to treatment participation. Similarly, many people with severe and persistent mental disorders often find themselves arrested for criminal offenses. Lenient disposition of their cases may be tied to treatment participation. In each of these contexts, the targeted patients face loss of liberty, property, or other valued interests if they fail to comply with prescribed treatment.

Mandated Treatment in the Social Welfare System

People with a disability, such as a serious mental disorder, may qualify under current federal or state laws in the United States to receive certain social welfare benefits. Two benefits to which some people who are found to be disabled by a mental disorder are entitled under current laws are monetary payments and subsidized housing.

Money as Leverage. Recipients of federal benefits in the form of Supplemental Security Income (SSI) or Social Security Disability Insurance (SSDI) typically receive checks made in their own names and make their own decisions about the use of the funds. The Social Security Act, however, provides for the appointment of a "representative payee" to receive the checks if it is determined to be in the beneficiary's best interests to do so. Last year, approximately 540,000 people in the United States with a mental disability received their benefits through a representative payee. One survey in Chicago indicated that the majority of patients who have a representative payee believe that there is a relationship between their adherence to treatment and whether they receive funds, and a substantial minority of patients believe that this relationship approaches quid pro quo (Hanrahan, Luchins, and Savage 1999).

Housing as Leverage. A survey conducted in 2001 found that there was not a single city or county in the United States in which a person with a mental disorder living solely on disability benefits could afford the fair market rent for a modest efficiency apartment (Edgar, O'Hara, and Smith 1999). The only alternative to publicly subsidizing housing for many people with a mental disorder, therefore, is homelessness. To avoid this outcome, the government provides a number of housing options in the community for people with a mental disorder that it does not provide to other citizens. No one questions that landlords can impose generally applicable requirements—such as paying rent, maintaining the premises in good condition, and not disturbing neighbors—on their tenants. The issue is whether landlords legally can and in fact do impose *additional*

requirements on tenants with mental disorder and whether any such requirements may pertain to treatment. Of the 600,000 people in the United
States with disabilities who in 2001 resided in housing subsidized by the
federal Department of Housing and Urban Development, the Technical
Assistance Collaborative estimates that approximately one-third qualified
for this subsidy due to mental disorder (A. O'Hara, personal communication, 2002). The only figures available on the number of people with
mental disorder who receive housing subsidies from a *state* government
in the United States are from Massachusetts. There, approximately 8,000
clients of the Department of Mental Health resided in subsidized housing
last year, with another 3,100 people on the waiting list (T. O'Leary, personal communication, 2002). The very little existing research on this topic
finds that subsidized housing is sometimes formally used as leverage to
assure adherence to mental health treatment in the community and may
be used much more often informally to the same end.

Mandated Treatment in the Judicial System

People with severe mental disorder are sometimes ordered to comply with
treatment by judges or by other officials acting in the shadow of judicial
authority (e.g., probation officers). Even in the absence of a judicial order,
patients may agree to adhere to treatment requirements to avoid an unfa-
vorable judicial order such as a sentence of incarceration. In all these
contexts, judicial authority to impose sanctions and curtail freedom provides the leverage for inducing treatment adherence.

Avoidance of Jail as Leverage.   Making the acceptance of mental health
treatment in the community a condition of sentencing a defendant to
probation rather than to jail has long been an accepted judicial practice,
and one that can affect many defendants. Of the 3,800,000 defendants
who were convicted and sentenced to probation last year in the United
States, between 8 and 12 percent (300,000–450,000 people) were estimated
to have a serious mental disorder.

Under what circumstances can the disposition of the criminal case of
a person with mental disorder be such that the person remains in the
community on the condition that he or she adheres to mental health
treatment? In other words, under what circumstances may the criminal
sanction be imposed if the person fails to adhere to mental health treatment
in the community? A judge in a general criminal court may:

(1) *grant bail, with a condition of bail being adherence to treatment.*
    If the person adheres to treatment, the person may remain on

bail; if the person does not adhere to treatment, bail will be violated and pretrial jail detention may be imposed.

(2) *defer prosecution conditionally*. If the person adheres to treatment, charges will be dismissed; if the person does not adhere to treatment, prosecution, possibly resulting in a jail sentence, may be initiated.

(3) *defer judgment conditionally*. If the person adheres to treatment, judgment will not be entered, the guilty plea will be withdrawn, and the record of conviction will be expunged. If the person does not adhere to treatment, judgment will be entered, and the person will be sentenced.

(4) *suspend sentence conditionally*. If the person adheres to treatment, the jail sentence that has been imposed will be suspended; if the person does not adhere to treatment, the jail sentence must be served.

(5) *sentence to probation, with a condition of probation being adherence to treatment*. If the person adheres to treatment, probation will remain in effect; if the person does not adhere to treatment, probation will be violated and a jail sentence may be imposed.

In addition to these options open to a general criminal court, a new type of specialized criminal court—called, appropriately, a "mental health court"—has recently been developed that makes even more explicit the link between sanctioning and treatment in the community. First established in Broward County, Florida, in 1997, mental health courts focus on the relatively low-level mentally ill offender who has had repeated contact with the criminal justice system. Adapted from the drug court model, a mental health court differs from a regular court in several respects: cases are heard on their own court calendar, separate from other cases, and are handled by their own specialized team of legal and mental health professionals; emphasis is put on implementing new working relationships between the criminal justice system and the mental health and social welfare systems; and defendants appearing before mental health courts generally receive intensive supervision in the community. These courts give prominence to the judge, who plays a much more active and directive role than the passive "umpire" role typically associated with judges in criminal court. Mental health courts appear to be burgeoning across the country. From one operating mental health court in 1997, there are approximately 45 in operation in 2003. And once a court is created, there is no shortage of business: the Broward County mental health court hears 800 new cases per year (Poythress et al. 2002).

Criminal Justice: Abnormality and Predation

In this section, I first consider those statutes, already in existence, that address the civil commitment of offenders who have been convicted of a sexually violent crime. I then review proposals, not yet enacted, to expand the scope of these statutes to include any form of violent crime.

Sexually Violent Offenders

The most influential case blending the criminal justice and mental health systems in recent years has been the U.S. Supreme Court's 1997 upholding of "sexually violent predator" statutes in *Kansas v. Hendricks* (521 U.S. 346 (1997)). Under those statutes, an offender, after being convicted of a specified sexual crime and serving the prison sentence associated with that criminal conviction, can be found to be a sexually violent predator. This finding can serve as the predicate for civil commitment to a mental hospital for an indefinite period. The Kansas Care and Treatment for Mentally Ill Persons Act defined a "sexually violent predator" as: "any person who has been convicted of or charged with a sexually violent offense and who suffers from a mental abnormality or personality disorder which makes the person likely to engage in the predatory acts of sexual violence" (§ 59–29a02(a)).

Justice Thomas, writing for the majority in this 5–4 decision, made clear that it was pivotal that the statute under review was *civil* in nature. "The categorization of a particular proceeding as civil or criminal 'is first of all a question of statutory construction.' Allen, 478 U.S. at 368. We must initially ascertain whether the legislature meant the statute to establish 'civil' proceedings. If so, we ordinarily defer to the legislature's stated intent." He continued:

> Here, Kansas' objective to create a civil proceeding is evidenced by its placement of the Sexually Violent Predator Act within the Kansas probate code, instead of the criminal code, as well as its description of the Act as creating a *"civil* commitment procedure." Kan. Stat. Ann., Article 29 (1994) ("Care and Treatment for Mentally Ill Persons") § 59–29a01 (emphasis added). Nothing on the face of the statute suggests that the legislature sought to create anything other than a civil commitment scheme designed to protect the public from harm. (*Kansas v. Hendricks*, 521 U.S. 346 [1997] at 361)

Justice Thomas elaborated on why the statute in question was properly categorized as civil rather than criminal:

> Commitment under the Act does not implicate either of the two primary objectives of criminal punishment: retribution or deterrence. The Act's purpose is not retributive because it does not affix culpability for prior criminal conduct. Instead, such conduct is used solely for evidentiary purposes, either to demonstrate that a "mental abnormality" exists or to support a finding of future dangerousness. . . . Nor can it be said that the legislature intended the Act to function as a deterrent. Those persons committed under the Act are, by definition, suffering from a "mental abnormality" or a "personality disorder" that prevents them from exercising adequate control over their behavior. Such persons are therefore unlikely to be deterred by the threat of confinement. (Ibid.)

Even Justice Breyer, writing for the four dissenters, noted that "Civil commitment of dangerous, mentally ill individuals by its very nature involves confinement and incapacitation. Yet 'civil commitment,' from a constitutional perspective, nonetheless remains civil" (ibid. at 380).

Five years later, in *Kansas v. Crane* (122 S.Ct. 867, 151 L.Ed.2d 856 (2002)), the Supreme Court reaffirmed the view that, in sexually violent predator cases, "the confinement at issue [is] civil, not criminal, confinement" (ibid. at 868). The Court in *Crane* held that proof of a complete inability to control one's behavior was not a constitutionally necessary prerequisite to being found to be a sexually violent predator and civilly committed to a hospital.

> It is enough to say that there must be proof of serious difficulty in controlling behavior. And this, when viewed in light of such features of the case as the nature of the psychiatric diagnosis, and the severity of the mental abnormality itself, must be sufficient to distinguish the dangerous sexual offender whose serious mental illness, abnormality, or disorder subjects him to civil commitment from the dangerous but typical recidivist convicted in an ordinary criminal case. (Ibid. at 870)

Fifteen states and the District of Columbia have now enacted sexually violent predator statutes modeled on the Kansas law upheld in *Hendricks* and in *Crane*, providing for the post-imprisonment civil commitment in a mental hospital of sex offenders who have a mental abnormality and who are assessed as having the risk factors that indicate a high risk of violent recidivism. As of mid-2002, 2,478 people had either been civilly committed to inpatient hospitalization as sexually violent predators (1,632 people) or were being detained as hospital inpatients awaiting a hearing for such commitment (846 people) (Fitch and Hammen 2002).

Hubbard v. Superior Court (969 P.2d 584 (1999)) is typical of the state cases that have followed *Hendricks*. In this case, the California Supreme Court upheld California's Sexually Violent Predator's Act (SVPA) against due process, equal protection, and ex post facto challenges. The "diagnosed mental disorder" necessary to trigger the act was defined verbatim as the "mental abnormality" posited by the Kansas statute that had been upheld by the U.S. Supreme Court in *Hendricks*. Expert witnesses had concluded that "Hubbard suffered from a diagnosable mental disorder, as set forth in the DSM-IV." More specifically, Hubbard's had received "a definite diagnosis of [DSM-IV code] 302.9, Paraphilia Not Otherwise Specified, Bondage, Rape and Sodomy of Adult Women, Severe" and a diagnosis of [DSM-IV code] 301.9, "Personality Disorder, Not Otherwise Specified, with Antisocial Traits."

Finding that the SVPA "establishes the requisite connection between impaired volitional control and the danger posed to the public," and that such a connection "permissibly circumscribes the class of persons eligible for commitment under the Act," the legislation was upheld. The court found it noteworthy that the legislature had declared its intent "to establish a non-punitive, civil commitment scheme covering persons who are to be viewed 'not as criminals, but as sick persons,'" and that "to this end, the maximum length of each commitment term is relatively brief—two years." A "relatively brief" two years that is renewable indefinitely, however.

Generally Violent Offenders

As Stephen Morse (1998, p. 264) has observed, "the problem that [*Hendricks*] presents is that the definition of mental abnormality the Court found acceptable cannot be logically limited to sexually violent predators. . . . Nothing would seem constitutionally to bar a state from defining a class of 'mentally abnormal violent predators,' or more broadly, 'mentally abnormal dangerous predators,' and for providing for involuntary commitment of the class at the end of a prison term."

Shortly after Morse wrote this, the Michigan State Senate passed, by a vote of 255 to 33, a "Violent Predator" statute (Senate Bill 0465 (2001)), that did precisely that. In Section 1061, the purpose of the statute was given:

> The legislature finds that a small but extremely dangerous group of violent predators exists who do not have a mental illness that renders them appropriate for the existing civil commitment process that is designed to provide treatment to individuals with serious mental illness.

The legislature also finds that the likelihood of a violent predator engaging in repeat acts of predatory violence is high. The legislature also finds that the prognosis for curing this small group of violent predators is poor, that the treatment needs of this population are very long-term, and that the treatment modalities for this population are very different from the traditional treatment modalities for individuals who are appropriate for commitment and treatment under this code.

"Mental abnormality" is defined under the statute exactly as it is in *Hendricks*. The statute, which authorizes indeterminate civil commitment to a mental hospital (with a reexamination "at least every 3 years," rather than the every two years specified in the California SVPA) is applicable only to persons convicted of a violent offense, who had previously been convicted of two or more murders or voluntary manslaughters. The bill still awaits action by the Michigan House.

The proposed Michigan Violent Predator statute represents the outer limit that legislators in the United States are—currently, at least—prepared to go in indefinitely detaining "dangerous" people who do not have a major mental disorder. Other countries may be prepared to go much farther. In particular, a joint "consultation paper" issued by the British Home Office and Department of Health, *Managing Dangerous People with Severe Personality Disorder: Proposals for Policy Development*, issued in July of 1999 (Home Office 1999), demonstrates the astonishing lengths to which the type of reasoning legitimized in *Hendricks* can be taken. The paper posits that:

> Personality disorder is a term used to describe a number of different conditions . . . [At one] end of the spectrum is a small group of people who are very seriously disordered and who pose a very high risk to the public. . . . The law as it stands fails to protect the public from the danger these people represent because in many cases they have to be allowed to return to the community even though they remain dangerous.(Ibid., p. 3)

This group is said to number "just over 2,000 people" in England and Wales (98% of whom are men). In the subsequent white paper, *Reforming the Mental Health Act, Part II: High Risk Patients* (Home Office 2000), the government more precisely estimated that "a total of between 2,100 and 2,400 men are dangerous and severely personality disordered (DSPD)" (§ 1.5).

Independent scholars have framed the figures differently. Based on an analysis of the risk assessment literature as applied to the British government estimates of the number of people with DSPD, Alec Buchanan and Morven Leese (2001, p. 1958) have concluded as follows:

> Six people with DSPD would have to be detained for a year to prevent one person from acting violently during that year. The overall estimate for sensitivity suggests that for every ten people with DSPD who would be violent, five would be identified and detained and five would be missed. The overall estimate for specificity suggests that for every ten people with DSPD who would not be violent, seven would be identified and released and three would be detained.

Like Hendricks's "mental abnormality," people with severe personality disorder are distinguished by having "poor control of impulses" (Home Office 2000, p. 5).Two "case studies" are offered in the white paper. One notes that the patient's harmful behavior is "compulsive," and the other that the patient "has a low threshold to violence" and "a psychopathic disorder." Neither case involved a major mental disorder.

Crucially, however, *Hendricks*—and the U.S. state cases that have followed it, such as *Hubbard*, and the U.S. proposals to extend it, such as the Michigan Violent Predator Statute—are addressed only to persons who have been convicted and imprisoned for certain specified violent crimes and are approaching the end of their prison sentences. The British proposal, in contrast, takes the position that "a minority of people with severe personality disorder may be assessed as presenting a high risk *but may not have been convicted of a recent serious offense*" (emphasis added) (Home Office 2000, p. 6). Such persons are to be referred for "specialist assessment" in a civil proceeding. "As with those charged with an offense, referral will only be available on the basis of prior psychiatric reports together with evidence of probable risk" (ibid.). In a passage that is difficult to characterize as anything other than Orwellian, the white paper states, regarding evidence against persons not changed with any criminal offense: "In time such evidence is likely to come most often from the local multi-agency public protection panels and risk panels that are being set up around the country to help in identifying those individuals who are a cause of real concern" (ibid.).

The paper mentions in a footnote (ibid., p. 13, note 10) that the "risk panels" referred to "are usually chaired by the police." The risk panels also "include representatives from probation, local social services, child protection groups, health, housing and if necessary other agencies."

Two options for protecting the community from Dangerous Severely Personality Disordered persons are put forth in the report. The first ("Option A") would maintain current statutory provisions, with changes including "removing the existing requirement of 'likely to benefit from hospital treatment' in the case of DSPD individuals detained in civil [commitment] proceedings," and "introducing new powers for compulsory supervision and recall of DSPD individuals following discharge from detention under civil proceedings" (ibid., p. 14). The second ("Option B") is even more radical:

> This option would create a new legal framework for detention of all DSPD individuals, based on the risk they present and their therapeutic needs, rather than whether they have been convicted of any offense. It would require the establishment of new specialist facilities for the assessment and subsequent management of DSPD individuals. These facilities would need to be identified as being clearly separated from existing prison and health services. . . . [This option] would provide the best means of ensuring that DSPD individuals were allocated to a facility fully meeting their specific needs, rather than on the basis of their offending history. (Ibid., p.18)

A wave of criticism from British psychiatrists, psychologists, and civil libertarians washed over the white papers summarized earlier. The Mental Health Bill that the Department of Health ultimately introduced into Parliament in June 2002 and that is currently under debate backed off from the most controversial of the white paper proposals ("Option B"). In particular, in the final bill "there is no separate legislation for 'DSPD.' . . . People with personality disorders will be treated in exactly the same way as patients with other mental disorders and will come under compulsory powers if they meet the same conditions for compulsion" (Department of Health 2002, p. 23). Accordingly, "mental disorder" is now defined in the Bill in so broad a manner as to subsume personality disorder: "'Mental disorder' means any disability or disorder of mind or brain which results in an impairment or disturbance of mental functioning" (Part 1, § 2(6)). The Consultation Document accompanying the Bill makes clear the criminal justice like nature of these changes in the Mental Health Act:

> The new legislation will allow for the detention of someone with mental disorder for as long as they pose a significant risk of serious harm to others as a result of their mental disorder, thereby meeting the conditions for compulsion. In some cases, where the mental disorder, and the behaviours arising from it are complex and difficult to manage, an individual may be detained in hospital for a long time. (Department of Health 2002, p. 23)

Finally, the Bill introduced into Parliament would for the first time allow people with mental disorder "to be subject to community-based treatment orders rather than detention in hospital." Directly apropos of the controversy surrounding the American debate on outpatient commitment, the Mental Health Alliance, an organization representing 50 consumer groups in England and Wales, promptly charged that "this Bill will actually make mental health services worse. It will backfire as forced treatment in the community will drive people away from seeking services. The new criteria for compulsion are far too wide."[2]

Violence Risk Assessment

As seen earlier, risk assessments of violence play a crucial "triggering" role in authorizing intervention by the mental health system in the lives of nonoffenders—whether in the form of inpatient commitment, outpatient commitment, or some other form of mandated community treatment—and in authorizing intervention by the criminal justice system in the lives of offenders—currently offenders who are sexually violent, but perhaps in the future offenders who commit nonsexual violence as well.

There are two basic approaches to the risk assessment of violence or of any other form of human behavior. One approach, called clinical prediction, relies on the subjective judgment of experienced human decision makers—typically, in the case of violence, psychologists and psychiatrists, but also parole board members or judges. The risk factors that are assessed in clinical prediction might vary from case to case, depending on which seem more relevant. These risk factors are then combined in an intuitive manner to generate an opinion about violence risk. The other approach, termed actuarial (or statistical) prediction, relies on explicit rules specifying which risk factors are to be measured, how those risk factors are to be scored, and how the scores are to be mathematically combined to yield an objective estimate of violence risk. Christopher Slobogin, writing almost 20 years ago, stated: "Read in their best light the data suggest that neither the clinical nor the actuarial method of prediction provides information that will permit an accurate designation of a 'high risk' group whose members have more than a forty to fifty percent chance of committing serious assaultive behavior" (1984, p. 126).

Recent research, reviewed later, confirms the continuing validity of Slobogin's claim regarding clinical prediction, but indicates that his conclusion regarding actuarial prediction is no longer valid. In this section, I consider clinical methods first, then actuarial ones.

Clinical Risk Assessment

I reviewed early research on the accuracy of clinicians at predicting violent behavior toward others in 1981. The conclusion of that review was that: "psychiatrists and psychologists are accurate in no more than one out of three predictions of violent behavior over a several-year period among institutionalized populations that had both committed violence in the past (and thus had high base rates for it) and who were diagnosed as mentally ill" (Monahan 1981 pp. 47–49).

Only two studies of the validity of clinicians' predictions of violence in the community have been published since that time. Sepejak et al. (1983, p. 181, note 12) studied court-ordered pretrial risk assessments and found that 39 percent of the defendants rated by clinicians as having a "medium" or "high" likelihood of being violent to others were reported to have committed a violent act during a two-year follow-up, compared to 26 percent of the defendants predicted to have a "low" likelihood of violence, a statistically significant difference, but not a large one in absolute terms.

In the second study, Lidz, Mulvey, and Gardner (1993) took as their subjects male and female patients being examined in the acute psychiatric emergency room of a large civil hospital. Psychiatrists and nurses were asked to assess potential patient violence toward others over the next six-month period. Violence was measured by official records, by patient self-report, and by the report of a collateral informant in the community (e.g., a family member). Patients who elicited professional concern regarding future violence were found to be significantly more likely to be violent after release (53 percent) than were patients who had not elicited such concern (36 percent). The accuracy of clinical prediction did not vary as a function of the patient's age or race. The accuracy of clinicians' predictions of male violence substantially exceeded chance levels, both for patients with and without a prior history of violent behavior. In contrast, the accuracy of clinicians' predictions of female violence did not differ from chance. While the actual rate of violent incidents among discharged female patients (46 percent) was higher than the rate among discharged male patients (42 percent), the clinicians had predicted that only 22 percent of the women would be violent, compared with predicting that 45 percent of the men would commit a violent act. The inaccuracy of clinicians at predicting violence among women appeared to be a function of the clinicians' serious underestimation of the base-rate of violence among mentally disordered women (perhaps due to an inappropriate extrapolation from the great gender differences in rates of violence among persons without mental disorder).

Actuarial Risk Assessment

The general superiority of statistical over clinical risk assessment in the behavioral sciences has been known for almost half a century (Meehl

1954; Swets, Dawes, and Monahan 2000). Despite this, and despite a long and successful history of actuarial risk assessment in bail and parole decision making in criminology, there have been only a few attempts in the past to develop actuarial tools for the specific task of assessing risk of violence to others among people with mental disorder. Recently, however, this situation has changed. Consider three actuarial violence risk assessment instruments developed for use with people with mental disorder. The first two will be described briefly and the third at greater length.

The Violence Risk Appraisal Guide

The Violence Risk Appraisal Guide (VRAG) (Quinsey et al. 1998) was developed on a sample of over 600 men from a maximum-security hospital in Canada, all charged with a serious criminal offense. Approximately 50 predictor variables were coded from institutional files. The criterion was any new criminal charge for a violent offense, or return to the institution for a similar act, over a time at risk in the community that averaged approximately seven years after discharge. A series of regression models identified 12 variables for inclusion in the VRAG, including the Hare Psychopathy Checklist Revised, elementary school maladjustment, and age at the time of the offense (which had a negative weight). When the scores on this actuarial instrument were dichotomized into "high" and "low," the results were that 55 percent of the group scoring high committed a new violent offense, compared with 19 percent of the group scoring low. A version of the VRAG specific to the prediction of sex offenses—the Sex Offender Risk Appraisal Guide (SORAG)—has also been developed.

The HCR-20

Douglas and Webster (1999) reviewed ongoing research on a structured clinical guide that can be scored in an actuarial manner to assess violence risk, the "HCR-20," which consists of 20 ratings addressing Historical, Clinical, or Risk management variables. The Historical items include previous violence, age at first violent incident, and substance abuse. The Clinical items include lack of insight, impulsivity, and unresponsiveness to treatment. The Risk Management items include "plans lack feasibility, lack of social support, and stress." Douglas and Webster reported data from a retrospective study with prisoners, finding that scores above the median on the HCR-20 increased the odds of past violence and antisocial behavior by an average of four times. In another study with civilly committed patients, Douglas et al. (1999) found that during a follow-up of approximately two years after discharge into the community, patients scoring above the HCR-20 median were six to 13 times more likely to be violent than those scoring below the median.

The MacArthur Violence Risk Assessment Study

As a final and more extended illustration of the use of actuarial approaches to improve the prediction of violence, the MacArthur Risk Assessment Study (Monahan et al. 2001b) assessed a large sample of male and female acute civil patients at several facilities on a wide variety of variables believed to be related to the occurrence of violence. The risk factors fall into four domains. One domain, "dispositional" variables, refers to the demographic factors of age, race, gender, and social class, as well as to personality variables (e.g., impulsivity and anger control) and neurological factors (e.g., head injury). A second domain, "historical" variables, includes significant events experienced by subjects in the past, such as family history, work history, mental hospitalization history, history of violence, and criminal and juvenile justice history. A third domain, "contextual" variables, refers to indices of current social supports, social networks, and stress, as well as to physical aspects of the environment, such as the presence of weapons. The final domain, "clinical" variables, includes types and symptoms of mental disorder, personality disorder, drug and alcohol abuse, and level of functioning. Community violence is measured during interviews with the patients and with a collateral conducted post-discharge in the community, as well as from a review of official records. Data are available for two time periods, the first 20 weeks after discharge and the first year after discharge.

The MacArthur Study developed what the researchers called an "Iterative Classification Tree." A classification tree approach to violence risk assessment is predicated upon an interactive and contingent model of violence, one that allows many different combinations of risk factors to classify a person as high or low risk. Whether a particular question is asked in any clinical assessment grounded in this approach depends on the answers given to each prior question by the person being evaluated. Based on a sequence established by the classification tree, a first question is asked of all persons being assessed. Contingent on the answer to that question, one or another second question is posed, and so on, until each person is classified into a category on the basis of violence risk. This contrasts with the usual approach to actuarial risk assessment in which a common set of questions is asked of everyone being assessed and every answer is weighted and summed to produce a score that can be used for purposes of categorization.

Finally, Monahan et al. (2001b) adopted an approach that combined the results of five prediction models generated by the Iterative Classification Tree methodology, each of which captures a different but important facet of the interactive relationship between the risk factors and violence. This combination of models produced results superior to any other actuarial violence risk assessment procedure reported in the literature to date. The researchers were able to place all patients into one of five risk classes for which the prevalence of violence during the first 20 weeks following discharge into the community varied between 1 percent and 76 percent (see figure 9.1).

The risk factors that frequently came into the classification trees that allowed the risk assessments depicted in figure 9.1 included prior arrests (both seriousness and frequency), demographic factors (age, male gender), being unemployed, being abused as a child (both seriousness and frequency), diagnosis (antisocial personality disorder, schizophrenia), whether one's father used drugs or was present in the home while the patient was a child, substance abuse, a lack of anger control, and violent fantasies. In the case of several of these variables, the relationship to violence was negative: people of older age, whose father was in the home while the patient was a child, or who had a diagnosis of schizophrenia (compared, for example, to a diagnosis of personality disorder) were significantly *less* likely to be violent than other patients. These and other risk factors have been combined in the first "violence risk assessment software," which is currently undergoing further testing in preparation for release for clinical use.

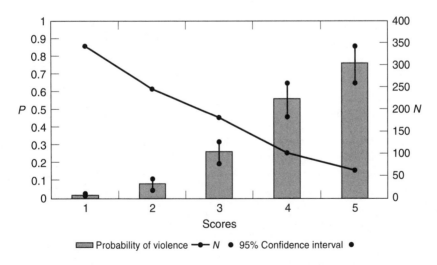

Fig. 9.1. Prevalence of violence during first 20 weeks following discharge.

From Risk Assessment to Risk Management

To trigger an intervention to manage—that is, to reduce—violence risk, as in the mental health or criminal justice interventions described earlier, it is necessary to apply a cutoff or "decision threshold" (Swets, Dawes, and Monahan 2000) to the estimates that risk assessments generate: if the risk estimate is below the decision threshold, then the contemplated action to manage risk is foregone, and if the estimate is at or above the decision threshold, then the contemplated action commences. The choice of decision threshold for managing risk, of course, is itself a decision, and one that in many circumstances belongs to policy makers, and not to the psychologists or psychiatrists who are assessing the risk.

Monahan and Silver (2003) recently reported a study that directly asked one set of policy makers—judges—where they would set the threshold for one type of risk management decision: whether or not to institute short-term civil commitment as a "danger to others" of a nonoffender with a serious mental disorder. The survey was conducted in the context of an actual violence risk assessment project, the MacArthur Risk Violence Risk Assessment Study, described earlier. Judges enrolled in the Graduate Program for Judges at the University of Virginia served as subjects. The judges had a mean of 10 years experience on the bench. Approximately 90 percent sat on state appellate courts at the time of the research (and many had been trial judges in the past).

The MacArthur Study was briefly described to the judges, and they were presented with the findings on the five final "risk classes" shown in figure 9.1. The judges were then asked the question:

> If this violence risk assessment software were administered to a person who was mentally disordered, and if the mental health professional who administered the software agreed with the estimate it produced, *what is the lowest likelihood of violence to others that you would accept* as fulfilling the "dangerousness" criterion for authorizing short-term civil commitment?

The response categories they were given to check off were the same as in the actual MacArthur Study: Group 1 (1 percent probability of violence), Group 2 (8 percent probability of violence), Group 3 (26 percent probability of violence), Group 4 (56 percent probability of violence), and Group 5 (76 percent probability of violence).

The results were clear: judges in this study drew a line between Risk Classes 2 and 3 as their cutoff for the risk management activity being contemplated. In the terms proposed by Swets, Dawes, and Monahan (2000), they chose Risk Class 3—a 26 percent likelihood of committing a violent act—as their decision threshold for short-term civil commitment as dangerous to others. That is, on average the judges were of the view that people with a serious mental disorder whose risk was assessed by the MacArthur instrument as being in Risk Classes 1 or 2 did not qualify for commitment, and that people with a serious mental disorder whose assessed risk placed them in Risk Classes 3, 4, or 5 did qualify for commitment. Of course, if the decision presented to the subjects had been different than short-term civil commitment (e.g., outpatient commitment), or if the type of violence being predicted had been different than the given illustration of battery with injury (e.g., sexual violence), or if the person had also been convicted of a crime, other decision thresholds might have been chosen.

The choice of a decision threshold has many and varied consequences. For example, the statistical characteristics associated with each possible decision threshold from the MacArthur Violence Risk Assessment Study are presented in table 9.1. If one applied the decision threshold of Risk Class 3 or higher to the data produced in the MacArthur Study, the risk assessment upon which the contemplated risk management activity was predicated (short-term civil commitment, in this case) would have a true positive rate of 44.0 percent (and therefore a false positive rate of 56.0 percent), a true negative rate of 96.1 percent (and therefore a false negative rate of 3.9 percent), a sensitivity of 86.9 and a specificity of 74.4. Slightly over three-quarters of the sample (76.8 percent) would be correctly classified as violent or nonviolent. If the risk management activity was completely successful at preventing the predicted violence, then 91.1 percent of all the violence committed by this sample of patients would be prevented. To accomplish this, however, it would be necessary to intervene in the lives of 37.1 percent of the patients (of whom more than half (56.0%) would not have been violent even without the intervention). To the extent that the risk management activity was less than completely successful, the percentage of all violence prevented would decline. If another decision threshold were chosen, these figures would change in the manner indicated in table 9.1.

The necessity for choosing a decision threshold for criminal justice or mental health risk management decisions, long implicit and therefore capable of being ignored in clinical risk assessment, is made apparent and unavoidable in actuarial prediction.

Conclusion

A blending of the criminal justice and mental health systems, which Norval Morris cautioned against 20 years ago, has begun in the United States,

Table 9.1. Statistical Characteristics Associated with Each Decision Threshold in the MacArthur Study (%)

Intervene if in class	True positive rate[a]	False positive rate	True negative rate	False negative rate	Sensitivity	Specificity	% of sample classified correctly	% of sample targeted	% of violent acts prevented[b]
1 or higher	18.7	81.3	na	na	100.0	0.0	18.7	100.0	100.0
2 or higher	28.9	71.1	98.8	1.2	97.7	44.4	54.4	63.5	98.9
3 or higher	44.0	56.0	96.1	3.9	86.9	74.4	76.8	37.1	91.0
4 or higher	63.6	36.4	90.8	9.2	59.7	92.1	86.0	17.6	67.3
5 only	76.2	23.8	85.4	14.6	27.3	98.0	84.8	6.7	33.5

[a]Equivalent to the positive predictive value (PPV)
[b]If the intervention was successful

and may be on the cusp of beginning in the United Kingdom. The state's police power is resurgent as the principal justification for the civil commitment of people with serious mental disorder, resulting in a significant loosening of libertarian-oriented standards for involuntary hospitalization and the first enforceable laws allowing for involuntary treatment in the community. Statutes authorizing the indefinite commitment in a mental hospital of offenders convicted of a sexually violent offense and believed to have a mental abnormality are flourishing and may be extended to those convicted of any form of violence.

This coming together of the criminal justice and mental health systems has been enabled by improvements in the professional technology of violence risk assessment. After decades of negative results on the predictive accuracy of clinical risk assessment, positive findings on the predictive accuracy of actuarial prediction have become more the rule than the exception. This, too, had been foreseen:

> One should not place great reliance on psychiatric predictions of social dangerousness until they have been expressed in the form of prediction tables, which are really only "experience tables," and which are available for critical testing by other than the predictor. The raconteurs, the narrators of the individual case history, may greatly contribute to our understanding of the dynamic interaction of individual and social processes, but such solitary insights can only in the most exceptional cases form the basis of prediction of social dangerousness on which the law should rely. Control over another man's life is too serious a matter to be posited on other than tested, evaluated, refined experience—on carefully validated prediction tables. (Morris 1970, p. 190)

Notes

1. Data are available at http://www.omh.state.ny.us/omhweb/kendra_web/kstatus_rpts/statewide.htm.
2. Data are available at (http://www.mentalhealth.org.uk/page.cfm?pagecode=PRNR0111).

References

Appelbaum, P. 1994. *Almost a Revolution: Mental Health Law and the Limits of Change.* New York: Oxford University Press.
——— 2001. "Thinking Carefully about Outpatient Commitment." *Psychiatric Services* 52:347–350.

Buchanan, A., and M. Leese. 2001. "Detention of People with Severe Personality Disorders: A Systematic Review." *The Lancet* 358:1955–1960.

Department of Health. 2002. Mental Health Bill, Consultation Document. London: Department of Health.

Douglas, K., and C. Webster. 1999. "The HCR-20 Violence Risk Assessment Scheme: Concurrent Validity in a Sample of Incarcerated Offenders." *Criminal Justice and Behavior* 26:3–19.

Douglas, K., J. Ogloff, T. Nicholls, and I. Grant. 1999. "Assessing Risk for Violence among Psychiatric Patients: The HCR-20 Violence Risk Assessment Scheme and the Psychopathy Checklist: Screening Version." *Journal of Consulting and Clinical Psychology* 67:917–930.

Edgar, E., A. O'Hara, and B. Smith. 1999. *Priced Out in 1998: The Housing Crisis for People with Disabilities*. Boston: Technical Assistance Collaborative.

Fitch, L., and D. Hammen. 2002. "Sex Offender Commitment in the United States." Presented at the Annual Meeting of the State Mental Health Program Directors, Forensic Directors Division, Meeting. Seattle.

Gerbasi, J., R. Bonnie, and R. Binder. 2000. "Resource Document on Mandatory Outpatient Treatment." *Journal of the American Academy of Psychiatry and Law,* 28:127–144.

Gostin, L. 2002. *Public Health Law: Power, Duty, Restraint*. Berkeley: University of California Press.

Grisso, T., and P. Appelbaum. 1998. *Assessing Competence to Consent to Treatment: A Guide for Physicians and Other Health Professionals*. New York: Oxford University Press.

Hanrahan, P., D. Luchins, and C. Savage. 1999. "Representative Payee Programs for Mentally Ill Persons in Illinois: Census Survey." Presented at the Institute for Psychiatric Services and the Annual Conference of the American Public Health Association.

Hiday, V., J. Swanson, M. Swartz, R. Borum, and H. Wagner. 2002. "An Exploration of Outpatient Commitment's Impact on Victimization of Persons with Severe Mental Illness." *American Journal of Psychiatry* 159:1403–1411.

Home Office. 1999. *Managing Dangerous People with Severe Personality Disorder*. London: Home Office.

——— 2000. *Reforming the Mental Health Act*. London: H.M. Stationery Office.

Jaffe, D. J. 1999. Speech to the National Alliance for the Mentally Ill.

Lidz, C., E. Mulvey, and W. Gardner. 1993. "The Accuracy of Predictions of Violence to Others." *Journal of the American Medical Association* 269:1007–1011.

Meehl, P. 1954. *Clinical versus Statistical Prediction*. Minneapolis: University of Minnesota Press.

Monahan, J. 1981. *The Clinical Prediction of Violent Behavior*. Washington, D.C.: Government Printing Office.

Monahan, J., and E. Silver. 2003. "Judicial Decision Thresholds for Violence Risk Management." *International Journal of Forensic Mental Health* 2:1–6.

Monahan, J., R. Bonnie, P. Appelbaum, P. Hyde, H. Steadman, and M. Swartz.

2001a. "Mandated Community Treatment: Beyond Outpatient Commitment." *Psychiatric Services* 52:1198–1205.

Monahan, J., H. Steadman, E. Silver, P. Appelbaum, P. Robbins, E. Mulvey, L. Roth, T. Grisso, and S. Banks. 2001b. *Rethinking Risk Assessment: The MacArthur Study of Mental Disorder and Violence.* New York: Oxford University Press.

Morris, N. 1970. *The Honest Politician's Guide to Crime Control.* Chicago: University of Chicago Press.

——— 1982. *Madness and the Criminal Law.* Chicago: University of Chicago Press.

Morse, S. 1998. "Fear of Danger, Flight from Culpability." *Psychology, Public Policy and Law* 4:250–267.

Pescosolido, B., J. Monahan, B. Link, A. Stueve, and S. Kikuzawa. 1999. "The Public's View of the Competence, Dangerousness and Need for Legal Coercion among Persons with Mental Illness." *American Journal of Public Health* 89: 1339–1345.

Poythress, N., J. Petrila, A. McGaha, and R. Boothroyd. 2002. "Perceived Coercion and Procedural Justice in the Broward Mental Health Court." *International Journal of Law and Psychiatry* 25:1–17.

Quinsey, V., G. Harris, M. Rice, and C. Cormier. 1998. *Violent Offenders: Appraising and Managing Risk.* Washington, D.C.: American Psychological Association.

Satel, S., and D. Jaffe. 1998. "Violent Fantasies." *National Review* 36–37.

Sepejak, D., R. Menzies, C. Webster, and F. Jensen. 1983. "Clinical Predictions of Dangerousness: Two-Year Follow-up of 408 Pre-trial Forensic Cases." *Bulletin of the American Academy of Psychiatry and the Law* 11:171–181.

Slobogin, C. 1984. "Dangerousness and Expertise." *University of Pennsylvania Law Review* 122:97–174.

Steadman, H., K. Gounis, D. Dennis, K. Hopper, B. Roche, M. Swartz, and P. Robbins. 2001. "Assessing the New York City Involuntary Outpatient Commitment Pilot Program." *Psychiatric Services* 52:330–336.

Swanson, J., M. Swartz, R. Borum, V. Hiday, H. Wagner, and B. Burns. 2000. "Involuntary Outpatient Commitment and Reduction of Violent Behaviour in Persons with Severe Mental Illness." *British Journal of Psychiatry* 176:324–331.

Swartz, M., and J. Monahan. 2001. "Introduction: Special Section on Involuntary Outpatient Commitment." *Psychiatric Services* 52:323–324.

Swartz, M., J. Swanson, H. Wagner, B. Burns, V. Hiday, and R. Borum. 1999. "Can Involuntary Outpatient Commitment Reduce Hospital Recidivism? Findings from a Randomized Trial in Severely Mentally Ill Individuals." *American Journal of Psychiatry* 156:1968–1975.

Swartz, M., J. Swanson, V. Hiday, H. Wagner, B. Burns, and R. Borum. 2001. "A Randomized Controlled Trial of Outpatient Commitment in North Carolina." *Psychiatric Services* 52:325–329.

Swets, J., R. Dawes, and J. Monahan. 2000. "Psychological Science can Improve Diagnostic Decisions." *Psychological Science in the Public Interest* 1:1–26.

Torrey, E., and M. Zdanowicz. 1998. "Why Deinstitutionalization Turned Deadly." *Wall Street Journal,* August 4.